ORIGINS OF SHAREHOLDER ADVOCACY

ORIGINS OF SHAREHOLDER ADVOCACY

Edited by

Jonathan GS Koppell

palgrave
macmillan

First published in 2011 by PALGRAVE MACMILLAN® in the
United States - a division of St. Martin's Press LLC, 175 Fifth Avenue,
New York, NY 10010.

Where this book is distributed in the UK, Europe and the rest of the
World, this is by Palgrave Macmillan, a division of Macmillan Publishers
Limited, registered in England, company number 785998, of
Houndmills, Basingstoke, Hampshire RG21 6XS.

Palgrave Macmillan is the global academic imprint of the above
companies and has companies and representatives throught the world.

Palgrave® and Macmillan® are registered trademarks in the United
States, the United Kingdom, Europe and other countries.

ISBN: 978–0–230–10732–8

Library of Congress Cataloging-in-Publication Data

Origins of shareholder advocacy / edited by
   Jonathan GS Koppell.
      p. cm.
   ISBN 978–0–230–10732–8
   1. Stockholders. 2. Corporations—Investor relations.
   I. Koppell, Jonathan GS
   HD2744.O75 2011
   306.3—dc22   2010027367

Design by Integra Software Services

First edition: January 2011

10 9 8 7 6 5 4 3 2 1

Printed in the United States of America.

For Uncle Ike

Contents

LIST OF FIGURES

ACKNOWLEDGMENTS

This volume is the direct result of a unique conference organized by the Millstein Center for Corporate Governance and Performance at the Yale School of Management. Commemorating the four-hundredth anniversary of Isaac Le Maire's protest on behalf of the shareholders of the Dutch East India Company, the conference brought together scholars from varied disciplines to examine the Origins of Shareholder Advocacy in a variety of contexts and eras.

The Millstein Center appreciates the support of four U.S., Dutch, and global institutions that served as partners in producing both the conference at Yale, held in November 2009, and a commemorative volume–Shareholder Rights at 400—that includes the first reprint and translation of Le Maire's petition as well as an essay by Paul Frentrop placing the Le Maire case in historical perspective. In addition to the ongoing support of the Yale School of Management, this project would not have been possible without the support of the IRRC Institute, APG Asset Management, Eumedion, and the International Corporate Governance Network. The project benefited greatly from the participation of various individuals, including those on the steering committee: Paul Frentrop, Head of Corporate Governance at APG; Joost Jonker, University of Utrecht; Abe de Jong, RSM Erasmus University; Randall Morck, University of Alberta; William Goetzmann, Geert Rouenhorst, and Jonathan Koppell, Yale School of Management; and Jon Lukomnik, Program Director at the IRRC Institute. Ira Millstein, Senior Associate Dean for Corporate Governance, oversees all programs of the Center.

The Center is especially grateful to all those who served as discussants at the conference and offered feedback to the authors, including Bruce Kogut, Columbia Law School; Karen Brenner, New York University; Arthur Pinto, Brooklyn Law School; Tamar Frankel, Boston University; Rick Antle, William Goetzmann, and Martijn Cremers, Yale School of Management; Timothy Guinnane, Yale Department of Economics; and Stephen Davis, Millstein Center for Corporate Governance and Performance.

Instrumental in organizing and administering the Origins of Shareholder Advocacy conference were the Millstein Center staff, including Milica Boskovic, Michele Grammatico, Crysta Collins, Jia Huang, and Michael Barton-Sweeney. Robert Bartholomew and Moonie Phantharat were especially helpful in preparing the manuscript for publication.

LIST OF CONTRIBUTORS

John H. Armour is Hogan Lovells Professor of Law and Finance, Oriel College, University of Oxford.

Brian R. Cheffins is S J Berwin Professor of Corporate Law, Faculty of Law, Cambridge University.

Stephen Davis is Executive Director of the Millstein Center for Corporate Governance and Performance, Yale School of Management.

Reza Dibadj is Professor of Law, University of San Francisco.

Abe de Jong is Professor of Corporate Finance, Rotterdam School of Management, Erasmus University and Professor of Financial Accounting, University of Groningen.

Johan Matthijs de Jongh is a Law Clerk in the Research Department of the Supreme Court of the Netherlands.

Oscar Gelderblom is Associate Professor of Economic and Social History group of Utrecht University.

William N. Goetzmann is the Edwin J. Beinecke Professor of Finance and Management Studies and Director, International Center for Finance at the Yale School of Management.

Yadira González de Lara is Assistant Professor of Economic History at the University of Valencia and Research Fellow, Prometeo Program at the University CEU-Cardenal Herrera.

Thomas Hall is Associate Professor of Economics and Finance at the Luter College of Business and Leadership, Christopher Newport University.

Joost Jonker is Associate Professor of Economic and Social History, Utrecht University.

Jonathan GS Koppell is Director of the School of Public Affairs at Arizona State University and Lattie and Elva Coor Presidential Chair.

Corrado Malberti is Associate Professor in Commercial Law, University of Luxembourg.

Randall Morck is Stephen A. Jarislowsky Distinguished Chair in Finance and University Professor in the Department of Finance and Management Science, University of Alberta.

Sebastien Pouget is Professor of Finance in the Institut d'Administration des Entreprises, University of Toulouse, and Visiting Professor at the Bendheim Center for Finance, Department of Economics, Princeton University.

Richard Sylla is Henry Kaufman Professor of the History of Financial Institutions and Markets, Department of Economics, Stern School of Business, New York University.

Andrew von Nordenflycht is Associate Professor in the Segal Graduate School of Business at Simon Fraser University.

Robert E. Wright is Nef Family Chair of Political Economy at Augustana College, South Dakota.

Fan Yang is Associate Professor at the Edwards School of Business, University of Saskatchewan.

CHAPTER 1

SHAREHOLDER ADVOCACY AND THE DEVELOPMENT OF THE CORPORATION: THE TIMELESS DILEMMAS OF AN AGE-OLD SOLUTION

Jonathan GS Koppell

Executives lining their own pockets! Corporate directors profiting from insider dealing! Cozy arrangements between business and government being exploited to eliminate competition! Shareholder lawsuits filed in protest—and counteraccusations that the agitators are simply promoting a nefarious short-selling scheme! Sounds like yet another sordid chapter in the financial crisis that gripped the world for two years. In fact, it is a 400-year-old story demonstrating that problems of corporate malfeasance are as old as the corporation itself. And, more specifically, it is a story that highlights the complex issues surrounding the active participation of shareholders in the governance of corporations.

On January 24, 1609, merchant-investor Isaac Le Maire sent an impassioned missive to Johan van Oldenbarnevelt, the most powerful politician in the United Provinces of the Netherlands, asking for relief from shareowner abuse at the Vereenigde Oost-Indische Compagnie (VOC), better know outside the Netherlands as the Dutch East India Company. It is, Le Maire wrote, "indefensible that a company board could, under whatever pretext, retain another's money for longer or use it in ways other than the latter wishes, for that would be a kind of tyranny."

Still, Le Maire's impassioned plea for the rights of VOC shareholders was rebuffed. The odds were stacked against him inasmuch as the state authorities to whom he was appealing had an interest in reaffirming the very power that Le Maire was challenging, an explanation that resonates quite loudly today. Le Maire drew notice in the annals of finance history for what he did next. He was an instigator of a notorious episode revolving around the short-selling of VOC shares. Isaac Le Maire and his defenders argued that this represented a last-ditch attempt to extract value for aggrieved shareholders, but his name remains associated with stock market skullduggery.

Le Maire's entreaty might be regarded as the first recorded shareholder lawsuit. As an early manifestation of the tension inherent in the corporate structure, it was neither the first nor certainly the last time that one group of shareholders felt they were being taken advantage of by management and other owners. Indeed, the role of shareholders has emerged as one of the most critical contemporary corporate governance issues. One conclusion reached by many analysts of the financial crisis that enveloped the globe for two years is that shareholders lack the tools to adequately police management and protect their interests. Policymakers in the United States and Europe are awash in proposals to bolster the tools of modern-day Le Maires. Shareholders would be given greater access to the proxy ballot, opportunities to express disapproval of executive compensation, and meaningful chances to reject nominations to the board of directors.

THE VALUE OF A HISTORICAL PERSPECTIVE

It is somewhat surprising that there has been little research done on the birth and evolution of shareowner participation in corporate governance. The Le Maire episode is not only a colorful historical anecdote, it offers a window onto an earlier era's treatment of seemingly intractable problems and an insight into current challenges. But it is only a single snapshot, leaving a vast reservoir of experiences from different parts of the world and different eras to be tapped. So in recognition of the four-hundredth anniversary of Isaac Le Maire's shareholder petition against the Dutch East India Company, the Yale School of Management's Millstein Center for Corporate Governance and Performance invited scholars to present original research on the origins and historical development of shareholder advocacy. The conference was not limited to studies of Isaac Le Maire or the Dutch East India Company. As the contributions to this volume indicate, the issues associated with shareholder participation in the governance of corporations predate the VOC episode.

The dearth of research on the origins of shareowner advocacy and investor rights may have been understandable when these were issues of secondary importance in modern capital markets (Dunlavy 2006, 1352). That is no longer the case. Shareholder participation is being offered as a critical, if often overlooked, element of corporate governance. Lucian Bebchuk has argued, for example, that shareholder challenges to incumbent directors are currently an impractical means of protecting value (2007). He has led the charge for changes in current practices that would make proxy contests more competitive (Bebchuk 2005, 2007). His critics have defended current practices and questioned his research, but the financial crisis has given his drive for reforming the proxy process new momentum (Lipton and Savitt 2007; Macey 2007).

Responding to entreaties from scholars, institutional investors, and civil society organizations, national lawmakers and regulators in the United States and Europe as well as international organizations such as the Financial Standards Board and the OECD are considering initiatives that would grant shareholders "say on pay," institutionalize majority-approval requirements for directors, and make proxies more accessible (Kirkpatrick 2009; Shorter 2009). They are hearing counterarguments from corporate entities and other interested parties, of course, who warn of the dangers of such changes. They point to abuses of shareholder power—including dominant shareholders using enhanced influence to serve their own interests at the expense of others—and the unintended consequences even well-intentioned reforms might have (Blair and Stout 1999; Anabtawi 2005).

Of course, there are modes of shareholder engagement other than elections. Recently, the methods of hedge funds and other managers of pools of capital that use their relationships with firms to enhance shareholder value have been scrutinized (Becht et al. 2008). Generally, in such situations, a single entity holds a dominant share or even takes a company private to obtain influence sufficient to dramatically reshape a firm (although a public sale of the company is typically envisioned as the means by which investors will realize their profits). The chapters in this volume do not emphasize this type of activism, the attention to the phenomenon underscores the extent to which an effective relationship among investors, corporate boards, and managers is now widely offered not just as a vital protection against malfeasance but as a prerequisite to good corporate performance, national economic status, healthy capital markets, and even social welfare.

By investigating the historical development of shareholder participation around the world, this collection of research not only sheds light on the origins of the institutions and methods with which share-holders are now attempting to protect their investments, it offers an opportunity to assess skeptically some of the claims offered by advocates and opponents of enhanced shareholder influence. Indeed, the Le Maire episode itself reflects the complexities of shareholder participation in corporate governance—its potential as a check on abuse of shareholders but also its possibilities as a tool of obstruction and profiteering.

As discussed in the chapters by Gelderblom, de Jong, and Jonker and de Jongh, the Dutch East India Company (VOC), in which Isaac Le Maire was a major shareholder, was more than a commercial enterprise. It also constituted an instrument in the Dutch geopolitical struggle with Spain and Portugal. As such it enjoyed a government-granted monopoly on certain trading routes and served state ends by establishing trading outposts in vital markets while staking out key shipping corridors as areas of Dutch influence and control. Le Maire's business ambitions were not satisfied by the VOC alone. In addition to pressing the company to expand its business, he pursued other ventures that would put him in competition with the VOC—including voyages to North America in search of the elusive Northwest Passage—to explore the commercial potential of transoceanic trade outside the sphere of the VOC's monopoly. So there was no shortage of tension leading to the shareholder complaints of 1609.

The emphasis of Le Maire's petition to van Oldenbarnevelt was not, in fact, the abuse of shareholders but rather the question of extending the VOC's government-granted monopoly. He argued that the VOC monopoly served neither commercial nor political interests because the company had failed to exploit the opportunities it already had been granted. And worse, by failing to generate revenue, the VOC lacked the capital to undertake new ventures and was destroying the value of shareholders' investment in the company. Rebuffed by the state for reasons explored in Chapter 2, Le Maire participated in an investment group that sold VOC short, an activity that was intended to discipline the company through the market or profit from securities manipulation (depending upon one's view of Isaac Le Maire). This prompted calls from VOC inside directors and management for government relief, which was granted. Short-selling was banned, and the company was relieved of its obligations to provide its shareholders with accounting of the company's business operations. This was accompanied by a divided payment presumably intended to mollify the discontented.

In so many respects, this story resonates today. It shows how the corporation, far from being a monolithic body with closely aligned interests, is a complex agglomeration of parties with some common and some conflicting goals. It shows how the power of the state to alter the rules at any moment is a huge wildcard in corporate governance, one coveted by adversaries, which can promote investment but also entrench powerful interests. And finally it shows that prosperity and robust return on investment can overwhelm even the most principled demands for better governance.

This collection of scholarly research, inspired by the four-hundredth anniversary of the Le Maire petition episode, provides an appropriate opportunity for a fresh examination of the earliest clashes between investors and corporate leaders. It promises insights into the current tumultuous debates that have the potential to reshape the market environment (as explored by Davis in the concluding chapter) and offers cautionary tales regarding the limitations of any corporate governance reform, including changes that enhance the potential of shareholder advocacy.

The book's historical and global approach to the study of shareholder participation is distinctive. The chapters address governance from the medieval to early industrial eras and consider markets as varied as the Netherlands, Venice, the United States, and China. The seemingly eclectic collection opens windows onto eras that are unfamiliar, offering an understanding of the origins of institutions that seem puzzling today and highlighting variation in investor rights in different markets (with attention to the causes and consequences of significant episodes in the history of shareholder activism). By looking at the contextual rationales behind features of the corporation that have persisted from bygone eras, we not only gain insight into the political, legal, and economic conditions that determine levels of shareholder participation but also implicit suggestions of contemporary practices that should be open to question. And although focused on shareholder advocacy, the assembled collection addresses issues that are of widespread interest to corporate governance scholars, practitioners, and policymakers, and the implications of variation in investor rights, including the connection between protection of investors and the development of capital markets (La Porta et al. 2000).

The historical comparative approach of this volume leads to two inescapable conclusions. First, the problems being addressed are truly universal. The corporate structure offers advantages that are undeniable but it introduces challenges as well. By separating the existence of an enterprise from its creators and managers, corporations encourage accumulation of capital for long-term investment on the scale necessary to build modern enterprises (Clark 1986). But, of course, the

corporation introduces its own set of problems. These are now famil-
iarly articulated as principal-agent problems, but the chapters in this
volume make clear they are as old as the corporate institution itself.

Second, reading descriptions of the corporate governance challenges that resonate deeply with contemporary events but were
encountered hundreds of years ago, in markets around the world, is
highly evocative. It suggests that the governance problems associated
with corporations are, on some level, "unsolvable." This might lead
some to throw their hands up in despair; if we cannot fix governance
then what is the point of our efforts? On the other hand, coming
face to face with hundreds of years of experience grappling with the
intractable challenges posed by the corporate structure should prompt
us to better analyze the trade-offs inherent in the design of any and
all governance regimes. Since there is no *pareto optimal* solution, our
energy is best devoted to understanding the compromises (and their
relative merits) associated with different approaches.

THE POTENTIAL AND LIMITS OF CORPORATE GOVERNANCE

This volume focuses on a particular aspect of corporate governance—
shareholder advocacy—that has received renewed attention in the last
few years. But precisely because increased shareholder participation
has been analyzed in the crucible of public policymaking, its proponents and detractors have offered polarized views. Those arguing for
expanded shareholder rights have latched onto the corporate abuses of
the last few years and argued that placing more power in the hands of
owners is the best corrective. Just as advocates of various governance
reforms (e.g., separation of CEO and Chairman of the Board) are
attempting to use the catastrophic events to build support for reforms
they have promoted for some time, proponents of greater shareholder
influence are want to take advantage of this crisis moment. There
is nothing wrong with this tactic. Indeed, the successful advocacy
group must be prepared for precisely this kind of window-opening
event (Kingdon 2003). There is a danger, however, that proponents
of governance reform may be overpromising.

On the other hand, detractors have not only questioned whether
this solution is effective, they point to the costs of empowering
shareholders, including the danger that companies will be driven to
prioritize immediate stock gains over growth and destroy long-term
value (the very antithesis of most shareholder rights advocates' intentions). And just as proponents are driven to amplify the positive effects
of enhanced shareholder power, opponents often stop just short of
promising Armageddon.

This collection offers a realistic take on shareholder participation that shows the truth and exaggeration in arguments for and against expanded shareholder advocacy on the basis of historical experience. Consider the Virginia Company of London (VCL), discussed by Thomas Hall in Chapter 6. The many conflicts of interests embedded in the corporate structure of the VCL make the abuse of shareholders that occurred appear a near certainty. Redemption seems to be found in the shareholder revolt and takeover led by Sir Edwin Sandys in 1619. Unfortunately, after replacing the conflict-of-interest ridden chief executive, Sandys proved to be a far less able manager than leader of dissident shareholders. Indeed, Sandys' egregious mismanagement—and efforts to hide its consequences—led to his own ouster and eventual dissolution of the firm.

No set of institutions can render corporate malfeasance or incompetence impossible. More problematic still is the implication that good corporate governance will lead to business success. It has been observed that many of the companies most troubled amidst the 2008 financial crisis had adopted recommended corporate governance features (Davis 2009). This does not suggest that these mechanisms are without value but it does reveal their limitations. It should go without saying, of course, that the well-governed company is not assured of prosperity. Still frequently one sees arguments for governance reform assailed by critics, who find a juicy example and sarcastically question, "If separating the Chairman and CEO is such a great idea, how come Acme Corp lost 250 billion dollars last year?" The reality is that well-governed companies sometimes make lousy business decisions and poorly governed firms sometimes strike gold. It should be clear already that there is nothing in these pages to suggest that enhanced shareholder participation *guarantees* business success, although the relationship between dysfunctional governance and poor performance does make itself known. Like the Virginia Company, the Compagnie des Indes (French East India Company) never seemed to overcome its internal battles, and this was reflected in its performance as discussed by Reza Dibadj in Chapter 8.

There is no fail-safe. There is no magic bullet. The chapters in this volume make both points perfectly clear. This book should be read therefore as a neutral evaluation of shareholder participation and corporate governance. With accounts representing different epochs and environments, it brings into relief the potential and limitations of shareholder participation in corporate governance but never stretches to make more of participation than the data justify or hides the negative implications of broadening participation.

One will find in these pages support for the general proposition that investor protection is good for economic development (La Porta et al.

2000; Chinn and Ito 2006). This seems true in contexts as different as thirteenth-century Venice, where a system of government-enforced *commenda* facilitated investment in ocean trade (analyzed by Yadira González de Lara in Chapter 5), and nineteenth-century China, where Shanxi banks achieved requisite stability to finance the overland tea trade (Randall Morck and Fan Yang in Chapter 9). Wright and Sylla argue in Chapter 11 that the high rates of incorporation in the early United States spurred rapid economic growth and can be traced to the protection afforded shareholders. Still the very case that inspired this volume offers reservations even on this point. Von Nordenflycht argues in Chapter 4 that we ought to properly see the establishment of the VOC as the first company with permanent capital as a massive expropriation; it was a taking effectuated by the government's decision to grant the company indefinite life rather than a triumph of corporate governance.

Beyond the general attention to shareholder participation that inspired this collection, several themes tie the chapters into a coherent whole. First, the full complexity of the principal-agent problem inherent in the corporate form is revealed in this volume. Conflict *among* shareholders is as problematic, if not more so, as tension between shareholders and management. Second, the historical role of the state in the establishment of the early corporate model and the accumulation of capital is a central feature in many of the analyses. At a time when the rise of sovereign wealth funds and emergency bailouts giving the U.S. government ownership stakes in automakers and insurance companies have brought issues surrounding government ownership to the fore, this issue has great relevance. Third, the contextual dependence of any governance regime is laid bare. Rules and regulations are only part of the picture. After reading the contributions to this volume, the importance of social, political, and economic variables is undeniable. Indeed, each of the episodes underscores in different ways the reality that corporations are fundamentally political organizations. They bring together parties with some shared and some divergent interests and in so doing create a powerful actor, one that has the potential to rival the state and its representatives.

PRINCIPAL-AGENT PROBLEMS

The corporation ought to make a short list of inventions that are essential to any explanation of the development of modern civilization. By moving beyond the sole proprietorship and partnership, the invention of the corporation made feasible the accumulation of capital necessary to build large technology-intensive enterprises. Moreover, the corporation divorced a business from its creators and owners; giving it a life of its own, endowing it with greater stability and permanence than its predecessors. With a corporate structure, individuals could buy and sell ownership stakes in firms relatively easily, making investment in commercial endeavors a more appealing and practical possibility. Introducing the idea of equity shares also made it possible to greatly expand participation in ownership—offering the benefits of capital investment to a wider swath of the population and effectively transforming more accumulated wealth into potential business capital.

Of course, the corporate form introduced a whole set of problems that were not features of traditional business models. In particular, the separation of share ownership and corporate control introduced a significant principal-agent challenge (Jensen and Meckling 1976; Fama 1980). Unlike business owners running their own firms, investors who entrust insiders with their capital must wonder whether insiders are maximizing profits or pursuing other ends that are not congruent with outside shareholders' interests. This dynamic has different manifestations. In the United States and the United Kingdom, the emphasis is on the principal-agent tension between shareholders and management, but elsewhere the insiders may be large blockholders (including controlling families) versus other shareholders (Morck 2005).

This dilemma is sometimes simplified as a matter of graft. Management—and other employees of the corporation—may be tempted to line their own pockets with company money or merchandise rather than passing profits onto the owners. Indeed, de Jongh reports in Chapter 3 an incident of a VOC director literally filling his pocket with a golden crucifix purloined from company inventory that was so heavy it ripped through the pants and fell to the floor! This problem exists in any business, of course, but if a sole owner is also directly engaged in the management of the business, it is her responsibility to prevent such malfeasance and it is easier to do so. Shareholders who are not engaged in management are at a distinct disadvantage relative to the insiders (managers or controlling owners), who may be tempted to dip into the till.

The principal-agent conflicts presented by the corporate form are more complicated and subtle, however, than simple thievery. Even sticking with the shareholder-management relationship, there are many ways in which the paid staff might not work with full dedication to the advancement of shareholder interests. For one thing, their effort may not be up to the level the investors expect, particularly over time. This problem is typically addressed by creating a set of incentives—stock options or other performance-based compensation—intended to align the interests of management and owner (Garen 1994). However, these fixes introduce new problems of information asymmetry. After all, the investor relies on management to report performance but how honest an assessment can one expect if those performance statistics determine compensation? So executive compensation introduces its own principal-agent problems (Bebchuk 2005). And, of course, how can the stockholder be confident that management will pursue an agenda that maximizes the long-term interests of the shareholder if it conflicts with the short-term gain of the leadership (e.g., a bigger bonus pool this year at the expense of future earnings).

There is no need to enumerate all such conflicts as they have been well documented and wrestled with many times over. Suffice it to say, the contributors to this volume document a variety of such issues. Among the issues confronted by VOC shareholders in the years *after* the Le Maire episode, the problem of insider directors remunerating themselves through related-party transactions was a concern; directors charged the company too much for supplies while buying imported commodities at bargain prices. The Virginia Company was plagued by the problem of management running their own ventures, and diverting resources to keep them healthy, whilst literally starving the firm. The Shanxi banks described by Morck and Yang generally avoided such problems but did so with methods that seem somewhat draconian by contemporary standards, including the potential enslavement of the wife and children of an employee found to be defrauding the company.

Less attention is typically given to other agency problems that are illustrated in the pages of this volume. Most notably, conflicting interests *among* shareholders is not emphasized even in contemporary analyses of corporate governance issues, even though seminal work in the field emphasized this crucial problem. It is a convenient simplification to see the shareholders in a publicly traded corporation as a monolithic bloc, unified by a shared concern about management run amok. There is, of course, an element of truth to this, but it is only part of the picture. In fact, shareholder interests are diverse (Anabtawi 2005). First, there is the reality that many of the shareholders are "insiders," creating the same conflicts discussed earlier. The VOC offers a paradigmatic case. Goetzmann and Pouget document early struggles with the concept of delegation of authority from passive owners to managing directors. By examining a lawsuit in fourteenth-century France stemming from some investors' objection to the decision of a director to take on debt, the authors show how governance evolves in response to the inherent uneasiness with the situation. Second, some owners may seek to enrich themselves at the expense of others. For instance, a bloc of shareholders may compel management to conduct a transaction with another company that hurts the firm and benefits the trading partner. Unthinkable unless it is added that this bloc of shareholders owns the trading partner and so, essentially, one set of shareholders is stealing from another. Du Pont's acquisition of a significant stake in General Motors for the purpose of securing contracts is perhaps the most memorable example of this problem. More recently, the Parmalat scandal involved a controlling family siphoning resources at the expense of shareholders and creditors (McCahery and Vermeulen 2005). Third, the investor profiles of sets of shareholders may simply be different, with one class looking for outsized returns with a high tolerance for risk, while others seek stability along with more modest profits. Or, in some cases, employees may own significant stakes in a company and prefer higher levels of employment and compensation to enhanced returns.

STATE ROLE IN ORIGINS OF THE CORPORATION

The problem of conflicting shareholder interests may never be more acute than when the state is one of the owners. At the dawn of the twenty-first century, the listing of state-owned enterprises in China and other countries with legacies of state ownership was the primary contemporary source of questions regarding the compatibility of the corporate governance doctrine with the realities of government-as-shareholder. Such concerns have not faded. Rather they have been given surprising resonance as the financial crisis led to unexpected government ownership of stakes in publicly traded companies in the United States.

In such situations, investors are naturally suspicious that the government has policy preferences related to company decision making that could trump pursuit of return to stockholders. Indeed, reports that the management of General Motors has been subject to political pressure regarding dealer closing and supplier relationships confirm this intuition (King 2009). Of course, one might see this problem as just another potential conflict among shareholder interests like those alluded to earlier. The critical difference here is that recourse is highly problematic. As Isaac Le Maire likely felt 400 years ago, appealing to the government as an aggrieved shareholder when the government itself is the source of the grievance hardly inspires a great deal of confidence in the outcome.

It may seem obvious that any collection of research focusing on the origins of the corporation would engage issues of state ownership. Although there is an ideologically motivated tendency to cast the state and the enterprise in adversarial terms, historians and other scholars have documented the essential role government played in the creation and proliferation of corporate bodies. Typically, of course, we focus on the state's role in formulating the legal framework for corporations to be created and governed, and chapters dealing with Venice and the early United States address this theme. But this collection also reminds us that government played a crucial role as investor and owner, across quite varied contexts but particularly in the area of transoceanic trade. Indeed, the governance institutions—and the patterns of shareholder participation—seem linked to state participation in the corporation at its seminal stages.

Conflict between state and corporate interests and objectives was clearly a major explanation for the repeated disputes among parties (including Le Maire) to the Dutch East India Company. The commercial purposes of ocean trading voyages were only a part of the equation for the governments sponsoring such missions. As discussed, the endeavors were also assertions of political power, with trading ports establishing territorial claims alongside commercial ones. This was true as well for the VCL and the French East India Company, as discussed by Hall and Dibadj, respectively, in their chapters.

The set of issues associated with government participation in these early corporations is distinctive and helps explain their structure. Protections for one set of shareholders may be sacrificed in order to gain another. So, as Gelderblom, de Jong, and Jonker explain in their analysis, the insulation of VOC directors from shareholders was actually an aberration in the context of governance norms of that era. This design may have ensured that the company would be a reliable agent of state political interests, but the insulation of self-dealing insiders was an unintentional, if acceptable, side effect. Unfortunately, the limited checks on the management of the firm may ultimately have undermined commercial success. Indeed, de Jongh suggests that the English East India Company, held up as a model by frustrated VOC shareholders, may ultimately have superseded the Dutch company because of its governance structure, at least in part.

One finishes this volume with the inescapable conclusion that the state cannot be regarded as just another owner. It offers capital with a set of objectives that is typically more multifaceted than other investors. Many of the chapters demonstrate how devastating government ownership can be for the commercial success of the enterprise and, of course, there are countless examples that could bolster the case. Critically, however, it is important to remember just why the state may be a *preferred* investor under some conditions and in some eras. Take the sovereign wealth funds that have been regarded with such suspicion in recent years. Many have actually been quite patient with their capital and, in most cases, provided greater latitude to management than other investors. This does not appear to be the case in the examples described in these pages.

Still the contributions do demonstrate that partnering with the state—even an intrusive state that demands much in the way of influence—offers potential advantages. Although government owners may extract a disproportionate share of profits or require pursuit of some nonbusiness objectives, the returns may be significantly greater as a result of state participation, thus making it a very worthwhile partnership. It is not surprising that across cases, governance objections tend to die down when profits rise. Indeed, as de Jongh reports, the repeated objections of VOC shareholders petered out when the guilders started flowing.

This dynamic seems timeless and helps explain the alacrity with which investors—even those who profess to prize corporate governance best practices—will line up to mix their capital with that of the Chinese state. Few would regard the government of the People's Republic as a strictly passive shareholder, but it is a business partner with a strong record of success in the Chinese market.

CONTEXT MATTERS

Just as state participation in the ownership of a corporation affects the nature of shareholder advocacy, environmental variables play a major role. Even the best solutions to principal-agent problems and other corporate governance dilemmas are effective only under the right circumstances. All the contributions to this volume provide insight into the contextual conditions—political, economic, and cultural—crucial to understanding the emergence, practices, and consequences of shareholder participation.

One can think of the composition of the shareholder population as one such element. We have already discussed the importance of state ownership, but there are numerous other issues. In his analysis of governance variation among early Italian companies, Malberti identifies concentration of ownership as a crucial variable explaining governance structure, including shareholder participation rights. Morck and Yang note that the relatively closed and homogenous society of Shanxi bankers provided an important governance mechanism. By creating enormous social costs for misbehavior, this context reduced the need for some shareholder safeguards.

The two chapters dealing with the most recent history also provide insight into the ways in which contextual conditions affect the corporation. Wright and Sylla argue that the early nineteenth-century American legal environment was directly linked to the very high rates of incorporation that they document. Companies could be started—and draw investment capital—because articles of incorporation could include voting practices and other modes of shareholder participation necessary to overcome agency concerns. Moreover, shareholders used these tools, sometimes electing new directors or investigating accounting practices, in the face of questionable dealings.

Armour and Cheffins investigate the incidence of offensive shareholder activism—investors taking significant stakes in underperforming companies with the intention of pushing for change—in the first half of the twentieth century. They argue that the conditions of the market meant that this tactic was not nearly as common as it is today and served different purposes. Specifically, this type of shareholder activism was a competitive tool of firms seeking to control companies in their own sector. By considering the distinctive aspects of the market for corporate control in that earlier era, the authors offer evidence for the more general point that the intricacies of institutional design cannot be examined in a vacuum.

This volume expands the range of variables to be considered in thinking about the efficacy of shareholder protection measures. The Venetian system, for example, hinged on the security afforded to merchants participating in state-protected trading convoys. As González de Lara points out in Chapter 5, had the naval security offered by the state been less effective, the incentive for businessmen to accept the governance arrangements required to participate might have been insufficient.

Adjustments to the corporate governance model introduced to avoid the principal-agent pitfalls embedded within the corporation are therefore accompanied by their own attendant complexities. These unintended consequences of shareholder advocacy and other governance features (e.g., abusive lawsuits, resistance to investments, greenmail) are introduced in each chapter, another connective tissue linking together these studies of very different eras.

SUMMARIES OF CHAPTERS

In the summaries of the chapters that follow, one gets a clear sense that the strands identified in this introductory chapter indeed cut across the various contributions. The chapters are organized into three sections. The first section, in keeping with the inspiration of the collection, has the Dutch East India Company as the object of analysis. The second section includes, a set of chapter looks more broadly at the particular problems of financing early international trade and the solutions offered by the corporate form. And finally, the third section includes chapters on the institutions of industrialization, including an insightful analysis of a fourtheenth century mill company in Toulouse and two chapters dealing with the early modern era and the emergence of contemporary practices of shareholder participation in the United States. In the concluding chapter, Stephen Davis connects the observations from these contributors to the contemporary debates over shareholder advocacy, particularly in the United States.

I. Dutch East India Company and the Shareholder as Aggrieved Party

The Dutch East India Company is widely regarded as the first modern corporation in the sense that it had a permanent capital base. The three contributions in the section offer new understanding of the company by explicating the governance context in which the Le Maire controversy took place, examining later conflict between directors and shareholders, and finally offering a new interpretation of the VOC's genesis, seeing in its origins not the seeds of good governance but rather something quite different.

"An Admiralty for Asia: Business Organization and the Evolution of Corporate Governance in the Dutch Republic, 1590–1640"
In Chapter 2, Oscar Gelderblom, Abe de Jong, and Joost Jonker provide much-needed contextual analysis to help better understand and interpret the significance of Isaac Le Maire's letter to Johan van Oldenbarnevelt of January 24, 1609. Widely recognized as the world's first joint-stock company, shares of the Dutch East India Company were actively traded and security ownership was dispersed over a broad and varied set of participants. Le Maire's pioneering shareholder activism was one of many events marking the evolution of corporate during the Golden Age of the Dutch Republic.

Business organization saw major innovations in the shape of the two intercontinental trading companies VOC (1602) and Dutch West India Company (WIC) (1621) and a few other, smaller, companies. The ways in which these companies were governed inspired vigorous debates over principles of corporate governance, first in 1609–1610, then during the early 1620s, and again during the 1640s. These early debates over the governance in joint-stock companies, and particularly the role of shareholders vis-à-vis the directors, provide interesting insights into the origins of shareholder rights and advocacy as well as into broader public debate and responses by directors and legislative bodies.

This chapter explores the issues raised in the seventeenth-century debates, and the extent to which they are still debated today, while delving deeply into the key court decisions concerning corporate governance. The authors connect the debate over the rights of VOC shareholders to the evolution of business organization, exploring whether the VOC controversies can be directly linked to this development. This analysis focuses on two major waves of joint-stock formation in the Dutch Republic: first, the creation of the Nordic, New Netherlands, and West-India Companies in 1612, 1614, and 1621, respectively, and then the 40-odd local companies that were launched during the 1720 stock market bubble in the Dutch Republic. The second part of this chapter uses records of Holland's High Court to consider the content of corporate governance questions before the court, the court's verdicts, and the impact of these decisions on corporate governance in Holland.

"Shareholder Activists Avant La Lettre: The "Complaining
Participants" in the Dutch East India Company, 1622–1625"
In Chapter 3, Johan Matthijs de Jongh focuses on a conflict between VOC shareholders and directors that arose more than ten years after the Le Maire fight, when the company's charter was extended in 1622. De Jongh traces the lack of shareholder rights in early corporations to their origins as "pre-companies" created to finance individual expeditions to the East Indies between 1594 and 1602. After each trip goods were sold, profits distributed to shareholders, and the company dissolved. Shareholders could not exercise control—the ships were at sea for most of the company's corporate existence—and since their capital was needed to finance the next trip, their interests could not be ignored.

Although the absence of shareholder control rights carried over to the VOC, the longer expected life introduced serious agency conflicts, explaining the various clashes that arose between the directors and the shareholders between 1602 and 1623. In 1622, when it came time to extend the 1602 Charter, the so called *dolerende participanten* (complaining participants or dissenting shareholders) accused the directors of abuses of power, including short-selling schemes and corrupt self-dealing. In published pamphlets that constitute the heart of this chapter, shareholders tried to mobilize public opinion, convince merchants not to invest in the VOC, and compel the government to guarantee more rights for VOC shareholders. They argued that shareholder approval was required for the VOC to borrow in capital markets and that large investors were entitled to vote on the appointment of new directors. They supported their arguments by referring to the corporate governance systems in the English East India Company and in the Dutch West India Company (incorporated at the same time).

This activism did result in charter revision, granting large investors the right to nominate director candidates and adding regulation of trading between the directors as well as a yearly dividend. In addition, a committee of nine shareholders was entrusted with overseeing the VOC directors. Known as the "Nine Gentlemen" (Heren IX), this supervisory body likely influenced the development of the two-tier board structure common in continental Europe.

"The Great Expropriation: Interpreting the Innovation of "Permanent Capital" at the Dutch East India Company"

The Dutch East India Company's transformation from a terminable to a permanent capital base has been seen as an important innovation in the development of the modern corporation, facilitating long-term specific investment. In Chapter 4, Andrew von Nordenflycht notes the dissonance of this observation with current research linking financial development to protection of outside investors. After all, the innovation at the heart of the VOC was achieved through a government-supported *expropriation* of outside shareholders. He suggests a new way to interpret this seminal episode in corporate development. While it did help the Dutch government achieve its political and economic goals of establishing a dominant position in Asia, it also entailed some downsides, partly in difficulties raising equity investment in additional national monopolies but especially in solidifying the Dutch East India Company as an exemplar of entrenchment and the political persistence of inefficient economic institutions. By contrast, the English East India Company developed permanent capital in a more investor-friendly way, without requiring a government expropriation, albeit in a longer time frame. Thus, while the Dutch East India Company's permanent capital bestowed an initial advantage, its coerced birth is consistent with the view that the

Company was an anomaly, rather than a direct ancestor of the public corporation. The English Company's evolution may have been the more important innovation for the development of the modern corporation.

II. Overcoming the Agency Challenge of Early Global Trade

"Institutions, Information, and Contracts: The Protection of Investor Rights in Late-Medieval Venice"

In late medieval Venice, the transition from the sea loan to the better risk-sharing *commenda* "contributed greatly to the fast growth of maritime trade" (Lopez 1976, 76), but this shift created a danger that investors' profits would be diverted by merchants. In Chapter 5, Yadira González de Lara explores this important transition from debt to equity. She finds that increased state regulation of trading voyages in a manner that facilitated the ex post verification of merchants' accounts enabled investors to present evidence in support of their claims to the courts and thus fostered the development of equity markets. Specifically, since about 1180, colonial governors progressively oversaw custom duties; administered warehouses and lodging facilities; enforced the use of Venetian measures, weights, and coins; and kept public records of various monopsony prices. In Venice, public brokers further registered all legal commodity sales by 1225. In addition, the Maritime Statutes of 1229, which codified the prevailing customs, required that a semipublic scribe register the number, weight, and owner of any merchandise loaded and unloaded in a ship. The ship's captain was made responsible for the merchandise registered with the scribe.

This explanation for the switch in contractual forms is novel in various respects. First, since the transition from the sea loan to the *commenda* was a widespread phenomenon, occurring under plausibly different institutional regimes in Barcelona, Genoa, Marseille, Venice, and most other Mediterranean localities, it is intuitive to attribute it to exogenous technological and/or information-related changes (Lane 1966; Lopez 1976; Williamson 2002). Yet, the evidence suggests that in late medieval Venice, contracts were shaped by endogenous institutional factors. Second, the Venetian institutional system seems to have differed from the private-order institutions highlighted by Greif [e.g., 2006] and others (e.g., Rosenberg and Birdzell, 1986) as having surmounted various contractual problems during this period of time. It appears that financial relations were largely enforced by the state and that private parties did not engage in informal monitoring of merchants themselves. On the contrary, colonial governors, public brokers, and ship scribes came to monitor trading ventures in all their phases, thereby generating and transmitting the information required to verify merchants' accounts. This account is consistent with literature postulating that legal rules and enforcement are essential parts of a broad system of corporate finance (e.g., La Porta et al. 1997, 1998). Like Lerner and Schoar (2005), it recognizes how the legal system constrains the ability of private parties to write contracts that are complex and state contingent, but it emphasizes the role of the state as an information-generation mechanism. The extent to which formal monitoring shapes the structure and performance of (equity) markets both in the past and today is thus highlighted.

"Shareholder Activism in the Virginia Company of London, 1606–1624"

Thomas Hall offers in Chapter 6 a case study of early shareholder advocacy, and its consequences, in the VCL. After explicating the initial development of the company, including its institutional structure, governance, and history, he focuses on two important episodes of substantial shareholder activism: first, the successful effort led by Sir Edwin Sandys to remove the firm's CEO ("treasurer") Sir Thomas Smith during 1618–1619, and second, the eventual counterreaction against Sandy's gross mismanagement that led to the dissolution of the firm in 1624.

Several dysfunctional corporate governance features of the VCL are analyzed and linked to the firm's poor performance and ultimate collapse. These include (1) various forms of managerial shirking and diversion such as the creation of a carve-out firm ("magazine") that resupplied the colony and diverted profits from the VCL, (2) the rule of one-shareholder-one-vote that created a wedge between control and cash-flow rights, (3) the ability of the ruling clique to deny the vote at shareholder meetings ("courts") to members of the opposing faction in the post-1618 period, and (4) misrepresentation by management to shareholders, including the brazen willingness of Sandys to conceal the horrific conditions in Virginia that resulted in large part from his malfeasance.

Using surviving (though incomplete) data on individual shareholders and their stakes, the chapter assesses the importance of shareholder motivation and the VCL's effect on subsequent joint-stock companies and its importance for reconsiderations of corporate governance. Attention is focused on the implications of the separation of control and cash-flow rights, the difficulties associated with dual public/private management, and the importance of how investor identity and a multitude of motivations can lead to dysfunctional corporate governance.

"Shareholders' Rights in the Early Italian Companies: Agency Problems and Legal Strategies"

The French Code de Commerce of 1807 is often treated as the starting point in the discussion of Italian corporate governance and the focus is generally on the family-dominated ownership structure that has characterized the country for the last 150 years (Aganin and Volpin 2005). In Chapter 7, Corrado Malberti argues that this convention overlooks the rich and varied pre-Italian history of corporations in the states that would be unified as "Italy" in 1865. Not only were companies influenced by the legal and economic situations of the pre-unitary states, they displayed significant common traits inspired by the well-known models of the Dutch and English East India companies. This chapter explores two different dimensions of the relationship between shareholders and directors in these early Italian companies on the basis of an original empirical examination of more than 100 corporate charters, dating from 1638 (the first known case of Italian public company) to 1808.

Malberti first assesses the balance of power between directors and shareholders to determine whether this relationship is best characterized as a dynamic interaction between (a) dispersed investors and managing shareholders, (b) dispersed investors and powerful managers, (c) concentrated investors and managing shareholders, (d) concentrated investors and powerful managers, or (e) majority and minority shareholders. The role of other constituencies in these early business entities is also investigated. Second, the agency problem between directors and shareholders is considered with emphasis on the governance tools provided by the charters of the early Italian companies (e.g., directors' constraints, rules, and standards), affiliation terms (entry and exit), appointment rights (selection and removal), decision rights (initiation and veto), and incentives (trusteeship and reward). This analysis offers a better understanding of the different managing and monitoring powers granted to shareholders and directors in the first Italian public companies. It is argued that, even at the beginning of the Italian "Società Anonima," the balance of powers between the different constituencies of business entities varied as a function of a company's shareholding structure. This provides insights on the current debate over the determinants of governance structures, on the potential and limits of legal transplants in company law, and on the current proposal to increase shareholders powers.

"Compagnie des Indes: Governance and Bailout"
In Chapter 8, Reza Dibadj considers the governance of the French Compagnie des Indes (Compagnie), aka the French East India Company, during two phases between 1763 and 1770. Two aspects of shareholder participation in the company are emphasized: first, the ongoing conflict between shareholders and managers; second, the tension between shareholders and state interest. The first phase, from the end of the Seven Years War in 1763 lasting until 1769, has direct parallels to today's important debates over shareholder advocacy. During this time, the shareholders of the Compagnie were pitted against insiders—notably, directors and syndics (managing agents)—for control of the company. As just one example, the shareholder advocates were deeply concerned about the money and perquisites the Compagnie's insiders had arrogated to themselves. Much is to be learned from the Compagnie's successes and mistakes, not to mention the colorful protagonists in the Compagnie's drama—Morellet, de Mairobert, and Necker, to name just a few.

The second phase, from 1769 until 1770 when the Compagnie was liquidated, is more unusual but equally enlightening. The French Controller-General sought to withdraw the Compagnie's monopolistic license and liquidate its assets, thereby allowing other players to compete on France's overseas trade routes. Debate regarding the policy-motivated state support for the Compagnie foreshadows today's struggle to determine how governments should support failed corporations, notably financial institutions in the current crisis. And the debate as to whether today's banks are "too big to fail" also echoes eighteenth-century France. Some argued that the Compagnie needed to be subsidized given its importance to France's strategic objectives; others, that the state should not be propping up a failing monopoly. More generally, the saga at the Compagnie broaches the broad issue of how government needs to manage the complex relationship between individuals as profit-maximizing shareholders and individuals as citizens who should be concerned with the greater good.

"The Rise and Fall of the Rishengchang Bank Model: Limiting Shareholder Influence to Attract Capital"
In Chapter 9, Randall Morck and Fan Yang offer a unique look at the national branch banking system developed in China during the

Qing dynasty. During the nineteenth century, these so-called native banks developed branch networks to provide traveling merchants, based in the inland province of Shanxi, with cash transfers in distant and often dangerous regions. Improbably this made the remote inland province China's paramount banking center of the time. The first and largest Shanxi bank, the Rising Sun Bank, developed unique corporate governance and contract enforcement systems that let it, and its imitators, flourish in a corrupt and essentially lawless commercial environment.

China's almost complete isolation from foreign influence at the time has led historians to posit a Chinese invention of modern banking. However, Shanxi merchants ran a tea trade north into Siberia, traveled to Moscow and St. Petersburg, and may well have observed Western banking there. Nonetheless, the Shanxi banks were unique. Some of the tools the bank used, such as making itself indispensable to the ruling elite, are well understood, but others are unique. Its corporate governance system entailed multiple classes of shares, with carefully structured voting rights for executive and nonexecutive investors. Nonexecutive investors, including the founding family, had voting rights to appoint new executives, but not over other business decisions, and perpetual dividend rights. Insider's shares had the same dividend plus votes in meetings advising the general manager on lending or other business decisions, and were swapped upon death or retirement for a third inheritable nonvoting equity class, dead shares, with a fixed expiry date. Augmented by contracts permitting the enslavement of insiders' wives and children, and their relatives' services as hostages, these governance mechanisms prevented insider fraud and propelled the banks to empire-wide dominance. Modern civil libertarians might question some of these governance innovations, but others provide lessons to modern corporations, regulators, and lawmakers.

III. Shareholder Rights and the Growth of Industrial Economies

A Shareholder Lawsuit in Fourteenth-Century Toulouse
The mills of Toulouse were organized as companies from at least the twelfth century, and the shareholders who owned them delegated operational and financial decisions to elected agents. In Chapter 10, William N. Goetzmann and Sebastien Pouget examine court records from a shareholder suit in the fourteenth century—centuries before Isaac Le Maire would rage against injustice—that suggests investors

sought to constrain management's ability to encumber the firm with debt.

An institutional solution to this problem appears to have been the development of a board of advisors who were empowered to approve major firm actions. These advisors also approved accounts and payments by the treasurer. Although the Toulouse mill companies persisted into the twentieth century as a consolidated public company called the Société Toulousaine du Bazacle, few historians regard it as a precursor to the modern corporation. Thus the distinctly modern issues of corporate control elucidated by this late medieval episode may suggest that institutional solutions to the problems of agency may arise spontaneously.

"Corporate Governance and Stockholder/Stakeholder Activism in the United States, 1790–1860: New Data and Perspectives"

By the early nineteenth century, the United States was home to more business corporations and more corporate capital than any other nation on earth. In Chapter 11, Robert E. Wright and Richard Sylla rely upon an original database that includes (almost) every business corporation chartered by U.S. state governments between 1790 and 1860. Contrary to assertions that an era of shareholder "democracy" gave way to "plutocracy," Wright and Sylla find that few corporate charters specified one vote for each shareholder. Rather, they typically specified one vote per share or stipulated some sort of "prudent mean" rule of graduated voting rights designed to empower small shareholders by limiting the voting rights of large blockholders.

The sheer numbers of pre-1860 U.S. corporations, tens of thousands as compared with tens or at most hundreds in other nations at the time, lead the authors to question recent claims that the American corporate form was less flexible than organizational forms offered to enterprises in Germany, France, and the United Kingdom. Corporate charters in the United States could be customized and (amended if need be) to advance the interests of the corporation, its shareholders, other stakeholders, and the state itself. Charter renewals and amendments allowed corporations to change, for example, their names, their number of directors, the amount of capital authorized and paid in, and their permissible range of activities. The state as stakeholder could use charters, charter renewals, and charter amendments to take an ownership stake in the corporation, set limits to corporate authority, change governance procedures, and obligate the corporation to extend financial and other forms of support to the state or its designees.

This chapter complements data analysis with examples of early U.S. corporate governance drawn from extensive archival research. Episodes of both quotidian and crisis-period corporate governance illuminate the quantitative results, and suggest that stockholder and stakeholder activism remained strong throughout the antebellum era. Records of securities prices allow the authors to show that early U.S. stockholders took advantage of the young nation's liquid securities markets to "vote with their feet," but often only after exhausting other options, including attempting to elect new directors and forming stockholder commissions to examine account books and corporate operations. Of course, companies sometimes failed due to governance shortcomings (e.g., insider expropriation of assets) but the U.S. corporate system appears to have worked fairly well with limited ongoing government supervision. Indeed, Wright and Sylla suggest that early leadership in developing and extending the corporate form of business organization was a key ingredient in the United States' differentially high rate of economic growth after 1790 (compared with earlier eras in American history and other leading nations).

"Origins of 'Offensive' Shareholder Activism in the United States"
In Chapter 12, John H. Armour and Brian R. Cheffins provide some historical context to better understand the shareholder activism of hedge funds, a major corporate governance phenomenon of the last few years. This recent wave of shareholder insurgency can be distinguished from the sort of activism in which traditional institutional investors engage, the authors argue, because it is "offensive" in nature; the hedge funds build up a stake in a company with the explicit goal of agitating for change.

Corporate governance analysts have yet to put this recent wave of shareholder insurgency in its proper analytical context, thus obscuring the factors that have influenced its emergence and hindering prediction of future trends. By examining the pattern of offensive shareholder activism in the United States before 1950, Armour and Cheffins try to identify the variables influencing the prevalence of offensive activism, using "the market for corporate influence" as a heuristic device to do so. They show that the motives of early activists differed from their contemporary cousins, reflecting their own firms' strategic objectives rather than an intention to "turn around" underperforming companies.

Contemporary issues in Shareholder Advocacy
In this concluding chapter, Stephen Davis looks at contemporary proposals to reform corporate governance—specifically to increase the

influence of shareholders—that have arisen in the wake of the financial crisis. While making the case for a historical study of corporate governance as a field of inquiry, he links the insights gained from the included chapters to the initiatives currently being considered in the U.S. Congress and around the world.

REFERENCES

Aganin, Alexander, and Volpin, Paolo. 2005. "The History of Corporate Ownership in Italy." In *A History of Corporate Governance Around the World: Family Business Groups to Professional Managers,* ed. R. Morck. Chicago: University of Chicago Press.

Anabtawi, Iman. 2005. "Some Skepticism about Increasing Shareholder Power." *UCLA Law Review* 53: 561.

Bebchuk, Lucian A. 2007. "The Myth of the Shareholder Franchise." *Virginia Law Review* 93 (3): 675–732.

Bebchuk, Lucian Arye. 2005. "The Case for Increasing Shareholder Power." *Harvard Law Review* 118 (3): 833–914.

Becht, Marco, Franks, Julian, Mayer, Colin, and Rossi, Stefano. 2008. "Returns to Shareholder Activism: Evidence from a Clinical Study of the Hermes UK Focus Fund." *Review of Financial Studies* 22 (8): 3093–3129.

Blair, Margaret M., and Stout, Lynn A. 1999. "Team Production in Business Organizations: An Introduction." *Journal of Corporate Law* 24 (V): 743–50.

Chinn, Menzie D., and Ito, Hiro. 2006. "What Matters for Financial Development? Capital Controls, Institutions, and Interactions." *Journal of Development Economics* 81 (1): 163–92.

Clark, Robert Charles. 1986. *Corporate Law.* Boston: Little, Brown.

Davis, Gerald. 2009. *Corporate Governance and the Financial Crisis* 2009 [cited November 28, 2009]. Available from http://webuser.bus.umich.edu/gfdavis/Presentations/Davis_Aspen_governance.pdf.

Dunlavy, Colleen A. 2006. "Social Conceptions of the Corporation: Insights from the History of Shareholder Voting Rights." *Washington & Lee Law Review* 63: 1347.

Fama, Eugene F. 1980. "Agency Problems and the Theory of the Firm." *Journal of Political Economy* 88 (2): 288.

Garen, John E. 1994. "Executive Compensation and Principal-Agent Theory." *The Journal of Political Economy* 102 (6): 1175–99.

Jensen, Michael C., and Meckling, William H. 1976. "Theory of the Firm: Managerial Behavior, Agency Costs and Ownership Structure." *Journal of Financial Economics* 3 (4): 305–60.

King, Neil Jr. 2009. "Politicians Butt In at Bailed-Out GM." *Wall Street Journal* A1.

Kingdon, John W. 2003. *Agendas, Alternatives, and Public Policies.* 2nd ed. New York: Longman.

Kirkpatrick, Grant. 2009. *The Corporate Governance Lessons from the Financial Crisis.* Paris: OECD.

La Porta, Rafael, Lopez-de-Silanes, Florencio, Shleifer, Andrei, and Vishny, Robert. 2000. "Investor Protection and Corporate Governance." *Journal of Financial Economics* 58 (1–2): 3–27.

Lipton, Martin, and Savitt, William. 2007. "The Many Myths of Lucian Bebchuk." *Virginia Law Review* 93 (3): 733–58.

Macey, Jonathan R. 2007. "Too Many Notes and Not Enough Votes: Lucian Bebchuk and Emperor Joseph II Kvetch about Contested Director Elections and Mozart's 'Seraglio.' " *Virginia Law Review* 93 (3): 759–72.

McCahery, Joseph A., and Vermeulen, Erik P. M. 2005. "Corporate Governance Crises and Related Party Transactions: A Post-Parmalat Agenda." In *Corporate Governance in Context Corporations, States, and Markets in Europe, Japan, and the US,* ed. K. J. Hopt, E. Wymeersch, H. Kanda and H. Baum. London: Oxford University Press.

Morck, Randall. 2005. *A History of Corporate Governance Around the World: Family Business Groups to Professional Managers.* Chicago: University of Chicago Press.

Shorter, Gary. 2009. *"Say on Pay" and Other Corporate Governance Reform Initiatives.* Washington, D.C.: Congressional Research Service.

PART I

THE DUTCH EAST INDIA COMPANY AND THE SHAREHOLDER AS AGGRIEVED PARTY

CHAPTER 2

AN ADMIRALTY FOR ASIA: BUSINESS ORGANIZATION AND THE EVOLUTION OF CORPORATE GOVERNANCE IN THE DUTCH REPUBLIC, 1590–1640

Oscar Gelderblom, Abe de Jong, and Joost Jonker

Isaac le Maire and conflicting conceptions about the corporate governance of the VOC[1]

INTRODUCTION

The Dutch East India Company (VOC) in 1602 showed many characteristics of modern corporations, including limited liability, freely transferable shares, and well-defined managerial functions. However, we challenge the notion of the VOC as the precursor of modern corporations to argue that the company was a hybrid, combining elements from traditional partnerships with a governance structure modeled on existing public-private partnerships. The company's charter reflected this hybrid structure in the preeminent position given to the Estates General as the VOC's main principal, to the detriment of shareholders' interests. Protests by Isaac le Maire and Willem Usselinx about the board's disregard for shareholders were rooted in a conviction that it ought to conform to traditional partnerships with their judicious balance between stakeholders' interests.

However, the perceived public interest of a strong military presence in Asia prevented shareholders' protests from changing the corporate governance.

The Dutch Republic's successful Asian trade during the seventeenth century is often considered a direct result of the creation, in 1602, of the Dutch East India Company with a permanent capital, freely transferable shares, a separation of ownership and management, the shielding of corporate assets from creditors, and a limited liability for shareholders and directors (van Brakel 1908, 1912; van der Heijden 1908; Den Heijer 2005; Gaastra 2009). These features enabled the company to set up permanent trading posts for administration, storage, and ships' maintenance; to coordinate the activities of employees working in a variety of locations; and to mobilize the resources for establishing a strong military presence in Asia. The long-lasting, capital-intensive commercial enterprise thus created and the huge profits it generated for most of its existence have led economic and legal historians to consider the governance structure of this company a necessary precondition for its economic success, and an important step in the evolution of the modern corporation.

During the early years, however, the company's policy and corporate governance attracted sharp criticism from shareholders. Within a few years a number of leading shareholders left the board because of disagreements over the direction of operations. In 1609 Isaac le Maire sent a long memo to the Republic's highest civil servant, Grand Pensionary Johan van Oldenbarnevelt, complaining about the board's highhanded and misguided policy.[2] Subsequently Le Maire attempted to force the board to change tack by launching his famous bear raid on VOC shares (van Dillen 1930). The debate over the formation of an Atlantic trade company, the West-Indische Compagnie (WIC), also shows a keen awareness that its corporate governance structure should be fundamentally different from that of the VOC. Indeed, the main advocate for a WIC, Willem Usselinx, hammered time and again on the need to give shareholders power over the companies they owned (van Rees 1868). Finally, during the 1620s disgruntled shareholders fought hard to get more power over policy, ultimately in vain (van Rees 1868, 144–172).

In this chapter, we want to take a fresh look at the supposed character of the VOC as a pioneering joint-stock limited liability company (*naamloze vennootschap* or NV in Dutch). Paul Frentrop's book already did important groundwork for this, but he took the foundation of the VOC in 1602 as his point of departure, whereas, to gain perspective, we would want to know what went on before and connect this with what came later (Frentrop 2003). Traditionally, the historiography of Dutch corporate development regards the VOC as the first example of an NV and sees this form of organization as crucial to the company's economic success. Scholars broadly agree about the legal pedigree of the VOC. The company was essentially a private partnership with additional features, such as the limited liability for directors and for shareholders derived from various older forms of business organization (van Brakel 1908, 1912, 1914, 1917; van der Heijden 1908, 1914; Steensgaard 1982; Asser 1983; De Vries and van der Woude 1997; Den Heijer 2005, 35–36; see however Lehmann 1895 and Mansvelt 1922). However, opinions differ as to the precise evolutionary path, that is, which feature emerged why, when, and whence, and about origins, motivations, and evolutions of particular features, such as limited liability.[3]

Moreover, we think that by looking at the relationship between agents and various principals within the company we can clear up the reigning confusion as to the provenance of these governance features, that is, where exactly the VOC fits in the evolutionary path of Dutch corporate law. The notion of agency dates at least back to Michael C. Jensen and William H. Mecking (1976), in which firms are described as "nexus of contracts." The agency literature models contracting and agency costs under assumptions of asymmetric information and divergent interests (an overview in Becht, Bolton and Röell 2003). Analyzing the VOC from this perspective gives us a better understanding of where exactly the VOC fits in the evolutionary path of Dutch corporate law.

Our analysis shows that the corporate governance norms that Le Maire and Usselinx wanted applied were common in other business organizations, such as the partnerships with additional features. The VOC deviated from these norms because of its essentially hybrid character as a private corporation entrusted with a public task, that is, taking the war against Spain overseas by establishing a colonial empire in Asia (van Brakel 1908, 20–22; van Rees 1868, 20–29; Steensgaard 1982, 244–247, Israel 1989, 70–72; De Vries and van der Woude 1997, 384–386; van Goor 2002; Den Heijer 2005, 67–68). This aim inspired a governance structure modeled on semipublic institutions such as the local admiralty boards, which coordinated the activities of the Dutch navy from the late sixteenth century onward; the water boards, which managed dikes and drainage; and the polder boards, which ran land reclamation projects (Fockema Andreae 1975, 26–30, 49–50, 114–116, 125, 139–140, 142; van Zwet 2009, 55–58, 76–84). Company directors therefore really faced two principals: the shareholders and the Estates General, the highest political institution in the Dutch Republic. With the investors' capital tied up for ten years and local elites dominating the general board of directors, the Estates General quickly emerged as the main principal. As a result, corporate governance features common at the time and common in modern corporations were sacrificed for political aims. Commercially oriented shareholders vilified the company's policy, but they were no match for the war-party with its control of the general board and direct access to the Estates General.

THE STRETCH OF TRADITIONAL PARTNERSHIPS

During the second half of the sixteenth century, merchants in Britain and the Habsburg Netherlands began to explore new markets in Russia, the Eastern Mediterranean, and the coast of West Africa. These ventures carried considerable risk because of violence at sea, stark fluctuations in supply and demand, and the difficult monitoring of partners and employees trading in the distant markets. To manage these risks, British and Dutch merchants amended existing partnership contracts with additional clauses about the purpose and duration of the venture, the capital invested by the partners, the division of work between them, and, for those who contributed labor rather than capital, their share in profits and losses. The earliest British trade with Guinea, for instance, was organized as temporary partnerships, which arranged a number of voyages counting two to five ships between 1553 and 1567. Upon their return, accounts were drawn up and any profits split as agreed in the contract (Scott 1968, 3–9). The Flemish merchants pioneering Antwerp's trade with Narva during the 1560s also set up temporary partnerships with a small number of participants. The duration of and the capital invested in these companies increased with the familiarity between the partners, but even close relatives apparently preferred contracts for a limited time period with a clearly defined purpose (Denucé 1938, xxii–xxvii; Brulez 1959, 363–365, 557–558; Wijnroks 2003, 65–105).

Specific-purpose partnerships, *compagnia* in Italian parlance, were ideally suited to fund commercial expeditions to poorly known destinations (Lazzareschi 1947, 11–13; Lopez and Raymond 1955, 175, 291; De Roover 1963, 139–140, 260–261; Lopez 1971, 74; Hunt 1994).[4] They could be established by private contract and, in its most restrictive form, comprised a single voyage only. Just like general partnerships, the partners in a *compagnia* remained severally and jointly liable for each others' actions as long as these actions were in accordance with the purpose and duration of the company contract (De Roover 1963, 142, 145). This emendation of the general partnership's rules had become accepted practice in Antwerp as early as

1537, for an accounting manual published in that year stated that "there is no difference between the rule of a partnership with specified duration (*metter tyt*) and without specified duration (*sonder tyt*), except that shares are taken for a certain period, and the revenue is calculated according to this share" (vanden Hoecke 1537, quoted in Goris 1925, 105n).

Partnerships also split tasks, for instance, when the partners were separated by distance, when they employed an agent elsewhere, or when the collaboration was just a sideline for one or more partners (Nanninga Uitterdijk 1904, 529; van Brakel 1912, 1914, 1917; Brulez 1959, 366–368). Merchants commonly had constantly shifting partnerships—some short term and for particular purposes, such as a single voyage or the joint handling of a cargo load, others for longer terms and broader purposes, say the trade in one commodity with a particular country. To minimize internal control problems arising from the division of labor, merchants used a range of solutions drawn from experience. Remuneration schemes were jigged to provide incentives, while partnership contracts stipulated the obligations of partners-managers toward the joint enterprise in broad terms, referring to a general obligation to manage a business and its administration in good faith, with due diligence, and in conformity with the usage of merchants. During the second half of the sixteenth century a very important form of limited liability developed for partnerships, in that principals could claim not to be liable for obligations that agents had incurred outside the partnership's purpose (van Brakel 1908, 161–170; van der Heijden 1908, 50–56; van Brakel 1914, 168–169; Riemersma 1952, 335–337; Asser 1983, 88–89, 95–103, 115–119).

Partnership contracts were enforced by customary law and mercantile usage. One key custom was the requirement for proper account keeping coupled to the acceptance of ledgers, account books, and supporting documentation such as bills, account extracts, and correspondence as legal proof in litigation (Gelderblom 2011). The status of legal proof made archives valuable, so contemporary depictions of merchant offices always show voluminous archives. The gradual adoption of double-entry bookkeeping, facilitated by the publishing of practical handbooks such as the manuals of Jan Ympyn (Antwerp 1543) and Claes Pietersz (Amsterdam 1576), made business accounts far more transparent and thus easier to check (Jonker and Sluyterman 2000, 18; Gelderblom 2011). Proper account keeping provided the basis for other self-evident norms. Business partners had full access to all documents at all times plus a mutual obligation to draw up comprehensive annual accounts. Such annual reckoning was so normal that contracts only mentioned exceptions, for instance, the settling of accounts after the liquidation of a shipping expedition of uncertain length, or after the number of years a particular venture would run (De Jonge 1862, 97 article 24; van Brakel 1914, 165, 179, 182–183, 184–185). Similarly, merchants keeping current accounts with each other customarily exchanged account extracts for approval.

At this stage, rulers in Britain and the Netherlands maintained some distance to new commercial ventures. Philip II left the Antwerp companies to their own devices as long as they did not harm the Spanish monopoly in the Americas. Nothing changed in 1577 when Calvinists took control of Antwerp's magistrate. In Britain, Queen Elizabeth did contribute ships to the first African voyages but her participation was considered no different from that of other investors. She also granted a corporate charter to the Muscovy Company in 1555 so its members could negotiate privileges in Russia. This did not alter the company's financial organization. The merchants continued to organize separate voyages liquidated on return. In 1581 this model was transplanted to the Mediterranean trade with the merger of the Levant Company and the Venice Company. Despite earning fees from incorporation, the Crown did not renew the Levant Company's charter. By 1592 the company functioned as a licensing agency that merely coordinated the protection of private trade (Scott 1968 II, 88).

Until the 1580s merchants in Holland had largely concentrated on trade between the Baltic and France, Spain, and Portugal. This trade was organized by individual merchants, small family partnerships, and shipping companies or *partenrederijen*. It is tempting to view these shipping companies as a distinct legal entity, but the term *partenrederij* is a nineteenth-century invention. The underlying contract was a partnership with a specific purpose, in this case the exploitation of a ship, and particular only in the arithmetical division of shares (1/2, 1/4, 1/8, etc.). The accounts of shipping companies were settled after a specific trip or after a trading season, following which participants were free to reinvest or not. As with all specific-purpose partnerships, the partners were jointly and severally liable for debts related to the purpose of the company, with one key exception. Any loss of cargo would be spread over all freight owners, while a total loss of the ship would free all shipping partners from any remaining claims on the company.[5] These two features of shipping companies appear to have been quite general in European maritime law, but in addition Dutch shipping partners enjoyed a particular form of limited liability. If the company faced claims exceeding the value of their investment, the partners could free themselves from having to pay the excess amount by abandoning their share. Participants in land reclamation ventures had the same right (Dekker and Baetens 2009, 65).

Following the fall of Antwerp in 1585, Amsterdam emerged as the new long-distance trade centre in the Low Countries. Antwerp merchants migrated north and continued their trade with Russia, the Levant, and Africa from the Dutch port. The Russia trade continued to be dominated by Antwerp firms, and the earliest voyages to Genoa and Venice in the 1590s were also organized by Flemish companies. Merchants in the long-distance trade were mostly left to their own devices, but to support the Levant trade the government sometimes supplied arms to individual ships, and it negotiated commercial privileges with the Ottoman sultan. The same was true for the Atlantic world. The early sugar expeditions to the Canaries, Madeira, and Brazil and the first voyages to West Africa were run by special-purpose partnerships, and the salt trade to the coast of Venezuela was done by shipping companies (Gelderblom 2000, 179–181; van Goor 2002, 18–23). Between 1593 and 1598 at least 30 ships sailed to West Africa from Amsterdam, Enkhuizen, Hoorn, Rotterdam, Middelburg, and Delft (van Goor 2002, 22; Den Heijer 2005, 31).

Surviving accounts reveal that investments in the African trade were typically made for one voyage, with the capital raised in advance and spent on the ship, its equipment, crew, armament, and merchandise (van Gelder 1916, 208; Unger 1940). A small number of partners coordinated the expedition, for which they received a small fee. Upon the return of the ship the same men notified the other participants, sold the cargo and sometimes also the ship, and distributed the proceeds among all their fellow investors.[6] The early success of these early African companies quickly raised concerns about increasing competition. In 1598 the eight companies then trading between Amsterdam and Africa decided to merge into a General Guinea Company so as to avoid competition, as director Jacques de Velaer explained to shareholder Daniël van der Meulen (Unger 1940, 208–209). The new company maintained the governance structure of the previous companies and organized single voyages only.

These ventures were all private enterprises, with little or no government involvement. The various companies sailing to Africa armed their own ships and sailed in convoy whenever possible; government support was initially limited to naval escorts in European waters for incoming and outgoing ships (van Gelder 1916, 241).[7] Until 1598 the companies were exempt from the customs duties levied by the admiralty boards that ran the navy, but once a regular trade had been established they had to contribute. In addition to this, Prince Maurice in 1596 and 1598 secretly supported two expeditions by the Antwerp merchant Balthasar de Moucheron to establish fortified trading posts on the Principe and São Tomé off the coast of Guinea. Both attempts failed, as did an expedition equipped by the Estates General in 1599.

THE EARLY VOYAGES TO ASIA

The government played a more active role in the trade with Asia (Den Heijer 2005, 21). Three successive attempts to find a northwestern passage to Asia were backed with public money supplementing private investment (*RSG* 1593–1595, 337, May 16, 1594). Officials also supported companies exploring the ordinary route to Asia via the Cape of Good Hope. The admiralties gave ordnance on loan, sold one or two ships on favorable terms, and granted exemption from customs duties (Den Heijer 2005, 29). In addition the admiralties provided regulations for coordinating the fleet and for securing discipline on board.[8] The early companies also borrowed ordnance from various cities, with the Estates General sometimes providing guarantees.[9] The funding of the early voyages to Asia was entirely a private matter, however, and organized as special-purpose partnerships. Between 1595 and 1601 a total of 66 ships sailed from Amsterdam, Middelburg, and Rotterdam to Asia.

Small groups of merchants formed these partnerships by drawing in relatives, business associates, and, for the first expedition, the entire crew of the four ships involved, since the company withheld two months' wages as venture capital (De Jonge 1862, 97, article 24). Though canvassed by directors and presumably attracted by their business standing, subscribers were not beholden to the directors but to the partnership.[10] The success of most early companies made them attractive propositions. The Amsterdam ventures did not lose a single ship, and merchants who invested in all expeditions earned an average annual return of 27 percent, stimulating shareholders to roll their profits from one voyage into the next. As with the other long-distance ventures, the directors rendered accounts and paid out the profits after each trip, before asking investors whether they wanted to take part in a new venture.[11]

The lead merchants each had a specific task in the company, for which they were remunerated with a percentage of the value of the money and goods handled.[12] The Amsterdam *Oude Compagnie* had four committees of managers or *bewindhebbers* respectively for equipping the ships, for hiring crew members, for purchasing supplies, and for the outgoing cargo. The tasks were assigned to directors on the basis of their knowledge and skills: local merchants took care of shipping matters, and two Antwerp traders were in charge of the ships' cargo. All directors were expected to help in unloading the spices on the ships' return, and some of them were charged with storing the leftover provisions and victuals.[13]

The directors' personal credit provided a vital ingredient to the early expeditions. They paid for supplies from their own purse and charged interest on these advances, or else obtained them with suppliers' credit.[14] Once shipments had returned from Asia, rebates on cash payments for spices bought provided additional liquidity.[15] Shareholders also advanced money to their company. In November 1601 the directors of the *Verenigde Amsterdamse Compagnie* paid interest to participants who paid their installments early.[16] They also borrowed to purchase specie for sending to Asia.[17] Such credit transactions reveal the limits of the partnerships that organized the early voyages. Because the participants were jointly and severally liable for company debts, the directors preferred to use their personal credit, which curtailed the total.[18]

Only a few shareholders managed the early companies, as the directors' resolutions for the Amsterdam *Oude Compagnie* show. The book does mention a general assembly on December 7, 1598, but since the remainder of the text concerns directors' decisions, this term probably did not mean a meeting of all shareholders.[19] However, some directors appear to have been more powerful than others. The *collegie*, a committee formed by the four directors responsible for recruitment, appears to have evolved into an executive committee.[20] The other three committees each ran their own business, but could turn to the *collegie* for solving difficulties.[21] This evolution seems to have caused disagreement. Several resolutions were needed to ensure that the appointment of the expedition's commanding officer, the shipmasters, and the principal merchants would be made jointly by all directors.[22] From at least 1599 an Amsterdam magistrate, Reynier Pauw, acted as president of the *collegie,* in which position he could convene the board of directors and probably also act in public on the company's behalf.[23]

The gradual articulation of governing large partnerships was taken a step further by the First United East India Company (*Eerste Verenigde Compagnie op Oost-Indië*), formed by a merger between Amsterdam's *Oude Compagnie* and a venture run by Flemish immigrants, the *Nieuwe Compagnie,* in 1601.[24] With no fewer than 23 directors, the new company needed stronger coordination. Pauw again acted as president of the *collegie,* which now had the authority to give instructions about interest payments on shareholders' installments and about the accounts to be rendered by the subcommittees.[25]

CONSOLIDATION: THE VOC

In the long-distance trade, merchants could not concentrate on business alone; they had to organize armed protection as well and thus break the state monopoly on violence. Amsterdam enabled companies to do this by keeping a rein on them through the magistrates on their boards, very much in the style of the admiralties. With the growing military and economic importance of the Asian trade, this arm's length governing no longer sufficed. In 1597 van Oldenbarnevelt started pushing for a consolidation because the continuing competition threatened to compromise the Dutch fight against Spain and Portugal in Asia (Den Heijer 2005, 41). The companies of Middelburg and Veere followed the Amsterdam example and merged into one *Verenigde Zeeuwse Compagnie* in 1600. The idea for a merger between all the companies, first considered in 1599, then reappeared, given new momentum by the emergence of the East India Company in Britain. Like the early Dutch companies, the British company organized single voyages, or a series of two or three voyages, but always with full accounts presented upon completion. A permanent joint-stock concern was only created in 1657, tied to clear rules about the accountability of its directors (Scott 1968 II, 128–132).

Negotiations between the Dutch companies took a long time because of conflicting demands. First, the Estates General wanted the merger to secure a strong Dutch presence in Asia. The hot rivalry between the *voorcompagnieën* undermined the country's fragile political unity and economic prosperity, and seriously limited the prospects of competing successfully against other Asian traders from Europe. By attacking the Luso-Hispanic overseas empire, a large, united company would also help in the ongoing war against the Spanish Habsburgs. Initially van Oldenbarnevelt thought of no more than two or three manned strongholds (van Deventer 1862, 301), but the Estates General wanted an offensive (van Brakel 1908, 20–21). Second, the Republic's political fragmentation meant that the merger terms needed careful tailoring to vested financial and commercial interests in the various towns and provinces concerned. The solution adopted mirrored the organization of the admiralties. The company was made up of six local chambers running operations and delegating directors to a central board. Third, all merchants active in the Asian trade needed to join if the new concern's monopoly was to work, and some were loath to give up their lucrative business. Balthasar de Moucheron, for instance, even set his own terms for joining and got them, only to walk out within a year over a policy disagreement (De Jonge 1862, 267, 282–283). Fourth, the directors of existing companies sought to protect their own positions as managers of a lucrative commercial enterprise. According to Willem Usselinx, a large merchant well versed in the intercontinental trade, the VOC charter was drafted by *bewindhebbers* bent on defending their own interests and the Estates General had allowed that to pass so as to achieve the desired merger (van Rees 1868, 410). An agreement was finally reached on March 20, 1602, after which the Estates General issued a charter granting a monopoly on the Asian trade for 21 years (Gaastra 2009, 21–23).

The VOC charter is often considered a blueprint for the governance structure of the company, perhaps even the founding act of the world's first corporation with modern features such as permanent capital, entity shielding, separation of ownership and management, freely transferable shares, and limited liability. We will discuss these features in more detail soon but want to emphasize two points here. First, the VOC's corporate governance must be understood by reading the charter in tandem with the preamble to the share subscription ledgers of the company's six local chambers. The merger negotiators probably drafted this text during the negotiations, for the two surviving copies are identical (Unger 1946–1948, 13–14; van Dillen 1958, 205–206).

The charter and the preamble served very different purposes and highlight the VOC's character as a hybrid—a private commercial company with superimposed public responsibilities. Shareholders were no party to the charter; this was a contract between the directors and the Estates General. Indeed, during the 1620s conflict with shareholders, the *bewindhebbers* even claimed that they, and not shareholders or the company, owned the charter.[26] The shareholders put their name under the preamble, thereby agreeing to put their money in the company for a period of ten years and to submit to its subscription conditions, which included a detailed procedure for transferring shares. Though investors would have known the terms of the charter, from the preamble the company looked like any other special-purpose partnership, a *compagnia* established with a specific purpose for a set number of years.

Second, the financial structure as laid down by the charter did not really differ from preceding long-distance trading partnerships. The VOC's capital was not intended to be permanent, but revolving in three consecutive and separate accounts: one for the 14 ships that sailed in 1602, one for the decade starting in April 1602, and one for the period 1612–1622. Shareholders in the 1602 expedition had the right to take their money back on its return (charter article 9).[27] Shareholders in the VOC received the right to have their money back on the presentation of full accounts for the first ten-year period in 1612 (article 7). These terms were not fundamentally different from the four-year turnover time of earlier expeditions to Asia, only longer. The longer timespan was probably the reason for defining a share transfer procedure, though the speed with which share trading developed after the VOC's launch suggests that a demand for easy transferability of shares had manifested itself before (Gelderblom and Jonker 2004).

AGENCY PROBLEMS IN THE VOC CHARTER

If the preamble made the VOC look like a customary partnership, the company's charter laid down an entirely different form: a judicious compromise between, on the one hand, a partnership, and existing public bodies on the other. The company had to have some form of public status, because of its political and military aims, and its monopoly. The concept of a government department for the Asian trade similar to the Spanish Casa de India, that is, an agency licensing private expeditions and financing warfare with the license revenues, was dropped during the merger talks for reasons unknown (De Jonge 1862, 257–261).[28] Amending the customary partnership to secure official influence on private business must have appeared the logical and obvious solution. This was exactly what the admiralties, water boards, and polder boards did: providing public goods by levying duties for their use. Those boards were administered jointly by representatives from the parties concerned and officials appointed by local authorities. Similar organizations were later set up for the Baltic and Levant trades (Veluwenkamp 2000, 183; van Tielhof 2002, 232–248).

With the VOC, however, the Estates General did not put representatives on the board of directors, but chose to anchor public control in the charter (Den Heijer 2005, 50). As a result, the charter showed a heavy imbalance between the three main stakeholders: the *bewindhebbers* or shareholder-directors; the investors, that is, the shareholders and bondholders; and the state in the form of the Estates General.

Out of the 46 charter articles, 29 dealt with various aspects of corporate governance and the stakeholders' positions.[29] It stands out that the Estates General meant to keep a tight rein; after all, the VOC received suzerain rights overseas, the right to wage war and make treaties.[30] Four corporate governance clauses tied the VOC closely to the authorities at various levels. Article 6 gave the Estates General powers to overrule the *bewindhebbers* or managing directors. Under articles 15 and 16 the company had to supply data about incoming goods and about sales revenues to the provincial and city authorities if their inhabitants had supplied 50,000 guilders capital or more. If those authorities chose to appoint someone to organize share subscriptions for the company, that agent had a right to full financial information so as to keep the authorities, but not the shareholders, informed. In the end these two clauses remained dead letters. Finally, article 26 gave the right to appoint directors to the provincial Estates.

A second feature that stands out is that the charter devoted attention to the VOC shareholders in only six of the 46 articles.[31] No. 10 laid down the subscription procedure. The charter said nothing about the shareholders' right to information or a right of representation on the board, presumably because the public interest of limiting the spread of sensitive information about war and other policy considerations weighed heavier than the private interests of shareholders. As for financial information, van Oldenbarnevelt had wanted annual statements of equipment costs and product sales followed by full accounts after ten years (van Deventer 1862, 303), but the charter only gave shareholders a right to full accounts in 1612. Two articles defined exit rights. In addition to the right to sell shares stipulated in the preamble to the subscription register, shareholders were given a general exit right after the 1612 accounts (No. 7), while as we have seen the shareholders in the 1602 expedition could opt out (No. 9). Article 14 detailed some conditions for the intracompany accounts and for the statutory accounts to be presented to shareholders in 1612, and No. 17 gave shareholders a right to a dividend once the available cash reached 5 percent of capital.[32] One curious article (No. 27) stipulated that small shareholders had the same rights as big ones when it came to sharing in the company's expected benefits. This was no doubt inserted to counter the existing practice, widely decried in the late 1590s, to carve up the sale of spices between the directors (van Dillen 1930, 358–359). The charter clearly envisaged the VOC raising debt, as other private-public partnerships did, and denied the directors commission on such transactions (No. 30), but said nothing about bondholders or the priority of their claims over those of shareholders in case of bankruptcy.

Thus there existed a quite wide discrepancy between the intentions of the subscription ledger preamble and the charter, the former reflecting the customary partnership of equals, the latter creating an entirely different structure in which the heavy hand of the state left shareholders with no influence at all. The shareholders must have known both texts, but we have no indications that they saw the potential problems that this discrepancy might raise. If anything, they presumably considered the involvement of the Estates General as a boost to the new company's chances of success in enforcing its lucrative monopoly. In addition, the prevailing informal nature of relations between managers and shareholders must have allayed any fears that they would be sidelined. The business communities of Dutch towns were close knit. A 1616 play by the popular playwright Brederode portrayed a busy Amsterdam merchant running about town talking to his shareholders between closing deals (Jonker and Sluyterman 2000, 68). Backed up by the limited duration of enterprises, such informal control mechanisms had worked well enough until then, and shareholders will have thought they would continue to do so.

THE PROMINENT POSITION OF THE DIRECTORS

As we have seen, the directors' function was a fairly recent corporate innovation in need of definition. The evolution from the first expedition to Asia in 1595, organized by nine Amsterdam merchants who had styled themselves as *bewindhebbers* different from the general body of shareholders, to the emergence of the executive committees chaired by Pauw had taken only six years. The emerging differentiation does not appear to have affected contemporary conceptions about the character of the association. Though separately remunerated for their managing tasks, the *bewindhebbers* continued to act as first among equals. One document refers to them as the agents of the participants, a point repeatedly emphasized by Usselinx as well (van Rees 1868, 416, 446, 448, 451; van Dillen 1930, 354). In 1620 Usselinx described the WIC, then still in the project stage, as a *gemeene rederije,* perhaps best translated as a joint enterprise, in which all shareholders enjoyed equal rights of election and appointment. Consequently the directors ought to be chosen by and from the shareholders; letting city councils appoint them violated that principle (van Rees 1868, 416).

One clear sign of a divide between directors and the other shareholders appeared in the articles of association of the first expedition in 1595. The text itself has not survived, but we know from a related set of regulations that the contract denied participants the right to demand full accounts from the directors until all goods had been sold, during which time the participants would also have to content themselves with such information as the board of directors was prepared to divulge.[33] These clauses about accounting and about information sharing clearly served to highlight the fact that the company, by force of circumstance, deviated from the customary norms of full disclosure and annual accounts to partners. Everyone had to wait for up to two years until the ships had returned to European waters and sent fast-sailing yachts ahead with news and data. Once that had happened directors presumably gave participants a rough idea of the results, if only so as to secure their support for another venture.[34]

However, the regulations also show a subtle change in the status of the company's shareholders. The ban on the crew selling their shares before the return to port suggests that the exclusion of shareholders from the day-to-day running of the business was matched by an exit option in the form of freely transferable shares, possibly tied to an obligation to give the company an offer of first refusal (De Jonge 1862, 97, article 24). The exit option does not appear to have been exercised very often in the case of the *voorcompagnieën,* but at the launch of the VOC the trading option was considered so normal that, as we have seen, the charter did not even mention it (van Dillen 1930, 355–356; Gelderblom and Jonker 2004).

Exit options were a normal feature in shipping companies, as often as not tied to a right of first refusal for the other shareholders, but they made sense for partnerships only if these had made a clear distinction between partner-managers, who could sign for the company, and sleeping partners, who could not. This type of company became quite common; in 1610 Le Maire managed a whaling company with seven shareholders who traded their shares (Hart 1976, 211–212). The separation of functions probably led to a wider application of the limited liability principle. Common shareholders could not only claim this if directors went beyond the purpose of the partnership, but also because they were no longer in direct managerial control. The shareholder-managers must also have enjoyed internal limited liability, that is, they could not be called on to pay more than their share, but they do not appear to have acquired limited external liability, that is, they remained personally liable for a company's obligations. In 1597 the prominent Rotterdam businessman Johan van der Veken petitioned the Estates General to release him from litigation over company debts since he ought not to be held personally liable for them, but we do not know whether his claim succeeded (De Jonge 1862, 239–240). The fact that article 42 of the VOC charter expressly exempted the directors from personal liability suggests that the point needed articulation and did not follow automatically. Not everyone picked this up immediately. The Delft chamber of the Noordsche Compagnie, a whaling company set up in 1614, had apparently not exempted its directors from personal liability. As a consequence, the company became embroiled in a court case about the payment of beer ordered for the company's ships during 1616 and 1617. The directors settled the case in 1625 by sharing the bill (van Brakel 1909, 305–306, 339–348).

By contrast, the VOC charter gave very extensive and detailed attention to the company's directors. No fewer than 22 of the 29 corporate governance clauses concern the *bewindhebbers* in one way or another.[35] Seven laid down the responsibilities of the board, the tasks and responsibilities of the individual directors, their oath of office, and their position as officials in having no personal liability for the company's debts (Nos. 2, 3, 6, 12, 27, 32, 33, 42). A further five detailed the directors' remuneration and reimbursement arrangements (Nos. 5, 28, 29, 30, 31). Finally, several articles reflected the difficult merger negotiations leading to the complicated structure of six chambers, one for each city or region that brought its *voorcompagnie* into the merger (Nos. 1, 2). The *bewindhebbers* of those companies became the directors of the VOC, and the charter named all 76 of them (Nos. 18–26). Once natural attrition had whittled this number down to 60, provincial Estates and city councils were to fill vacancies from a list of candidates proposed by the company. In an important deviation from normal practice in the Republic, directors sat for life, surprisingly so, given the rotation schemes and limited appointment terms common to similar appointments.[36] Each chamber delegated a set number of its directors to the regular meetings of the 17-strong executive committee.

The attention devoted to the directors was the outcome of several factors. First, the charter was drafted by a committee of directors from the *voorcompagnieën* keen to keep their hold on a lucrative enterprise and at the same time concerned with the risk of incurring unknown liabilities arising out of a company with an unusually long lifespan (*RSH* 1602–1603, 295–297; De Jonge 1865, 262–281). Second, as officers in a state-sponsored enterprise, the directors would occupy newly created semipublic functions of major importance, if only because their position was unique in spanning the whole Republic, not just one of its constituent provinces. No other business enjoyed excise privileges for the whole of the country (No. 41) or possessed the right to apprehend sailors on the run wherever it found them (No. 43).

Third, reasons of state appear to have weighed very heavily indeed. With 12 articles detailing the relations between the company and the Estates General or other authorities, the state really acted as the second principal for the directors as their agents and determined the balance of power within the company.[37]

AN ADMIRALTY FOR ASIA

Though the importance of the VOC as a semipublic enterprise has been emphasized before in the literature, the agency theory framework highlights the extent to which this biased the company's corporate governance. Together with delegates from the various *voorcompagnieën*, representatives from the Estates General formed part of the committee that drafted the charter and that gave progress reports to the Estates; van Oldenbarnevelt himself addressed the first meeting and chaired the last one (van Deventer 1862, 303; De Jonge 1862, 262–281; Israel 1989, 70). Reasons of state, the desire to take the war to the Luso-Hispanic overseas empire and grab a Dutch empire there, brought the company into being and determined the way in which it was run in two ways, direct and indirect. First, in return for the monopoly plus other privileges and concessions such as the suzerain rights and tax breaks, the state received direct benefits: a small lump sum plus a range of instruments to guide policy.[38] The provincial Estates appointed new *bewindhebbers* (No. 26), a right that Holland transferred to the magistrates of cities with a VOC chamber (Gaastra 2009, 21). The Estates General could override board decisions (No. 6). Regional and local authorities could appoint agents to monitor the company (Nos. 15–16). As we have seen this failed to happen initially, though some provinces later succeeded in obtaining board representation (Gaastra 2009, 32). In addition the company had to submit reports about returning fleets to the Republic's admiralties and the commanding officer had to report in person to the Estates General (Nos. 36, 45).

These articles amounted to a strong injunction forcing *bewindhebbers* to give priority to the Estates General's wishes to the detriment of shareholders' interests, both via monitoring and bonding. Though the *bewindhebbers* possessed an obvious information advantage over any other stakeholder in the VOC, they had a clear incentive to share this with the state, but not with the shareholders. The state could, and did, help them in numerous ways, large and small: providing ships and ordnance, promulgating sanctions to speed up tardy share subscriptions, providing financial assistance and tax benefits, and issuing regulations for trading the company's shares, which included a ban on short selling after Le Maire's raid.[39] From 1609 the company received an annual subsidy of 20,000 guilders, rising to 300,000 guilders by 1615 (De Jong 2005, 82, table 3.5). Delegates from the *bewindhebbers* frequently attended the Estates General's meetings: to supply information, to give expert advice on a range of issues, or to get something done.[40]

As for the indirect ways, the system for filling vacancies provided the authorities with strong leverage over the board. Giving the power to appoint directors to local authorities meant ensuring that board members would be "one of them," recruited from candidates suitable for public office, that is, men adhering to Calvinism, the dominant religion, and fully aware that their career and the social position of their family depended on their success in maintaining the status quo. Rather than economic appointments, the directors' positions became social and political assets, part of the glue binding the elite. As a result, ties between magistrates and the VOC board were close indeed; as a rule, two or even three of Amsterdam's four mayors doubled as VOC directors (Gelderblom 1999, 246–247; Gaastra 2009, 32). It seems reasonable to assume that the directors' interests included personal wealth maximization via transactions with the VOC (tunneling) and via direct expropriation. Examples of both surfaced over time, one of them in Le Maire's petition. However, the patronage opportunities offered by their access to board seats were probably as important in guiding the behavior of directors.

Compared with that the shareholders' position was very weak. The charter handed most governing rights to the Estates General, created a fundamental misalignment of directors' and shareholders' interests, and provided only the barest minimum of checks on managerial behavior. Directors were required to keep a minimum shareholding as a guarantee for their oath of office and by extension for the proper conduct of their staff (Nos. 28, 33). As investors, bondholders and shareholders were jointly entitled to the financial surplus of the VOC's operations. The charter gave no provisions at all to solve the potential conflict between competing claims of shareholders and bondholders. We know no more than that the *bewindhebbers* appear to have used bonds to favor preferred investors, who were keen on them because of the regular interest payments and good rates. Consequently we do not know either to what extent the VOC shareholders were residual claimants with respect to the bondholders. As we have noted, the shareholders' statutory right to dividends if revenues amounted to 5 percent of capital was ignored, and they had very limited information and no voting rights. However, share trading gave investors a very convenient exit option.

From a pure agency perspective, the weak position of shareholders opened an enormous potential for the expropriation of wealth from investors by the Estates General and the directors. Some of the ways in which that happened have already been noted; others follow, and still more surfaced during the 1620s struggle with discontented shareholders, as shown elsewhere in this volume. One would expect investors to price protect against these agency costs, but poor data mean that we cannot really see whether they did. The VOC's shares were fairly rapidly subscribed and are reported to have traded substantially above par for some time after. The fact that the board asked the Estates General to prod tardy subscription payers suggests that some investors may have had second thoughts, but there simply is insufficient evidence one way or another. Share prices seem to have fluctuated with the general outlook of the company, that is, news from Asia and rumors about dividend payments; to what extent agency issues had an impact, we simply cannot say.

CONFLICTING CONCEPTIONS

Firmly in control of the company, the Estates General steered operations toward mounting war in Asia. During 1601–1602 successive expeditions had already engaged in skirmishes with Spanish and Portuguese ships; now the ongoing fight in Europe would be taken overseas with the express intention of, as van Oldenbarnevelt put it, bleeding the Spanish resources (van Deventer 1862, 311–313; van Brakel 1908, 20–21). Accordingly, the admiral on the first expedition sent out received secret instructions, to be opened only after passing the Cape of Good Hope, for aggressive action going way beyond van Oldenbarnevelt's original couple of fortresses.[41] It had been clear all along that the VOC would engage in war overseas; that was precisely the reason why three directors of the Amsterdam company declined to join its board (Gaastra 2009, 30). But the scale of operations that the Estates General demanded went much further than anticipated.

Consequently these demands soon created serious friction. The Estates General had to warn the company repeatedly to heed its instructions about a vigorous pursuit of the war (*RSG* 1604–1606, 224–225 (1604), 501–502 (1605)). The VOC retaliated by presenting a bill for fortresses, soldiers, and armament maintained at the behest of the state, which resulted in a regular subsidy (*RSG* 1607–1609, 696, 896 (1609), De Jong 2005, 82, table 3.5). Two prominent directors and large shareholders resigned from the board shortly after each other: De Moucheron in 1603 and Le Maire in 1605, probably driven by despair over the company's commercial prospects as a result of its military operations. Both attempted to move back into the Asian trade one way or the other, by sponsoring the launch of trade companies abroad or by organizing naval expeditions to explore routes not covered in the VOC charter. These resignations prompted the VOC board in 1606 to ask the Estates General for an injunction against directors giving up their seats.[42] Another prominent shareholder, Pieter Lintgens, sold out because, as a Baptist, he had conscientious objections to the VOC's warfare; he also attempted to found a company abroad.[43] By 1608 a disappointed VOC admiral strongly advised his successor not to try and combine business with war, since this was impossible. Realizing this, the VOC board changed priorities and put war before trade (De Jonge 1865, 233–240; van Brakel 1908, 21–22).

As a result the VOC's commercial operations made little headway and no dividends were being paid, all the more galling since the 1602 expedition started showering dividends three years later on the shareholders who had wisely opted not to let their share be subsumed into the VOC.[44] This must have caused uproar among the rest, who now knew that large amounts of money were coming in without being paid out. Combined with continuing bad news from Asia, the discontent over dividends appears to have pushed the company's share price from 140 percent in 1605 down to 80 in 1606 (De Jonge 1865, 69). By 1610 and possibly a little earlier, the board considered the VOC's prospects to be so poor that it petitioned the Estates General to waive the accounts due in April 1612, fearing that disclosure would lead to a precipitous withdrawal of capital.[45] The Estates initially resisted, demanding full accounts over the first ten-year period, annual accounts for the second ten-year period, the public advertising of sales, plus access to board meetings for selected members to represent shareholders' interests (*RSG* 1610–1612, 604, 703). A decision was only taken in November 1613, when the Estates General, not wanting to weaken the VOC any further, authorized the company to continue without presenting accounts (*RSG* 1613–1616, 153, 154–155, 156, van Rees 1868, 47). It was only with this decision, taken in flagrant contravention of the charter, that the company's capital became permanent, a momentous corporate innovation effected by state intervention. A subtle shift in terminology suggests that, at more or less the same time, the board also sought to redefine the position of the shareholders toward the company. Initially shares were known as *partijen,* that is, literally parts in the company similar to the parts shipowners held in a ship, and together the holders of parts or *participanten* formed the company. From 1606, however, the VOC started substituting the term *actie* or action-in-law for *partijen,* signifying that the holders were no longer considered a part of the company, but outside owners of a right to dividends (Colenbrander 1901, 386–387). Moreover, it looks as if directors tailored the amount of the company's first dividend payments during 1610–1612 to acquit themselves of all claims from shareholders to be part of the company. Totaling 162.5 percent by 1612, this amount neatly represented the paid-up capital plus the going rate of 6.25 percent interest a year during ten years, so directors could argue they no longer owed shareholders anything.

The experiences with the VOC were so disappointing overall that the initial plans to set up a similar company for the Atlantic trade envisaged a radically different corporate governance structure. In 1606 the Estates of Holland circulated a draft charter for a West India Company

(WIC) (for the text see Meijer 1986, 50–59). The overall structure of the proposed company was to resemble that of the VOC. A single-tier board of *bewindhebbers* headed the company, with day-to-day decisions delegated to a committee of 17. In the VOC this board operated more or less independently, but the draft charter envisaged giving the WIC shareholders power over it in two ways. First, the *bewindhebbers* would no longer be appointed by city councils or provincial Estates, but elected by and from shareholders with a minimum holding of 2,000–4,000 guilders, depending on the chamber in which they had invested. A third of the *bewindhebbers* would seek reelection every two years (Meijer 1986, 55, articles 17–19). Usselinx, as keen an advocate of shareholders' rights as Le Maire but more articulate and persistent, saw regular board elections by shareholders as a guarantee that directors would not act as masters of other people's money, like they did in the VOC, but as agents, as they should (van Rees 1868, 448, 451; Jameson 1887; Ligtenberg 1914). Second, the large shareholders would elect a supervisory board of *hoofdparticipanten* or leading shareholders to audit the accounts and discuss policy with the *bewindhebbers*, the first manifestation of the two-tier board so characteristic of Dutch corporate governance today (Meijer 1986, 55–56, articles 21, 23–26).[46] The draft also proposed keeping separate accounts for the commercial activities and for warfare, and presenting full accounts every six years. Finally shareholders would get a dividend if profits reached 10 percent of capital, as originally proposed for the VOC but lowered to 5 percent in the charter, which latter threshold had clearly proved too low (De Jonge 1862, 266, 273; Meijer 1986, 56, article 22,).[47] Even Le Maire's scathing profit estimate of no more than 2.3 million guilders over seven years meant that the company ought to have paid the statutory dividend in most years and thus had formally transgressed its charter, giving shareholders another legitimate cause for complaint (*Shareholder Rights at 400*, 45). The figure was therefore doubled so the WIC could conserve cash.

The company sketched in the 1606 blueprint was intended to function in tandem with a public body governing trade and warfare, the link between the two being provided by a board member appointed by the Estates General.[48] Clearly official thinking now accepted the undesirability of combining politics with business and consequently split the two tasks over separate bodies. This new insight and the consequent greater weight given to shareholders' interests can only be understood as an attempt to remedy perceived shortcomings in the VOC charter of four years before. It shows that a more balanced model of corporate governance giving more power to the shareholders was not only conceivable, but in fact conceived. The fact that the

Estates of Holland issued the draft also shows that these shortcomings were sufficiently serious to warrant official attention.[49]

Le Maire's 1609 diatribe and innovative bear raid on the VOC shares of the same year thus formed part of a groundswell of discontent. Indeed, Le Maire's criticism about corporate governance appears quite muted, all the more remarkable for the fact that he continued to hold 85,000 guilders worth of shares, which he sold only during 1610, presumably to fulfill obligations arising from his bear raid.[50] He subordinated his corporate governance criticism to his main concern, that the VOC's monopoly should be restricted and not, as the board wanted, extended. Big merchants such as he and De Moucheron were keen to get the scope of the intercontinental trade widened and chafed at the unremunerative VOC monopoly. But perhaps Le Maire also decided to focus the main thrust of his arguments on what he wanted to achieve most, because he realized that demands for corporate governance changes stood little chance since the Estates General would unlikely alter a structure designed in its favor. Moreover, at a time when immigrants from the Southern Netherlands like De Moucheron, Lintgens, and Le Maire were slowly but surely sidelined by the Hollands majority, calls for more power coming from that corner were unlikely to be popular, whereas claims for free and fair trade opportunities would attract a wide audience (Gelderblom 1999).

Whatever his motives, Le Maire concentrated on his objections to the VOC board's business policy and discussed only three main corporate governance complaints (*Shareholder Rights* 2009). First, the company's rising debt burden cut into the shareholders' profits, so that no dividends had yet been paid and were unlikely to be paid before the 1612 accounts (*Shareholder Rights* 2009, 39, 40, 42, 45). Second, the dictatorial board refused to take advice or hear arguments. Third, the directors enriched themselves to the detriment of shareholders while trying to get the obligation to publish accounts waived (*Shareholder Rights* 2009, 39, 400–41, 45). The complaints amounted to a bill for the woeful impotence of shareholders: this had brought the latent conflict of interest between bondholders and shareholders to the fore and allowed the directors to get away with milking the company, which without public scrutiny of the accounts would continue indefinitely.

In combination with the sweeping proposals of the 1606 WIC draft statutes, Le Maire's complaints show that contemporaries were acutely aware of the VOC charter's failings. Yet nothing was done. The Estates General duly lifted the company's obligation to publish accounts and subsequent drafts for a WIC charter reverted to the VOC model, omitting the clauses on shareholder representation. Clearly the main principal wanted to keep a tight hold over its companies and ignored other interests.

Conclusions

During the sixteenth century traditional partnerships evolved to meet new commercial demands in the scale and scope of business in the Low Countries. The flexible legal system enabled existing forms such as the shipping company and the partnership to adapt by developing arrangements to safeguard the interests of stakeholders and third parties, redefining liabilities, and solving emerging agency issues. Tried and tested in the developing long-distance trade of Antwerp and subsequently Amsterdam, this framework proved sufficiently flexible to accommodate the biggest challenge, the overseas trade with Asia.

At first sight the VOC was a natural shoot off these old roots, and not a revolutionary innovation. Other companies had pioneered the joint-stock principle, the separation of ownership and management, limited liability, tradable shares, and capital pledged for long periods of time. Yet the VOC differed materially from its predecessors: by its size, scope of operations, purpose, durability and by the creation of a lively securities trade. The company's corporate governance structure also differed materially as a result of its need to combine colonial warfare with trade. As a compromise between existing commercial interests, reasons of state, and the business models available at the time, its governance model in fact came closest to other private-public partnerships in the Republic such as the admiralty boards. The deficiencies of this construction were quickly recognized, but never remedied. With the war against Spain and colonial conquest in full swing, reasons of state would not allow that, and turning the *bewindhebbers* positions into a key instrument for social and political advancement created a powerful lobby group firmly defending the status quo.

The very modern character of the equity market that emerged with the establishment of the VOC in 1602 has led legal and economic historians to overlook the deviant nature of the company's governance structure. The VOC represented the culmination of a long evolution of corporate organization in several key respects: limited liability, freely transferable shares and securities trading, and a better definition of management functions and responsibilities. In those respects the company is a worthy precursor of modern corporations and Dutch limited liability companies. However, the VOC's corporate governance was a clear step backward, a deviation from both the preceding evolution and contemporary conceptions of business organization and accountability. Directors appointed by outsiders and sitting for life were an anomaly, as was the disregard for shareholders' rights to information, but they became the norm in the VOC, over vociferous protests from shareholders and prominent businessmen such as Le Maire and Usselinx, because reasons of state overrode the interests of private investors. Like the company's permanent capital, its corporate governance model was the consequence of state intervention, not of a quest for greater economic efficiency.

NOTES

1. We are indebted to Matthijs de Jongh and Judith Pollman for pointing us to sources that helped to shape the argument of this chapter, and to the participants of conferences and seminars at Yale, Antwerp University, the University of Amsterdam, Utrecht University, and CalTech for their constructive comments. Rienk Wegener Sleeswijk made us understand the precise legal character of early shipping companies; Ailsa Röell gave very useful detailed comments.

2. The original documents lie in the Dutch National Archives, the Hague (henceforth NA) 3.01.14 van Oldenbarnevelt no. 3123. Cf. De Jonge 1865, 364–378, and Haak and Veenendaal 1962, 293–294 for transcriptions. An English translation in *Shareholder Rights* 2009.

3. According to De Vries and van der Woude 1997, 385, the directors of the predecessors did not enjoy third-party limited liability, whereas Den Heijer 2005, 35–36, thinks they did.

4. To be sure, this kind of adaptation of the general partnership can be traced back to the Justinian code: Zimmerman 1990, 457–459.

5. Maritime law also provided for an equal distribution of damages among all freighters in case the cargo of only some of them was damaged or lost (thrown overboard) in order to save the ship: Schöffer 1956.

6. For most participants it would have been easy to establish with their own eyes when and in what condition ships returned, but managers usually informed those living elsewhere by letter: van Gelder 1916, Unger 1940.

7. Ships from different companies coordinated their operations so as to maximize mutual security. In 1601 two captains, one from Rotterdam and one from Amsterdam, signed a contract of agreeing on a joint return voyage with mutual assistance and defense, secured on their ships and with penalties for noncompliance of up to 1,000 guilders: Unger 1940, 214–217.

8. NA 1.04.01 Inv. Nrs. 3 and 4, printed in De Jonge 1862, 204–212, 249–253.

9. NA 1.04.01, Inv. Nr. 27, fol. 4v (November 30, 1598), fol. 12v (September 2, 1599); fol. 30 (September 3, 1600); NA 1.04.01 Inv. Nr 29, fol. 2 (October 13, 1601).

10. NA 1.04.01 Inv. Nr. 27, fol. 45v (December 30, 1600). See for a discussion about the relationship between shareholders, directors, and the company van Dillen 1930, 353–354. That they did have a direct relation with the company is clear from De Jonge 1862, 97, article 24.

11. See, for instance, for the fifth voyage: NA 1.04.01, Inv. Nr. 27, fol. 34 (August 12, 1600).

12. NA 1.04.01, Inv. Nr. 27, fol. 2 (November 16, 1598); compare a resolution on the submission of accounts by individual directors in NA 1.04.01 Inv. Nr.28, fol. 7 (October 4, 1600).

13. On storage: NA 1.04.01. Inv. Nr. 28, fol. 1 (July 19, 1599): on Texel: NA 1.04.01, Inv. Nr. 27, fol. 29 (June 12, 1600). See also: NA 1.04.01 Inv. Nr.29, fol. 2 (October 13, 1601), fol. 3 (October 29, 1601).

14. NA 1.04.01, Inv. Nr. 89. See also Inv. Nr. 27, fol. 5 (January 4, 1599). At times the directors also personally took financial risks for the company. In July 1600, for instance, six directors together insured, until its moment of sailing, a newly bought ship for 10,000 guilders. In the end the policy ran until July 1601: NA 1.04. 01 Inv. Nr. 27, fol. 29v (July 7, 1600); fol. 30v-31, April 16, 1601.

15. Amsterdam's *Oude Compagnie* set the rate for these rebates at 8–9 percent in 1599 (NA. 1.04.01, Inv. Nr 27, fol. 16v (October 7, 1599); Inv. Nr. 28, fol. 7 (October 7, 1599) and 8 percent in 1600 and 1601 (NA 1.04.01, Inv. Nr. 27, fol. 34 (August 12, 1600); NA 1.04.01 Inv. Nr. 29, fol. 10 (October 2, 1601).

16. NA 1.04.01, Inv. Nr 29, fol. 4 (November 26, 1601).

17. NA 1.04.01, Inv. Nr 29, fol. 4 (November 15, 1601).

18. See, for instance, NA 1.04.01 Inv. Nr. 1 (December 3, 1594) for the directors of Amsterdam's *Oude Compagnie* assuming joint and several liability for cannon borrowed on the company's behalf, printed in De Jonge 1862, 239–242.

19. "Adi 7 december ao 98 is bovengemelde [… ?] geschut in die generale vergaederynghe en spetialijcken die bewynthebberen daer op geroepen, gheproponeert, en oock by alle geaccepteert en geapprobeert," NA. 1.04.01 Inv. Nr. 27, fol. 4v (December 7, 1598). Other general meetings are noted on December 14 and February 25, but the addition of "ter presentie van alle die bewynthebberen, alleenlyck absent synde [namen]" (with all directors present, only [named individuals] being absent) appears to suggest that the meeting were for directors only (NA. 1.04.01 Inv. Nr. 27, fols. 5 and 6). By August 1599 the term "general meeting" stands for a meeting of the directors: "vergaderinge vande generale bewinthebbers" (NA 1.04.01, Inv. Nr. 27, fol. 12v). The power shift from the shareholders to the directors is exquisitely illustrated by a subtle mistake in the draft minutes about directors each paying part of a bill for cannon. Having started the word participant, the writer crossed this beginning out and replaced it with "bewynthebber" or director: "Aen 7 december ao 98 is gearresteert dat yder bewynthebber zal tot zynen laste neemen voor reeckenynghe van tgeresikeerde gheschut die somme

van seshondertenvyfftyck gl corent," NA. 1.04.01 Inv. Nr. 27, fol. 4v (December 7, 1598).

20. NA 1.04.01, Inv. Nr. 28, fol. 5 (August 23, 1599). On March 1, 1599, "vergaderingynge van die colleganten en diverse der bewyn-thebberen" (NA 1.04.01, Inv. Nr. 27, fol. 6). See also: NA 1.04.01, Inv. Nr 28, fol. 6 (August 30, 1599).

21. NA 1.04.01 Inv. Nr. 28, fol. 5: "Dat ijegelick particulier Collegie vol-comen macht heeft om aff te doen t'geene aen haer werck dependeert ende swaricheyt maeckende, ofte onder haer discorderrende, vermo-gen den Raedt vant Collegie te hulpe te nemen." This clause is added to the resolution of August 23, 1599, in a different handwriting, so the exact date remains uncertain.

22. NA 1.04.01, Inv. Nr. 27 fol. 22v (January 11, 1600) fol. 33 (July 25, 1600); See also: NA 1.04.01 Inv. Nr. 28, fol. 19 (January 11, 1600). See also the resolution, struck out in the draft index, stating that all directors regardless of their specific tasks had equal voting power (NA 1.04.01, Inv. Nr. 27, fol. 2 (November 16, 1598).

23. NA 1.04.01, Inv. Nr. 27, fol. 6 (February 25, 1599), fol. 17 (October 9, 1599); NA 1.04.01 Inv. Nr. 28, fol. 5 (August 23, 1599), fol. 8 (October 9, 2009). See also Witteveen 2002, 40.

24. NA. 1.04.01 Inv. Nr. 27, fol. 20v (November 15, 1599).

25. NA 1.04.01, Inv. Nr. 29, fol. 4 (November 15, 1601, April 2, 1602).

26. Pamphlet Knuttel No. 3347, *Tegen-vertooch bij eenighe lief-hebbers vande waarheyt ende haer Vaderlandt ende mede participanten vande Oost-Indische Compagnie aen de Ed. Hoog. Moog. heeren Staten Generael*, 1622.

27. We follow the text of the 1602 charter as printed in van der Chys 1857, 118–135. An English translation may be found in Gepken-Jager, van Solingen, and Timmerman 2005, and on http://www.australiaonthemap.org.au/content/view/50/59.

28. The proposal for a Casa de India structure probably dated from 1600 or 1601. The 1602 merger talks initially appear to have envisaged the executive committee of XVII *bewindhebbers* as a semipublic board for the Asian trade, though without shareholder representation, but this idea no longer appeared in the second draft: De Jonge 1862, 262, 272. However, the final document summarizing the outcome of the talks still referred to the company's board as a "gemeene collegie van den Oost-Indischen handel," that is, a general board for the trade with East India, De Jonge 1862, 278, van Deventer 1862, 301. As late as 1622 Usselinx still pleaded for a public board charged with run-ning the Asian trade and headed by the stadtholder: van Rees 1868, 424–427, 455. Alexander Bick is preparing a PhD thesis at Princeton on the WIC's governance.

29. We counted charter articles 2, 3, 5, 6, 7, 8, 9, 10, 12, 14, 15, 16, 17, 18–23, 24–25, 26, 27, 28, 29, 30, 31, 32, 33, and 42 as dealing with aspects of corporate governance.

30. Van der Chys 1857, 130, article 35. Senior VOC officers therefore had to swear an oath of allegiance to both the company and the Estates General.

31. Van der Chys 1857, 118–135, counting articles 7, 9, 10, 14, and 17.

32. The initial document and the second draft drawn up by the merger committee had specified a threshold of 10 percent: De Jonge 1862, 266, 273.

33. De Jonge 1862, 97, article 24 of the regulations concerning the expedition crew, referring to the contract between the participants.

34. This was already the case with the first expedition: van Dillen 1930, 355–356.

35. Van der Chys 1857, 118–135, counting articles 2, 3, 5, 6, 12, 18–23, 24–25, 26, 27, 28, 29, 30, 31, 32, 33, and 42.

36. Cf. Usselinx' comments comparing the *bewindhebbers* to the boards of orphanages, church wards, and hospitals in van Rees 1868, 417.

37. Van der Chys 1857, 118–135, counting articles 6, 15–16, 26, 34–36, 38, 39, 41, 44, 45.

38. Van der Chys 1857, 118–135, counting articles 6, 15–16, 26, 34–36, 38, 39, 41, 44, 45.

39. For examples from the company's early years, see *RSG* 1604–1606, 501 (borrowing warships and ordnance), pp. 501–502 (sanctions for late paying shareholders), 805 (new admonition to tardy shareholders), 808 (renewed publication of the monopoly and the penalties for disobeying it), 809 (ban on VOC crew to enlist in foreign service); *RSG* 1607–1609, 306 (official share transfer procedure and renewed sanctions for late paying shareholders), 307 (loans of cannon and ammunition), 729 (instructions to the ambassador in Paris to do everything in his power to frustrate the French plans for an Asian trading company), 896 (supply of ammunition and guns worth 25,000 guilders for the defense of forts). From 1609 the Estates General gave the company a regular annual assistance of 100,000 guilders in cash, on military costs that the company claimed in 1610 to amount to 420,000 guilders: *RSG* 1610–1612, 254; cf. 507 for the tax benefit granted in return for a loan of 250,000 guilders that the company had given to the state during 1605–1606, and 511 for a gift of spices from the directors to the members of the Estates General. Cf. Den Heijer 2005, 55, putting the first subsidy only in 1611, whereas it is clear from the resolutions that this was two years before. For the ban on naked shorting *RSG* 1610–1612, 16–17 and 44; this was promulgated on February 27, cf. van Dillen 1930, 68–69.

40. For instance, *RSG* 1602–1603, 88, 299 (consulting the Estates General on a successor to De Moucheron as director), 297–298 (various administrative issues on getting the company started up); *RSG* 1604–1606, 223–224 (forming a committee of directors to advise the Estates General on Spain's position in Asia), 506 (discussing the equipment of new warships); *RSG* 1607–1609, 11 (coordinating naval matters between the admiralties and the company),

12–13 (discussing the commander of a next expedition), 893–895 (discussions whether or not to include Asia in the truce with Spain); *RSG* 1610–1612, 694 (latest news from Asia).

41. "Secrete Instructie den Admiral van der Hagen gegeven," NA 1.11.01.01 Inv. Nr 255, fol. 71–74; printed in De Jonge 1865, 163. Cf. van Brakel 1908, 21.

42. *RSG* 1604–1606, 806; the request was refused, the Estates General instructing the board to fill any vacancies as laid down in the charter.

43. Van Rees 1868, 29, 31, 33–34. The efforts by De Moucheron and Lintgens to set up trading companies abroad inspired the VOC board to have Le Maire swear an oath that he would not compete with the company; this did not, however, deter him.

44. Van Rees 1868, 27: from 1605 to 1610 respectively 15, 75, 40, 20, 25, 50 percent for a total of 225. Van Rees erroneously attributes these dividends to the VOC, which paid its first dividend only in 1610. Article 9 gave shareholders in the last expedition of the *voor-compagnieën* the right to opt out. The Delft shareholder W.J. Dedel had clearly done this and, having received 130 percent by 1607, he sold his share: Colenbrander 1901, 386–387.

45. The published resolutions of the Estates General do not show when the board first requested the lifting of this obligation, but the Frisian Estates considered the request during 1610 and asked the Estates General in April 1611 to turn it down: *RSG* 1610–1612, 359.

46. According to Usselinx, the *hoofdparticipanten* were later dropped at the instigation of representatives from the country's main ports, that is, *bewindhebbers* from the VOC who feared that they would have to introduce a similar structure: van Rees 1868, 411, 423.

47. Usselinx considered 10 percent inadvisable and thought apparently that no figure should be mentioned: van Rees 1868, 452.

48. Information kindly provided by Alexander Bick from his ongoing research.

49. For subsequent convoluted developments surrounding the WIC see Den Heijer 2005, 45–50. Usselinx's complaint about WIC draft reflecting the repression of shareholders as practiced by the VOC quoted in van Rees 1868, 409.

50. NA 1.04.02 Inv. Nr. 7060, ledger of shareholders fols. 90, 102, 114, 121, 182–191, 193–194, 196, 198, 201.

REFERENCES

Asser, Willem Daniël Hendrik. 1983. *In solidum of pro parte, een onderzoek naar de ontwikkelingsgeschiedenis van de hoofdelijke en gedeelde aansprakelijkheid van vennoten tegenover derden.* Leiden: Brill.

Becht, Marco, Bolton, Patrick and Röell, Ailsa. 2003. "Corporate Governance and Control." In *Handbook of the Economics of Finance,* ed. G.M. Constantinides, M. Harris and R. Stulz, 1–109. Amsterdam: Elsevier.

Brakel, Simon van. 1908. *De Hollandsche handelscompagnieën der zeventiende eeuw, hun ontstaan, hunne inrichting.* The Hague: Nijhoff.

Brakel, Simon van. 1909. Vroedschapsresolutiën, sententiën en notarieele acten betreffende de Noordsche Compagnie. *Bijdragen en mededeelingen van het Historisch Genootschap 30*: 255–400.

Brakel, Simon van. 1912. Bijdrage tot de geschiedenis der naamlooze vennootschap. *Rechtsgeleerd magazijn* 31: 261–306.

Brakel, Simon van. 1914. Ontbrekende schakels in ons vennootschapsrecht. In *Rechtshistorische opstellen aangeboden aan mr. S.J. Fockema Andreae,* 153–194. Haarlem: Bohn.

Brakel, Simon van. 1917. Vennootschapsvormen in Holland gedurende de zeventiende eeuw. *Rechtsgeleerd magazijn* 36: 1–30, 145–189.

Brulez, Wilfrid. 1959. *De firma Della Faille en de internationale handel van Vlaamse firma's in de 16e eeuw.* Brussels: Koninklijke Vlaamse Academie.

Chys, Jacobus Anne van der. 1857. *Geschiedenis der stichting van de Vereenigde O.I. Compagnie en der maatregelen van de Nederlandsche regering betreffende de vaart op Oost-Indië, welke aan deze stichting voorafgingen.* Leiden: Engels.

Colenbrander, Herman Theodoor. 1901. Über das erste Auftreten des Wortes "Aktie" in den Niederlanden. *Zeitschrift für das gesamte Handelsrecht* 50: 383–387.

Dekker, Cornelis, and Baetens, Ronald. 2009. *Geld in het water, Antwerps en Mechels kapitaal in Zuid-Beveland na de stormvloeden in de 16e eeuw.* Hilversum: Verloren.

Denucé, Jan. 1938. *De Hanze en de Antwerpsche handelscompagnieën op de Oostzeelanden.* Antwerpen: De Sikkel.

De Roover, Raymond. 1963. *The Rise and Decline of the Medici Bank 1397–1494.* Cambridge, Mass: Harvard University Press.

Deventer, Marinus Lodewijk van. 1862. *Gedenkstukken van Johan van Oldenbarnevelt en zijn tijd, II, 1593–1602.* The Hague: Nijhoff.

Dillen, Johannes Gerard van. 1930. Isaac le Maire en de handel in actiën der Oost-Indische Compagnie. *Economisch-historisch jaarboek* 16: 1–165.

Dillen, Johannes Gerard van. 1958. *Het oudste aandeelhoudersregister van de Kamer Amsterdam der Oost-Indische Compagnie.* The Hague: Nijhoff.

Fockema Andreae, Sybrandus Johannes. 1975. *De Nederlandse staat onder de Republiek.* Amsterdam: Noord-Hollandsche Uitgevers Maatschappij. 7th edition.

Frentrop, Paul. 2003. *A History of Corporate Governance, 1602–2002.* Brussels: Deminor.

Gaastra, Femme. 2009. *De geschiedenis van de VOC.* Zutphen: Walburg Pers, 7th edition.

Gelder, Hendrik Enno van. 1916. Scheepsrekeningen van enkele der vroegste Guineavaarten. *Economisch Historisch Jaarboek* 2: 239–57.

Gelderblom, Oscar C. 1999. De deelname van Zuid-Nederlandse kooplieden aan het openbare leven van Amsterdam (1578–1650). In *Ondernemers en bestuurders, economie en politiek in de Noordelijke Nederlanden in de late Middeleeuwen en de Vroegmoderne Tijd,* ed. Clé Lesger and Leo Noordegraaf, 237–258. Amsterdam: NEHA.

Gelderblom, Oscar C. 2000. *Zuid-Nederlandse kooplieden en de opkomst van de Amsterdamse stapelmarkt 1578–1630.* Hilversum: Verloren.

Gelderblom, Oscar C., and Joost P.B. Jonker. 2004. Completing a Financial Revolution, the Finance of the Dutch East India Trade and the Rise of the Amsterdam Capital Market, 1595–1612. *Journal of Economic History* 64: 641–672.

Gelderblom, Oscar C. 2011. *The Freedom of Merchants, the Institutional Foundations of International Trade in the Low Countries, 1250–1650.* Princeton: Princeton University Press.

Gepken-Jager, Ella, van Solingen, Gerard and Timmerman, Levinus. 2005. *VOC 1602–2002: 400 Years of Company Law.* Deventer: Kluwer.

Goor, Jur van. 2002. De Verenigde Oost-Indische Compagnie in de historiografie, imperialist en multinational. In *De Verenigde Oost-Indische Compagnie tussen oorlog en diplomatie,* ed. Gerrit Knaap and Ger Teitler, 9–33. Leiden: KITLV.

Goris, Jan Albert. 1925. *Étude sur les colonies marchandes mériodinales (Portugais, Espagnols, Italiens) à Anvers de 1488- à 1567. Contribution à l'histoire des débuts du capitalisme moderne.* Louvain: Librairie Universitaire.

Haak, Simon, and Veenendaal, Augustus. eds. 1962. *Johan van Oldenbarnevelt, bescheiden betreffende zijn staatkundig beleid en zijn familie 1570–1620, II, 1602–1613.* The Hague: Nijhoff.

Harris, Ron. 2000. *Industrializing English Law. Entrepreneurship and Business Organization, 1720–1844.* Cambridge: Cambridge University Press.

Hart, Simon. 1976. *De eerste Nederlandse tochten ter walvisvaart. In Geschrift en getal, een keuze uit de demografisch-, economisch- en sociaal-historische studiën op grond van Amsterdamse archivalia, 1600–1800, 209–246.* Dordrecht: Historische Vereniging Holland.

Heijden, Egidius Johannes Josephus van der. 1908. *De ontwikkeling van de naamlooze vennootschap in Nederland vóór de codificatie.* Amsterdam: van der Vecht.

Heijden, Egidius Johannes Josephus van der. 1914. Over den juridischen oorsprong der Naamlooze Vennootschap. In *Rechtshistorische opstellen aangeboden aan mr. S.J. Fockema Andreae,* 132–152. Haarlem: Bohn.

Heijer, Henk den. 2005. *De geoctrooieerde compagnie, de VOC en de WIC als voorlopers van de naamloze vennootschap.* Deventer: Kluwer.

Hoecke, Gielis vanden. 1537/1545. *Een sonderlinghe boeck in dye edel conste arithmetica: met veel schoone perfecte regulen als Die numeracie vanden ghetale metten specien int gheheele ende int ghebroken... / Ghecalculeert ende versaemt met grooter naersticheyt bi Gielis vanden Hoecke, En geprent Thantwerpen op die Lombaerde veste. By mi Symon Cock.* Antwerpen.

Hunt, Edwin S. 1994. *The Medieval Super-Companies. A Study of the Peruzzi Company of Florence.* Cambridge: Cambridge University Press.

Israel, Jonathan. 1989. *Dutch Primacy in World Trade.* Oxford: Oxford University Press.

Jameson, John F. 1887. *Willem Usselincx*. New York: Putnam.

Jensen, Michael C., and William H. Meckling. 1976. Theory of the Firm: Managerial Behavior, Agency Costs and Ownership Structure. *Journal of Financial Economics* 3 (No. 4): 305–360.

Jonge, Jan Karel Jakob de. 1862. *De opkomst van het Nederlandsch gezag in Oost-Indië (1595–1811)*, vol I. The Hague: Nijhoff.

Jonge, Jan Karel Jakob de. 1865. *De opkomst van het Nederlandsch gezag in Oost-Indië (1595–1811)*, vol III. The Hague: Nijhoff.

Jong, Michiel de. 2005. *"Staat van oorlog": wapenbedrijf en militaire hervorming in de Republiek der Verenigde Nederlanden, 1585–1621*. Hilversum: Verloren.

Jonker, Joost P.B., andSluyterman, Keetie E. 2000. *At Home on the World Markets, Dutch Trading Houses from the 16th Century to the Present*. The Hague: SDU.

Lazzareschi, Eugenio. 1947. *Libro della Communità dei Mercanti Lucchesi in Bruges*. Milan: Malfasi.

Lehmann, Karolus. 1895. *Die geschichtliche Entwicklung des Aktienrechts bis zum Code de Commerce*. Berlin: Heymann.

Ligtenberg, Clara. 1914. *Willem Usselincx*. Utrecht: Oosthoek.

Lopez, Robert S. 1971.*The Commercial Revolution of the Middle Ages, 950–1350*. Englewood Cliffs: Prentice-Hall.

Lopez, Robert S., and Irving W. Raymond. 1955. *Medieval Trade in the Mediterranean World*. New York: Columbia University Press.

Mansvelt, Willem Maurits Frederik. 1922. *Rechtsvorm en financieel beheer bij de VOC*. Amsterdam: Swets & Zeitlinger.

Meijer, A.C. 1986. "Liefhebbers des Vaderlandts ende beminders van de commercie," de plannen tot oprichting van een Generale Westindische Compagnie gedurende de jaren 1606–1609. *Archief, mededelingen van het Koninklijk Zeeuwsch Genootschap der Wetenschappen*: 21–72.

Nanninga Uitterdijk, J. 1904. *Een Kamper handelshuis te Lissabon 1572–1594, handelscorrespondentie, rekeningen en bescheiden*. Zwolle: Tijl.

Rees, Otto van. 1868. *Geschiedenis der koloniale politiek van de Republiek der Vereenigde Nederlanden*. Utrecht: Kemink.

Riemersma, Jelle. 1952. Trading and Shipping Associations in 16th Century Holland. *Tijdschrift voor geschiedenis* 65: 330–338.

Resolutien Staten Generaal (RSG), consulted online at http://www.inghist. nl/retroboeken/statengeneraal/

Schöffer, Ivo. 1956. De vonnissen in averij grosse van de Kamer van Assurantie en Avarij te Amsterdam in de 18e eeuw. Onderzoek naar hun economisch-historische waarde voor de geschiedenis van handel en scheepvaart van Amsterdam op de Oostzee 1700–1770. *Economisch-Historisch Jaarboek* 26: 73–132.

Scott, William Robert. 1968. *The Constitution and Finance of English, Scottish, and Irish Joint-Stock Companies to 1720*. Gloucester Mass: P. Smith.

Shareholder Rights at 400, Commemorating Isaac le Maire and the First Recorded Expression of Investor Advocacy 2009. S.l.: APG.

Steensgaard, Niels. 1982. The Dutch East India Company as an Institutional Innovation. In *Dutch Capitalism and World Capitalism,* ed. Maurice Aymard, 235–257. Cambridge: Cambridge University Press.

Tielhof, Milja van. 2002. *The "Mother of All Trades." The Baltic Grain Trade in Amsterdam from the Late 16th to the Early 19th Century.* Leiden: Brill.

Unger, Willem Sybrand. 1940. Nieuwe gegevens betreffende het begin der vaart op Guinea. *Economisch Historisch Jaarboek* 21: 194–217.

Unger, Willem Sybrand. 1946–1948. Het inschrijvingsregister van de Kamer Zeeland der Verenigde Oost-Indische Compagnie. *Economisch Historisch Jaarboek* 24: 1–33.

Veluwenkamp, Jan Willem. 2002. *Archangel. Nederlandse ondernemers in Rusland 1550–1785.* Amsterdam: Balans.

Vries, Jan de, and Ad van der Woude. 1997. *The First Modern Economy, Success, Failure, and Perseverance of the Dutch Economy, 1500–1815.* Cambridge: Cambridge University Press.

Wijnroks, Eric. 2003. *Handel tussen Rusland en de Nederlanden, 1560–1640.* Hilversum: Verloren.

Witteveen, Menno. 2002. *Een onderneming van landsbelang. De oprichting van de Verenigde Oost-Indische Compagnie in 1602.* Amsterdam: Amsterdam University Press.

Zimmermann, Reinhard. 1990. *The Law of Obligations. Roman Foundations of the Civilian Tradition.* Oxford: Clarendon.

Zwet, Han van. 2009. *Lofwaerdighe dijckagies en miserabele polders, een financiële analyse van landaanwinningsprojecten in Hollands Noorderkwartier, 1597–1643.* Hilversum: Verloren.

CHAPTER 3

SHAREHOLDER ACTIVISTS
AVANT LA LETTRE: THE
"COMPLAINING PARTICIPANTS"
IN THE DUTCH EAST INDIA
COMPANY, 1622–1625

Johan Matthijs de Jongh

Redde Rationem Villicationis Tuae! **Give an Account of Your Stewardship!** There was a rich man whose steward was accused of wasting his possessions. So he called him in and asked him, "What is this that I hear about you? Give an account of your stewardship, because you cannot be manager any longer" (Luke 16. 1–2).[1]

Agency problems that arise from separating ownership and control are considerably older than their analyses in Berle and Means' *Modern Corporation & Private Property* (1932). This is evident in the biblical quotation, cited in 1622 by complaining shareholders of the Dutch East India Company (Verenigde Oost-Indische Compagnie, or VOC). The VOC, incorporated in 1602, dominated trade with the East Indies throughout the seventeenth century. It was gradually outstripped in the eighteenth century by the English East India Company (EIC), which had been incorporated in 1600. Unlike the EIC, the share capital of the VOC was *de facto* permanent as from its incorporation and VOC shares were already traded on the stock exchange in the first decade of the seventeenth century (e.g., Gelderblom and Jonker 2004). Although it was easy for the participants in the VOC (as shareholders were called at the time) to sell their shares, they had no control rights at all; the VOC never held a shareholders' meeting.

The absence of control rights did not impair the ability of VOC participants to actually express their opinions. From 1622–1625, the so-called *dolerende participanten* or *doleanten* (complaining[2] participants) caused quite a stir when they protested against the self-enrichment and inefficient management by the directors. Echoing many of the complaints articulated by Isaac le Maire in 1609, they accused the directors of using their powers primarily in their own interests. To put an end to this, the complaining participants, who jointly held almost 40 percent of the share capital (van Rees 1868, 148), demanded more influence in the VOC. The conflict between participants and directors was fought out in the public arena by way of a pamphlet battle (Knuttel 1978, 3345–3356 and 3585b).

Like the Le Maire controversy discussed in the previous chapter, the shareholder activism of 1622–1625 provides a window onto early challenges in corporate governance. First, it is an interesting illustration of the agency problems that arise if shareholders in a publicly traded company remain deprived of information and have no control rights. Second, the conflict is significant from the viewpoint of legal history. The outcome of the conflict was an important moment in the history of Dutch corporate law: it was acknowledged for the first time, at any rate theoretically, that shareholders in a listed company are more than just financiers of an enterprise, that they are also entitled to a voice, for example, in the appointment of directors.[3] Furthermore, the so-called two-tier board may well have its roots in this conflict. In companies with a two-tier board, the supervisory board is charged with oversee and advising the board of directors, which is composed only of executive directors.

This chapter is structured as follows. First, the Charter (*Octrooi*) of the VOC is examined with particular attention to the position of its shareholders. In this section, I also attempt to find an explanation for the participants' lack of control and look briefly back at shareholder activism before 1622. Second, the participants' complaints about the course of affairs at the VOC are explicated based on original analysis of various pamphlets published at the time of the controversy.[4] This section also provides an overview of the response by the directors and the outcome of the conflict, which resulted in an amendment to the Charter.

THE POSITION OF THE PARTICIPANTS UNDER THE 1602 CHARTER

Internal Organization of the VOC

The VOC can be considered a type of merger of several shipping companies, the so-called precompanies, which traded with the East Indies between 1594 and 1602. The precompanies were incorporated for the duration of one voyage, after which they were liquidated and the proceeds divided among the participants. The first precompany returned from the Indies in 1597. Although this company was not a success from a commercial perspective, it had proved that sailing to Asia was possible and had opened a new trade route to the East Indies (Gaastra 2009, 15). This immediately resulted in the formation of various precompanies in different cities in Holland and Zeeland, the two western provinces of the Netherlands. Within a few years, the Netherlands acquired a leading position in the trade with the East Indies and forced the Portuguese into second place (Gaastra 2009, 17–18).

The incorporation of multiple precompanies led to sharp competition, which caused the purchase prices in the Indies to rise and the market prices in the Netherlands to fall. Moreover, skirmishes with the Spaniards and Portuguese could not be ruled out. Both the merchants of the precompanies and the States General[5] therefore had an interest in having the precompanies merge into a united East India Company, which would be granted a monopoly on trade.

In the Charter of 1602,[6] the States General granted the VOC a trade monopoly on the East Indies for 21 years. It conferred certain public powers on the VOC, for example, to conclude treaties on behalf of the States General, build forts, enforce public order, and appoint judicial officers. The preamble to the Charter explicitly mentions that the VOC shall "promote the interests and the wellbeing of the United Netherlands as well as the interests of all the inhabitants." The numerous public duties and powers illustrate that the VOC was in fact a semipublic company, rather than a purely private enterprise that simply sought profit maximization.[7] As the Dutch were in a war of independence against the Spanish rule, one of the principal objects of the VOC was to weaken the Spanish and Portuguese overseas.

The Charter also regulated the internal relationships of the VOC. It provided that policy outlines had to be determined by a board known as the *Heren XVII* (the Lords XVII). The Lords XVII could turn over a specific matter to the States General for elucidation and decision if the Lords XVII were unable to reach agreement on matters of considerable importance. Although major decisions were made by the Lords XVII, their implementation and the day-to-day management was carried out by the local directors. These were employed at one of the six separate branches, called chambers. The VOC had chambers in Amsterdam, Rotterdam, Delft, Hoorn, and Enkhuizen, all trading cities in the province of Holland, as well as in the province of Zeeland. All chambers were former headquarters of the precompanies. Power was thus largely decentralized in the VOC. The Board of the Lords XVII was composed of the directors of the different chambers. Only major shareholders were eligible for directorships. In case of a vacancy, the directors of the chamber in question had a right to make a binding nomination of three candidates. Appointments were made by the States of the relevant province. In 1602, however, the States of Holland delegated the right of appointment to the mayors of the five cities in question (Den Heijer 2005, 111). The Charter of 1602 did not contain a provision on the basis of which directors could be dismissed. They were appointed for life.

The position of participants was limited to that of providers of capital, without any control rights being attached to their "shareholdership." The VOC did not have a body that showed any similarity to the modern day general meeting of shareholders. Although the Charter did not provide anything about this, it must be assumed that the internal liability of participants was limited to the level of the contribution promised by them. Participants were not liable to creditors of the VOC for debts of the VOC. The participants were also entitled to dividend distributions as soon as 5 percent of the proceeds from the return had been cashed. These distributions were initially considered advances on the intended liquidation of the VOC, which, as was the intention when the Charter was drafted, had been incorporated for 21 years. This provision, however, was never complied with because it soon became evident that the VOC was not a temporary organization and had to make expensive, lasting investments in the East Indies. According to the Charter, a general audit would be made after 10 and 20 years. The participants could then withdraw their money from the company if they wished so. In the meantime, they could freely transfer their shares. This enabled the emergence of a stock market trade in shares almost immediately after the incorporation (Gelderblom and Jonker 2004).

Explanation for the Participants' Lack of Control

The participants' lack of control can be explained by the organization of the precompanies that were formed for the duration of a single voyage. As the ships were at sea for most of the existence of a precompany, control by participants was no simple matter. After the ships returned, the proceeds were divided and the company liquidated. Participants could then decide whether or not to invest in a following company. Consequently, despite the lack of formal control, the directors could not simply ignore the participants' interests. Finally, the presumption is justified that most participants in the precompanies were not very interested in control rights, given the expected profits.

The incorporation of the VOC had no effect on the participants control or lack thereof. Participants were not involved in the negotiations on the Charter between the directors of the precompanies and the States General and the directors had no reason to impair their own status by granting them control rights. Neither had the States General; the public interests of a company at war against the Portuguese and Spanish could well conflict with the interests of private investors. Moreover, given the abundance of capital at the beginning of the seventeenth century due to the rapid economic developments in the 1590s, there was no market incentive to grant control rights to participants in order to attract investment (Israel 2008, 337 et seq.).

Activism During the First Charter: Isaäc Le Maire

The drafters of the Charter presumably did not fully realize that the VOC was faced with challenges that the precompanies did not have. The longer horizon required long-term investments and the development of a long-term strategy. For instance, much money was spent on setting up a network of trading posts throughout Asia for intra-Asiatic trade. This was necessary, because there were not enough markets in Asia for European goods. What's more, funds were used in the battle against the Portuguese and Spaniards in the East Indies (Den Heijer 2005, 65). Furthermore, the strong position of the directors, the indefinite time for which they were appointed and the fact that the Charter obliged them to conduct a financial audit only after 10 and 21 years did expose them to temptations that did not yet exist before. Because of this, the high expectations aroused by the profits of some of the precompanies were not met in the first 20 years of the VOC's existence.

The disappointing profits and absence of dividend distributions resulted in great dissatisfaction on the part of one of the major participants of the VOC, Isaäc le Maire.[8] This former Amsterdam director was forced to resign in 1605, presumably because he was suspected of fraud (van Dillen 1930, 3 et seq.). The monopoly of the VOC, as well as a non-competition clause he had signed, however, prevented him from setting up a competing Dutch company (van Dillen 1930, 4).

For this reason, Le Maire held secret talks consecutively with Hudson and with King Henri IV about the formation of a competing company (van Dillen 1930, 5 et seq.; Frentrop 2002, 78 et seq.).[9] Given his competing plans, Le Maire had every interest in the investors withdrawing their money from the VOC after ten years as provided by the Charter. On January 24, 1609, in a remonstrance, addressed to van Oldenbarnevelt, he denounced the "impotence" of the Company:[10] Le Maire argued that the VOC sent out too few ships, had to borrow money due to severe losses, did not make any discoveries and, above all, did not make enough use of the Charter, as a result of which the "beneficial navigation lies down as if dead and buried." Le Maire protested vehemently against the endeavor of the directors to have the first ten-year financial statements merge into the second ten-year financial statements and to deny the right of the investors to withdraw their money in 1612. He therefore requested that the VOC would act in accordance with the Charter, so that participants could withdraw their money if they wished so.

After Le Maire's request was rejected, Le Maire incorporated the *Groote Compagnie,* which engaged in short speculations on a large scale (Frentrop 2002, 79; Den Heijer 2005, 99). Le Maire hoped that, if the share prices would fall below par value, investors would ask their money back in 1612. This would require the VOC to be liquidated and would give Le Maire himself the opportunity to set up new trading companies. The *Groote Compagnie* did not hesitate to spread false rumors and to commit fraud (van Dillen 1930, 23).

The *Groote Compagnie's* short speculations were initially successful: the price fell from 212 percent in 1607 to 126 percent in 1609 (Gaastra 2009, 27). But they did not have the intended result: in spite of the clear wordings of the Charter, the VOC did not conduct an audit and investors were not granted the opportunity to withdraw their money. In addition, the States General issued a ban on naked short selling (*Groot Placaet-boek I,* columns 553 et seq.; van Dillen 1930, 15 et seq.; Frentrop 2002, 80 et seq.).

There is no doubt that the directors' course of action violated the Charter. It deprived the participants of the few of their disciplinary mechanisms: a financial audit and the right to withdraw their money. It is therefore well conceivable that the deprivation of this disciplinary mechanism made it more difficult for the directors to resist the temptation to enrich themselves in the following decade. On the other hand, it cannot be ruled out that not giving the participants the opportunity to withdraw their money enabled the directors to strengthen the position of the VOC with respect to the EIC. The EIC did not have any permanent share capital at that time, which was one of the reasons it was considerably less financially strong than the VOC (Gaastra 2009, 24).[11]

Le Maire's short speculations nevertheless resulted in dividends being distributed for the first time in 1610. Given the lack of liquid assets, it was decided that dividends would be distributed in mace.[12] A second distribution followed soon afterward, largely in kind and a small part in cash (Den Heijer 2005, 87–88; Gaastra 2009, 23). That distribution in cash was made only on condition that the payments in kind were accepted. Several participants objected to the distributions in kind as these led to decline in market prices.[13] And other that did not object to the distributions in kind *per se,* but rather to that the market price by which they were calculated was too high therefore making the payments far less than they seemed to be. These participants later received a payment in cash at the same level in 1612, 1613, and 1618 (Den Heijer 2005, 88). In total, during the first Charter, 200 percent of the nominal capital was distributed, which, based on a correct valuation of goods distributed in kind, comes down to about 7.5 percent a year (Frentrop 2002, 83).

SHAREHOLDER ACTIVISM BY PAMPHLET: THE PROTEST OF COMPLAINING PARTICIPANTS

Most of the participants may have begrudgingly accepted the fact that the directors did not conduct an audit in 1612, but when no audit was conducted once again ten years later, a heated conflict arose between directors and participants. The VOC offered almost ideal circumstances for a maximization of agency costs and conflicts of interest. First, the directors considered the States General, rather than the participants, as their first principal (De Jong, Gelderblom, and Jonker). Unlike the participants, the States General had sufficient methods in order to ensure that the public interest was taken into account by the directors. As shown by De Jong, Gelderblom, and Jonker in Chapter 2, there were numerous personal links between the directors and the local, provincial, and governmental authorities. Second, the remuneration structure as provided in the 1602 Charter introduced new conflicts. Third, under the 1602 Charter, no new disciplinary mechanisms were put in place in order to counterbalance the disappearance of the disciplinary mechanism of a liquidation of a pre-company after every voyage. Fourth, the few disciplinary mechanisms that were supposed to be in place—the rendering of a financial account and the opportunity to withdraw money after ten years—had proven ineffective due to the backing of the directors by the public authorities during Le Maire's activism.

As a result, there were practically no disciplinary mechanisms in place which could serve the participants' interests: they were not involved in the appointment of directors, who were appointed for life. Neither did the participants have any other control rights. The directors could not be held personally liable and had a monopoly on information. Although shareholders could sell their shares, there was no market for corporate control. Furthermore, the share market was essentially not regulated and self dealing was not explicitly prohibited. If one takes into account that no dividends had been declared after 1620 and the share price had gone down from 250 percent in 1620 to 165 percent in 1622 (van Rees 1868, 147), one can easily conclude that the participants were locked in.

Unlike Le Maire, the complaining participants were not aiming to put an end to the VOC. They explicitly did not propose their fellow shareholders to withdraw their money in accordance with the Charter. Rather, their activism was aimed at ending abuses and changing the internal balance of power. The public nature of the activism by the complaining participants was an essential part of their strategy. The complaining participants attempted to exert influence on the negotiations between directors and the States General on the extension of the Charter. By publishing various anonymous polemic pamphlets, they not only aimed at mobilizing the public opinion against the VOC, but also at preventing money from being invested in the Dutch West India Company (West-Indische Compagnie or WIC). In 1621, the WIC had been granted a Charter to trade with North and South America and was collecting funds from investors. The complaining participants probably attempted to stop people from investing in order to make the States General more receptive to their objections (Frentrop 2002, 101). This strategy proved effective, because subscription for shares of the WIC ran with much difficulty, even though the WIC Charter of June 1621 granted more control rights to participants than the VOC Charter of 1602. The limited interest of shareholders resulted in expansion of the WIC's trade monopoly in June 1622 and strengthening of the position of WIC participants on February 13 and June 21, 1623. These amendments of the WIC Charter coincided with the activism of the complaining participants. There is also a close connection between the incorporation of the WIC and the amendment of the VOC Charter with respect to content: the complaining participants sometimes derived inspiration from the WIC Charter, while some demands by the participants were not met at the VOC, but were at the WIC.

The incorporation of the WIC also proved to be an independent source of conflicts between the directors and the complaining participants. The reason for this was that the directors intended to participate in the WIC for one million guilders in order to obtain control in the WIC as well. The complaining participants protested vehemently against this decision, as they would then indirectly participate in the WIC against their will.[14]

The main complaints brought up in the pamphlets can be roughly divided into three categories: (i) failure to comply with the obligation under the Charter to render a financial account, (ii) self-enrichment and conflicts of interest, and (iii) participants' lack of control rights. After these are considered, attention is focused on the complaining participants' demanded amendments to the Charter and the directors' response. Finally, the actual Charter amendments in 1622 and 1623 are discussed as well as activism after the amendment of the Charter.

No Rendering of Financial Account

The immediate reason for the activism was the fact that the directors had refused for the second time to render account of their management and financial results:

There has been no audit. Everything has remained obscure and they haven't come up with anything but procrastination and excuses instead of the accounts book, which, as we suspect, they had smeared with bacon and which was eaten by the dogs. It is said that only someone who has something to conceal hides. But an honest rendering of account can, of course, bear the light of day. When our ancestors Adam and Eve hid and tried to conceal themselves behind fig leaves, they were unable to account to God for taking bites of the apple. Now the Complaining Participants set everyone thinking whether all suspicion can be removed in this way from the hearts of pious people.[15]

Anger was strengthened by the fact that not only the second financial statements and audit failed to materialize, but that directors had also requested the States General to extend the Charter by 50 years:

For instance, they did not allow the Participants to attend the annual audit, so they would not be able to solve the mystery how the directors had suddenly become so wealthy (...). They even requested to have the Charter extended by 50 years, so they could hold their well-paid jobs longer and only conduct a general audit for the participants' grandchildren in the next world.[16]

The complaining participants were therefore of the opinion that a proper audit should be conducted before a decision could be made to extend the Charter:

You Honorable Gentlemen can conclude from the above that the participants have good grounds to complain about the directors and demand a proper audit from them before their directorships can be continued. Because their good or bad administration will be evident from such an audit. It will then be evident as well how absurdly and shamelessly they have discharged their duties, which is the reason they first request extension of the Charter before they have proved that their administration is in order by conducting an audit. This shows, however, that they are trying to avoid a proper audit and are attempting to obtain an extension of the Charter by promising to conduct an audit afterwards. At that time, they will have enough possibilities to drag their feet, so no audit will ever follow again. This is in conflict with the custom of all right-minded agents or administrators who are charged with administering other people's property (such as the directors) and who are prepared to render account at any time to the satisfaction of their principals as often as their principals ask them to do so, so as not to harbor any suspicions or mistrust. Because an honest person highly values his honor and good name and cannot bear the thought that people think ill of him. The directors apparently do not pay much attention to their good name, as long as they can simply continue to have other people's goods at their disposal, which Your Honorable Authority should not allow (...).[17]

Conflicts of Interest

The complaining participants extensively complained about the wealth of the directors, which contrasted with the low dividends that had been paid out to the participants. Their wealth had appeared so suddenly, that it looked "like mushrooms that have grown overnight."[18] Amongst others, they accused the directors of self-dealing, insider trading, abuse of the remuneration rules and stealing from the company.

Self-Dealing

Many conflicts of interest occurred because directors purchased goods from the VOC at too low prices. I quote a passage from the *Vertooch* ("Remonstrance") and the *Tweede Nootwendiger Discours* ("Second, More Necessary Discourse"):

They have also permitted themselves to purchase the goods of the participants from each other, which is contrary to the custom of everyone who administers other people's property. The fact that they provide one another with benefits can be concluded from the following. Sometimes, when they are going to sell a batch of silk goods and have earmarked these for merchants, they first sell these goods to one another without waiting for or listening to these merchants, at a price that is one third less than the price these merchants would be willing to pay for them. Subsequently, the director, who bought the goods from his partners resells the goods immediately to the same merchants at a price that is one third higher than what he had paid for them, which enables him to earn 33% on the goods without investing money or running a risk. In that way, without undertaking a long and dangerous voyage to the East Indies, directors can make a very profitable voyage to the East Indies in just a few hours.[19]

Another director purchased a batch of indigo privately for 29 *stuivers*, of which it is not only said that a more profitable purchase had never been made before, because it was under market value. But because the director who made the purchase was also angry with his fellow directors (the sellers), he received a few thousand pound discount outright. In that way, they were said to have enriched one another at other people's expense.[20]

In the *Tegen-vertooch* ("Counter Remonstrance"), the directors replied that the Charter does not expressly prohibit directors from trading with the Company and they denied abusing their position.[21] This did not convince the author of the *Nootwendich Discours*. To substantiate his assertion that directors may not trade with the Company, he first of all relies on general principles of reasonableness and fairness (*bona fides*). In addition, he looks for similar situations in which someone in his capacity as trustee manages property that does not belong to him personally. He argues that a trustee may not engage in self-dealing or may do so only under stringent conditions:

It shall be enough that the directors are well paid and that they can imagine being gentlemen. Of course, they will argue that self-dealing is not expressly forbidden under the VOC Charter. However, I will then reply that the fact that something is not expressly forbidden, does not lead to the conclusion that it is allowed. One should take into account the fairness or unfairness of the specific case and then consider whether it is allowed or not. As the whole world considers self-dealing as unfair, it is expressly forbidden under the Charter of the Dutch West India Company. Equally, the Lords of the Admiralty are not allowed to trade with the Navy. Guardians and "*curatores bonis*" may not purchase goods that have been given in custody, unless by public auction, which may also be allowed in the case of the VOC. One can see that it violates the spirit of the Charter. Unfortunately, the profits that the directors enjoy as a result of self-dealing have disabled their power of judgment, as a result of which, just because of their silliness, these pious persons did not understand the spirit of the Charter, and therefore simply sought their own profits and would like to continue to do so.[22]

Information Asymmetries and Insider Trading

The directors' monopoly on information gave them a special position on the stock market, which was barely regulated. According to the participants, the directors made devious use of their information advantage. As the VOC did not publish financial accounts, investors often bought or sold their shares on the basis of rumors on the market. According to the participants, the directors spread false rumors among the unsuspecting public, depending on their long or short positions and their intentions to buy or sell:

> It is known that they can pull the wool over the participants' eyes and tell them anything they want, by which they constantly deal them a blind card. Sometimes they present Company matters optimistically to induce the participants to purchase shares. Then they make it seem as if matters are going badly again to frighten the participants, so that they can buy shares at a cheap price in order to meet their short obligations at the expiration date. By doing so, they ruin the participants and ultimately draw everything to themselves as absolute rulers of the East Indies. Oh shameless servants. It is time for the Gentlemen of the States General to take the matter in hand (...)![23]

There seem to have been some grounds for the accusations, because the directors did not deny that they traded in shares.[24] Without dealing with the accusation that they spread false rumors, the directors only asserted that it was evident from the pamphlets that the complaining participants were just as greedy as they accused the directors of being. If the directors did indeed engage in short speculations, just like Le Maire in 1609, this means that the directors could have a personal interest in the share price going down for at least a certain period. It is hard to imagine a more serious agency problem! It is therefore not surprising that the participants protested against this special form of conflict of interest:

> One can also imagine how the directors attempt to make profits at the expense of the participants when they sell more shares in the Company than they own. In this way, they intensely long for the misfortune of the Company so they can repurchase the shares cheaply at the expiration date, in order to make profits on the Company's losses. One can imagine how much such directors promote the prosperity of the Company (...).[25]

Directors' Remuneration as a Source of Agency Conflicts

Conflicting interests between directors and the VOC were aggravated further by the way in which directors were remunerated. According to the Charter, the total salary of directors amounted to 1 percent of the equipping and 1 percent of the profits. This amount was subsequently divided among the directors of the various chambers. This provision not only aimed at profit maximization, but also included an incentive to maximize the turnover. It created various possibilities for abuse. First, the provision that salaries were determined per chamber, rather than per director, sometimes resulted in vacant directors' positions not being filled so that the earnings could be divided among fewer directors.[26] Second, the fact that the directors' pay was higher the more the costs of equipping a ship rose, certainly did not contribute to an economical purchasing policy. Moreover, if a director sold equipment goods to the Company at too high a price, he could enjoy a double advantage.[27] This was done on a large scale, according to the *Nootwendich Discours*:

We will now discuss the supply for shipping equipment. Here, our well paid directors are playing dirty tricks (...); they have found a secret route to the goldmines. That route, however, does not lead though the Strait of Magellan, where they wasted the capital of the company. Rather, they sell salt beef, cables, ropes, anchors, wine, bread, biscuit rusk (even if the rusk has already made a previous trip), beans, peas, groats, they are constructing ships, providing artillery, powder and shots, etc. Each of the directors sells something in order to maximize his profits (...). But why, my dearest Gentlemen, doesn't the company organize a public auction, why doesn't it purchase the goods from anybody who is willing to accept the lowest price? This may save one third of the construction costs of the ships.[28]

The provision on the directors' commissions also resulted in the VOC having much too big ships built:

It is difficult to estimate how much loss the Company has suffered by building so many large and expensive ships: each chamber tries to build the largest ships in order to equip them with a lot of goods and make huge profits so that it can earn a large commission. This could have been done with cheaper ships and the money used in trade or to pay back loans. Those large, expensive ships were then used partially in the East Indies even to transport wood and stones for the construction of Fort Jacatra.[29] Some ships were lost in the process, which means that half of the large ships would have sufficed for the trade between the East Indies and here.[30]

More Self-Enrichment

A certain director is portrayed in a sarcastic manner, for whom the regular fee was not enough and who was accused of literally putting items of the VOC into his own pocket. This concerned a gold crucifix that was part of the inventory of a *kraak*, a certain type of sailing ship that the VOC had captured. The pants pocket proved unable to withstand the weight of the crucifix, according to the *Tweede Nootwendiger Discours* that reported this "exhibitionistic self-enrichment":

During the inspection of the goods belonging to a ship that had been captured by the company, a certain Director put a gold chain with a heavy gold crucifix in his pocket. As one should always give one's neighbor the benefit of the doubt, I believe this director only thought he was putting his handkerchief in his pocket. Due to the heavy weight, however, his pocket tore open and the gold crucifix, including a part of the chain was hanging out of his trousers. His fellow director, feeling pity for him that he was not able to bear his own cross, realized that anybody could see his groin and told him that his shirt was hanging out of his trousers. The director blushed to the roots of his hair, but then simply took up his crucifix and walked away. You directors, you wipe your mouth while telling us that you didn't eat![31]

Control Rights: The EIC as an Example for the VOC

The complaining participants not only wanted to stop the violations of the Charter and to diminish agency problems, they also demanded major institutional changes. They actually sought to invert the balance of power within the VOC so that they could exercise control over the directors and the company's course of affairs. In order to make their claim, the complaining participants referred to several other trading companies in which the investors exercised control over their agents, such as the *factorijvennootschap,* a very common limited partnership-like company in which the silent partners had a dominant position. They also refer to the governance of the EIC, which was characterized by a strong members' organization.[32] In a full-fledged shareholders' meeting, EIC shareholders enjoyed extensive information and approval rights. They appointed annually a board of directors, composed of a governor, his deputy, and 24 committees, and determined their salaries. It is therefore not surprising that the complaining participants held up the internal organization of the EIC, as well as the governance of the WIC and Portuguese and Spanish companies, as an example:

The complaining participants are not slaves, but free people in free countries. They only ask to be allowed to appoint administrators of their goods themselves, to whom they entrust such administration. That this request is not unfair is evident from the fact that even the King of Spain gives merchants who sail to the East Indies and Spanish merchants who trade with the West Indies the opportunity to appoint the agents or bookkeepers of their goods to whom they themselves entrust such management. In England as well, one sees that the participants in the EIC have the most to say: they remain masters of their own goods and each year appoint and dismiss from their midst as they see fit a Governor, his deputy and the Court of 24 Committees, as well as an auditor. And each shareholder is entitled to inspect the books and merchandise and see how the goods are converted to cash. This is evident from a certificate from the English East Indies Board, of which the complaining participants have obtained an authentic copy. Does this not turn you pale, oh shameless directors! Or does no red blood flow through your veins? But neither law nor reason can make you change your minds. Other countries set the standard and you remain stuck in your old ways. You do not follow any good examples. It appears that although greed has not blinded you, it has indeed made you insensitive and leprous.[33]

The participants' wish to be more involved in the internal affairs of the VOC is also clear from a passage from the *Tweede Nootwendiger Discours*. It was argued that the participants should be entitled to approve a resolution by the directors to take out loans, which was considered very risky in that time:

The directors should not needlessly have taken out an interest-bearing loan of 77 tons of gold, with as subsequent justification that the directors hoped that this would enable them to set up a profitable trade in silk. They should have been certain of this before assuming such a burden without the advice or knowledge of the participants. Furthermore, it is very doubtful that they were authorized and had good reasons to do so, because each participant has invested as much as he himself was willing to risk. Participants did not invest that which the directors borrowed over and above this as they saw fit, without an express mandate. In that way, they could indeed ruin all participants and the whole Company and allow them to go bankrupt. The participants therefore request that this unlimited power to burden the Company henceforth be limited, unless the directors jointly and severally guarantee such loans. *Nam factum cuique suum, non adversario nocere debet ff. De Reg. Iur.*[34] The directors are not authorized to do so, except with the advice, in accordance with the will and with the prior knowledge of the participants, their principals. The participants are thus not satisfied with such frivolous excuses and stories that the loan was communicated to His Princely Excellency [Stadtholder Prince Maurice of Orange] and the Honorable Gentlemen of the States General. Why don't you say that you have spoken to the participants who have a direct interest in this and did not approve it after you had brought it to their attention (or do you imagine that it is far beneath your station to consult with your lords and masters about your business)? Why do you, directors, put forth a fallacy? For the Prince and Honorable Gentlemen of the States General rely exclusively on the information you give them and, what's more, they understand nothing about commerce. They can therefore be easily misled when one presents matters to them otherwise than they are. In short, you obtained permission by devious means. So their permission cannot protect you, nor can it remove the power of the participants' arguments. Furthermore, the participants have never understood that, by contributing their own money to the Company, they turned themselves into children of the court and that henceforth, their own funds would be at the disposal of His Princely Excellency and the Honorable Gentlemen of the States General. (. . .) Isaiah speaks about this as follows in Chapter 5:[35] Shame on you who add house to house and join field to field, until not an acre remains, and you are left to dwell alone in the land.[36]

There was no change in response to this argument when the VOC Charter was amended, but one can be found in the WIC Charter that was supplemented on June 22, 1623. It provides "the Company may not withdraw any interest-bearing funds or deposits except with the advice and consent of the majority of directors and principal participants."

Proposals to Revise the Charter

In the short term, the participants wanted a dividend distribution in the form of cloves[37] and an audit in conformity with the provisions of the Charter. The complaining participants also wanted to reduce the risk of conflicts of interests by changing the remuneration policy:

[We request] that instead of a commission, the directors be paid a fair fee, for which they must fully and accurately perform the tasks with which they are charged, in order to prevent the unseemly greed on which the overabundant equipping of ships and sending of goods is based.[38]

As pointed out earlier, they also demanded certain institutional changes. Their initial proposals were nonetheless moderate by current standards. For example, they only proposed that the *principal* participants, that is, participants who are eligible for a directorship on the basis of their interest, must have influence on the appointments. Moreover, the complaining participants did not demand a direct right of appointment; they requested only a nomination for appointment. Nor did they request that the participants be given the right to dismiss directors in the interim. Their proposal, which also appeared in several altered forms in other pamphlets,[39] essentially comes down to the introduction of a kind of staggered board, from which several directors would retire periodically:

Regarding the amendment of the Charter, the participants request first of all that the directors will no longer remain for an indefinite time but that a fourth of them will retire and another fourth every two years. The participants also request that the principal participants be allowed to make a nomination for appointment, and that the appointment be made by the Gentlemen of the States of the province in question.[40]

Furthermore, the participants wanted more supervision to be exercised over the directors' management. For this purpose, they requested that a delegation of principal participants be allowed to inspect the books and be assigned supervisory duties. Account should be rendered annually to this Board. The *Kort Onderricht* (Short Instruction) desired, for instance[41]

that supervisory directors be appointed from the ranks of principal participants, who maintain day-to-day supervision of the accounts before grass grows over them. We request that a general audit report be made available to them annually, and that another general audit be prepared within six or more years, so that the directors can hold their offices with honor and without causing a scandal![42]

The Directors' Response

Thus far hardly any attention has been devoted to the directors' response to the participants' complaints. Not only were fewer pamphlets published on behalf of the directors, the pamphlets produced are less interesting from a corporate governance perspective because the incumbent directors had an interest in maintaining the *status quo*. The directors extensively argued that the pamphlets damaged the directors' reputation.[43] To the extent the directors dealt with the substance of the participants' pamphlets,[44] they emphasized that the VOC, as a semipublic company also had to take into account the public interest of the Netherlands. (The same argument was offered in response to complaining shareholders of the French East India Company as discussed in Chapter 8). According to the directors, the VOC had been very profitable for both the Netherlands and the participants and had meanwhile repaid part of its debts.[45] They cited various mitigating circumstances to explain the lower than expected earnings.[46] For instance, the war in Germany (now known as 30 Years' War, 1618–1648) supposedly impeded the sale of spices, and the VOC alleged to have waged expensive sea battles with the English, because they would otherwise have been driven out of the Indies.

The directors promised an audit in the next year,[47] but also stressed how complicated it was to prepare an audit when ships were far from the Netherlands conducting the continuous intra-Asiatic trade between 30 locations.[48] Finally, the directors do not fail to point out that the participants' pamphlet battle seriously harmed the

WIC.[49] This shows that the participants' only real weapon—refusal to subscribe for shares of the WIC—was effective.

The directors rather seem to rely on their close links with the governmental authorities instead (e.g., the directors of the Chamber of Middelburg were appointed by local or provincial authorities). Many VOC directors were also mayor, member of a town council, or were otherwise part of the local or provincial oligarchic elite (*regentenklasse*).[50] Some directors were member of the States of Holland or Zeeland, or even a representative of their province in the States General.[51]

This explains why the States of Holland were the directors' closest ally. For instance, the States of Holland prohibited the complaining participants from going to court in order to claim their rights under the old Charter.[52] The States of Holland also issued a ban on the *Nootwendich Discours*.[53] A reward of 400 guilders was offered to the person who could identify the author or printer.

It seems as if the suppression of the *Nootwendich Discours* did not come as a surprise to its author; this pamphlet already declared at the end *in libera republica, liberas oportet esse linguas* (In a free republic, speech should also be free). The ban did not make much of an impression: the *Nootwendich Discours* was reprinted twice under a different title.[54] In addition, the *Tweede Nootwendiger Discours,* published soon afterward, was scornfully dated in *In't Jaar Een-en-twintich, der Onghedane Rekeninge* (The twenty-first year for which no accounts were rendered). The *Tweede Nootwendiger Discours* presumes that the directors will indeed

rage like oil on a fire. A furious man trips over his own feet and would give four hundred guilders to find out the author's name and take revenge on the one he despises. They should think twice before they decide to find the author, because, if he were found, he would prove and substantiate and maintain all this and even more.[55]

The scornful polemic did not take away that the close relations and personal unions between the directors and the members of the States of Holland posed the participants for a serious dilemma: on the one hand, they complained about the misconduct by the directors, and on the other hand, they respectfully requested the same persons to stop their bad practices.[56]

The Charter of 1623

The Charter was amended by the States General, composed of representatives of each of the seven provinces of the Netherlands. The

VOC directors were strongly backed by the representatives of the powerful province of Holland in which five of the six VOC Chambers were situated. Representatives of the other provinces, however, were apparently somewhat more receptive to the participants' complaints.[57] This enabled the States General to act as an an intermediary in the negotiations between the directors and the complaining participants. These negotiations resulted in some demands having been met in the decision of the States General on December 22, 1622, to extend the Charter by 21 years as of 1623.[58] At least on paper.

This Charter confirmed that an audit would still be conducted; it would be presented in a public meeting "with open doors and windows" to representatives of the States General. According to the Charter, the incumbent directors would retire pursuant to a complicated rotation schedule. The newly appointed directors were to retire three years from the time all directors were replaced and would be eligible for reappointment only three years later. Pursuant to the new Charter, the participants would be convened in the event of a vacancy. This meeting would then designate a number[59] of principal participants who, together with the remaining directors of the chamber in question, would be allowed to nominate three candidates, all principal participants. The States of the province or the mayor of the city in question would then appoint the directors.[60] To prevent nepotism, it was no longer allowed to nominate close relations of directors.

In order to put an end to the self-enrichment of the directors, they were allowed to deliver goods only after approval from the public authorities. Directors were allowed to purchase goods from the Company only if these goods had fixed prices or were purchased at a public auction. The granting of discounts or postponements of payment was prohibited. The remuneration structure was adjusted in such a way that the directors would receive a joint remuneration of 1 percent of the profits.[61] In this way, the remuneration no longer depended partly on the value of the equipping of ships.[62]

Finally, the directors were placed under the supervision of a board of *Heren IX* (Lords IX), composed of sworn principal participants from the different Chambers. The Lords IX examined the annual balance sheet and were granted a right of advice in respect of important decisions by the Lords XVII. The Lords IX were bound by strict secrecy.[63] This supervisory body was expected to promote the interests of the (principal) participants who, just as under the first Charter, remained at a distance from the Board of Directors.

The States General had announced these amendments to the Charter without agreement having been reached between the participants and directors. Both the activism and the negotiations were therefore continued following extension of the Charter. On the advice of Stadtholder Prince Maurice, the States General resolved on March 13, 1623, to ultimately adjust the Charter in several places "to remove all further questions and disputes."[64] According to these adjustments, the participants were allowed to appoint a certain number of auditors who would have the right to inspect the underlying audit documents. The Lords IX were now allowed to attend all meetings of the Lords XVII. They also obtained a right to give advice on decisions concerning the sending and equipping of ships, sale of goods, and distribution of dividends. They were also entitled to inspect the correspondence with the East Indies and to inspect the warehouses. Last but not least, it was provided that, in principle, distributions would be made to participants each year.

Activism after the Prolongation of the Charter

The participants still didn't agree.[65] As a compromise, they promised that their activism would come to an end, if two demands would be met. Their first demand, a further regulation of insider trading and short speculations, was met within a few days: on April 1, 1623, the States General resolved to confirm the existing ban on naked short selling.[66] Their second request was initially delayed and finally never met. The participants demanded the Lords IX to get a decisive vote, rather than an advisory vote in the meetings of the Lords XVII.[67] The supreme governing body of the VOC would then *de facto* become a one-tier board, consisting of 17 executive directors, appointed by the local or provincial authorities upon a joint nomination by the principal participants and the directors, and of nine nonexecutive directors, directly appointed by the same principal participants. This proposal would not only dilute the voting rights of the incumbent 17 directors, it would also slightly weaken the position of the powerful Chamber of Amsterdam.[68] It is also for this reason why the Amsterdam directors opposed against the second demand.[69]

The Amsterdam directors—many of whom were also city magistrates—apparently exercised their influence in the States of Holland. Holland, on its turn, delayed and finally vetoed the second demand of the complaining participants. It is remarkable, however, that each of the other six provinces that were represented in the States General supported this demand.[70] This shows that the complaining participants enjoyed quite some support in the Netherlands, even on the highest political level.

In the mean time, the appointment of the Lords IX gave rise to further quarrels.[71] The Amsterdam directors, for instance, refused their cooperation to invite all principal participants, which would appoint four members of the Lords IX. Instead, the directors invited only some allied participants, which then appointed the Amsterdam representatives in the Lords IX.[72]

Furthermore, some provisions in the amended Charter were not complied with. For instance, according to the Charter, the delivery of goods by the directors to the VOC required the prior approval by the public authorities like the city magistrates. As many of the directors were city magistrates themselves, the directors could continue insider trading as they did before, at least according to the complaining participants.[73] Moreover, new directors would not by far be appointed always in accordance with the amended Charter.[74] In performing their supervisory duties, the Lords IX often took account of their own ambitions to become future directors.

A final source of conflicts was the financial audit. The 1623 Charter provided that the auditors that were appointed by the principal participants had the right to inspect all underlying documents. The settlement became a continuing story of refusal to grant access to the books, delay by the Amsterdam directors, apparently lost documents, admonitions by the States General and refusal by the Amsterdam directors to follow the instructions of the States General.[75] Finally, in 1624 the Amsterdam directors simply removed all books and declared the matter closed.[76]

How did the activism by the complaining participants come to an end? It actually fizzled out like a damp squib. In the course of 1625, the States General needed the support of the VOC in order to solve two issues with England and France.[77] National interest therefore required the States General to support the VOC in its conflict with the complaining participants. They therefore stopped exerting pressure on the directors to render the accounts. The participants must have acknowledged that any further protests would be useless.

CONCLUSION

All this does not alter the fact that the pamphlet battle was significant for the development of corporate law. The conflict forms an early, well-documented example of agency problems, which can arise due to the separation of ownership and control. In their pamphlets, the complaining participants raised corporate governance issues that are still relevant today, like self-dealing, insider trading, board remuneration, self-enrichment, and board independence. The activists stressed the importance of fiduciary duties of directors and of control and information rights for shareholders. Furthermore, the pamphlets illustrate the internal conflicts of interests that can arise if a semipublic enterprise has to serve both the public interest and the interests of investors.

As a result of the pamphlet battle, at least theoretically, a limited degree of control by major shareholders in a listed company was recognized for the first time. This would be exercised indirectly by a body composed of representatives of the principal participants. As the corporate governance of the VOC would serve as an example for many other continental European trading companies in the seventeenth century, the importance of the activism by the complaining participants was certainly not limited to the Netherlands.[78]

According to current standards, the Charter of 1623 would be faced with many protests from shareholders and would create a breeding ground for a "new round" of shareholder activism. This, however, did not happen: until its bankruptcy in 1799 the internal organization was not significantly changed. The silencing of the shareholder protest can be explained mainly by the fact that faulty corporate governance did not appear to prevent commercial success. Ironically, the beginning of the 1620s mark the beginning of an era of prosperity for the VOC.[79] Precisely in 1622, the Banda Islands were conquered and the VOC obtained a monopoly on the trade in nutmeg and mace, followed in the next decades by a monopoly on the trade in cloves and cinnamon. Furthermore, the VOC profited substantially from intra-Asian trade, particularly through access to Japan as of 1639. In short, abundant dividends flowed in and share prices gradually rose. Then as now, the surest way to curtail shareholder activism is to deliver outsize returns.

NOTES

1. Luke 16:1–2. Quoted in *Tweede Nootwendiger Discours, 13.*
2. *Dolerende participanten* can also be translated into *dissenting* or *aggrieved* participants.
3. Partnership-like companies or companies that resembled private limited companies often did, of course, have meetings in which investors had a voice; these companies, however, were different due to their smaller scale and limited exit opportunities of the partners/investors.
4. See also (Frentrop 2002, 88 et seq.) (van Rees 1868, 144 et seq.) (van der Heijden 1908, 61 et seq.) and (van Brakel 1908, 129 et seq.).
5. At the time the Charter was granted, the Republic of the Seven United Provinces was involved in a battle for independence from Spanish

rule, which resulted in international recognition of the Republic in 1648. This Republic can be considered a type of confederation of independent provinces that had delegated limited powers to a central body, the States General, for example, in relation to foreign policy. All provinces had one vote in this body. The Southern Netherlands—now Belgium, Luxembourg, and parts of Northern France—remained under Spanish rule (Israel 2008).

6. *Groot Placaet-Boek I,* column 530 et seq. A transcription of the text and its English translation have been published in Gepken-Jager et al. (eds.) 2005.
7. This issue is extensively dealt with by Gelderblom, De Jong and Jonker in Chapter 2
8. For extensive treatment of Le Maire's shareholder activism: (van Dillen 1930; Frentrop 2002, 76 et seq.; Frentrop 2009).
9. The discussions were discovered in Paris by the Dutch diplomat van Aerssen. The plans for a French company also failed owing to the murder of Henri IV in 1610.
10. For an English translation, see: (Frentrop, Jonker, and Davis 2009).
11. See also (Gelderblom 2009, 232–240), who gives various other explanations of the fact that the VOC had fewer funding problems than the EIC.
12. The announced distribution made the price go up again, which caused serious financial problems for the short speculators (van Dillen 1930, 22 et seq.).
13. The directors might have intended this, in order to force the English off the market (Frentrop 2002, 83).
14. Van Rees 1868, 148; *Nootwendich Discours,* 27.
15. *Nootwendich Discours,* 6.
16. *Vertooch,* 7–8.
17. *Vertooch,* 10.
18. *Nootwendich Discours,* 13.
19. *Vertooch,* 7.
20. *Tweede Nootwendiger Discours,* 70.
21. *Tegen-vertooch,* 4–5.
22. *Nootwendich Discours,* 13.
23. *Nootwendich Discours,* 17.
24. *Tegen-vertooch,* 6–7.
25. *Korte Aenwysinge,* 6.
26. Van Brakel 1908, 133.
27. According to the *Eyndelijcke Iustificatie,* 7 (Final Justification), the goods that were sold by the directors to the VOC were sometimes even not measured, weighed, or counted (see also van Rees 1868, 150).
28. *Nootwendich Discours,* 14–15.
29. In 1618, Governor General J.P. Coen decided that the VOC had to build a fort in Jakatra—now Jakarta. Coen brutally broke the resistance of the local Prince Sriwijaya, burned down the city and

then chased out the English. In 1619 Coen decided to reconstruct Jakatra, meanwhile renamed Batavia, and build a much larger fort. The complaining participants refer here to the expenses involved in this reconstruction.

30. *Korte Aenwysinge,* 7.
31. *Tweede Nootwendiger Discours,* 74.
32. About the EIC: Harris 2005; Chaudhuri 1965; Scott II, 89 et seq.
33. *Nootwendich Discours,* 29–30. See also Frentrop 2002, 95.
34. Because a person's own acts should harm the person acting himself, not his opposite party (Dig. 50,17,155).
35. Isaiah 5:8 (New English Bible).
36. *Tweede Nootwendiger Discours,* 34–45 (*cf.* also *Naerder Aenwysinghe,* 4).
37. Roelevink 1983, nos. 4655, 4690B, 4702, 4704, 4707, 4712, and 4765; *Nootwendich Discours,* 39.
38. *Tweede Nootwendiger Discours,* 25.
39. For instance, the *Nootwendich Discours* demands that one third of the directors should retire every two years. *Kort Onderricht,* 6 and *Tweede Nootwendiger Discours,* 25, however, take a tougher position and argue that the participants should be able to elect the directors directly. The *Nootwendich Discours* also contains the proposal that participants who jointly represent 1/60 of the capital each be allowed to appoint a director.
40. *Copye van eenen brieff* (Copy of a letter), 5.
41. The *Kort Onderricht,* 6 demanded "that the participants should absolutely be allowed to choose their own directors and have free disposition over their goods as they see fit." This is also stated in the *Tweede Nootwendiger Discours.*
42. *Kort Onderricht,* 6–7. The *Tweede Nootwendiger Discours,* 25 also demanded "that principal participants be allowed on a daily basis to inspect the accounts of all equipping of ships and all goods purchased and sold."
43. *Tegen-vertooch,* 4 et seq.
44. *Tegen-vertooch*; *Derde Discours.*
45. *Derde Discours,* 4–5, 9.
46. *Tegen-vertooch,* 7–8.
47. *Derde Discours,* 7.
48. *Derde Discours,* 7–8.
49. *Derde Discours,* 2–3, 10 et seq. This investment stoppage might also have been based on investors' objections relating to the colonial and military role assigned in part to the WIC.
50. Den Heijer 2005, 110 et seq.; Gaastra 2009, 28 et seq.
51. In the States General, each of the seven provinces could cast one vote. In theory, decisions were taken unanimously; however, in practice, the States General were dominated by the powerful province of Holland.
52. Van Rees 1868, 155; Frentrop 2002, 97–98.
53. *Placcaet,* 3.

54. Van Rees 1868, 157.
55. *Tweede Nootwendiger Discours,* 96.
56. The *Tweede Nootwendiger Discours* repeatedly shows that the complaining participants were well aware of this dilemma. See also van Rees 1868, 159 et seq.
57. Van Rees 1868, 162; Thyspf 3026. On the other hand, the States General were clearly irritated by the polemic tone of the *Tweede Nootwendiger Discours* (Roelevink 1983, 4737; Roelevink 1989, 95, 298).
58. *Groot Placaet-Boek I,* column 537 et seq.; Roelevink 1983, no. 4712, 4714.
59. The number matches the number of directors in the chamber in question, not counting the retiring director.
60. On this point, there is a close connection with the WIC Charter. It initially provided that directors and principal participants would be allowed to make a joint nomination for appointment. The complaining participants based their demands regarding the appointment of directors partly on this provision. The amendment of February 16, 1623, to the WIC Charter was subsequently influenced in turn by the activism of the complaining participants, in view of the provision that the nomination would be made exclusively by the *principal* participants. Lastly, the amendment of June 21, 1623, to the WIC Charter provides that the principal participants may also appoint some directors directly.
61. Ships, artillery, inventory and borrowed money were not allowed to be counted.
62. As of 1647, the directors would receive only a fixed remuneration (Gepken-Jager 2005, 67).
63. Pursuant to Articles 4 and 5 of the amendment to the WIC Charter on June 21, 1623, a similar supervisory body was to be established at the WIC.
64. *Groot Placaet-Boek I,* column 543 et seq.; Roelevink 1989, no. 490.
65. Thyspf 3023 and 3120.
66. Thyspf 3026, 6. The resolution, published in *Groot Placaet-Boek I,* column 555 *et seq.* also contained some regulation on future transactions, the registration of encumbered shares and the settlement of share transactions.
67. Thsypf 3026, 5.
68. More than half of the share capital had been subscribed for in the Amsterdam Chamber, but it had only eight representatives in the Lords XVII, so that Amsterdam could not control this meeting. Four members of the Lords IX were appointed by the principal participants of Amsterdam. If the request of the complaining participants had been met, "Amsterdam" would have 12 votes in the combined body of 26 directors. Amsterdam would then always need two additional votes instead of one in order to impose its will on the VOC.
69. Thyspf 3126, 9.

70. Thyspf 3026.
71. For disagreement on the appointment of representatives of the principal participants of Delft and Rotterdam, see Thyspf 3031.
72. One of these four representatives even resigned, after he became aware that the election process was not organized in a proper way. (Thyspf 3119; Thyspf 3118, 4–5. See also van Rees 1868, 168.)
73. Thyspf 3027, 9.
74. Gaastra 2009, 29 et seq.
75. Thyspf 3121; Thyspf 3123.
76. Thyspf 3122.
77. The VOC had captured two French ships. The diplomatic relationship with France would be seriously damaged if the VOC refused to pay damages. In England, Dutch diplomats had drawn a number of bills of exchange on the VOC. The States General urged the VOC to accept these bills (van Rees 1868, 169).
78. Gepken-Jager et al. (eds.) 2005.
79. Den Heijer 2005, 88.

References

Chaudhuri, K.N. *The English East India Company. The Study of an Early Joint-Stock Company 1600–1640*, London: Frank Cass & Co, 1965.
Copye van eenen brieff; Knuttel 1978, no. 3346.
den Heijer, H.J. *De geoctrooieerde Compagnie*, Deventer: Kluwer 2005.
Derde Discours; Knuttel 1978, no. 3351.
Frentrop, P.M.L. *Corporate Governance 1602–2002. Ondernemingen en hun aandeelhouders sinds de VOC*, Amsterdam: Prometheus 2002.
Frentrop, P. "The First Known Shareholder Activist: The Colorful Life and Times of Isaac le Maire (1559–1624)" in: Frentrop/Jonker/Davis 2009, 11–26.
Frentrop, P., Jonker, J., and Davis S. 2009, *Shareholder Rights at 400. Commemorating Isaac Le Maire and the First Recorded Expression of Investor Advocacy*, The Hague: Remix business communications 2009.
Gaastra, F.S. *Geschiedenis van de VOC*, Zutphen: Walburg Pers 2009.
Gelderblom, O. "The Organization of Long-Distance Trade in England and the Dutch Republic," in: O. Gelderblom (ed.), *The Political Economy of the Dutch Republic*, Surrey: Ashgate 2009.
Gelderblom, O., and Jonker, J. "Completing a Financial Revolution. The Finance of the Dutch East India Trade and the Rise of the Amsterdam Capital Market, 1595–1612," *The Journal of Economic History*, 64/3 (2004), 641–672.
Gepken-Jager, E. *Verenigde Oost-Indische Compagnie (VOC). The Dutch East India Company*, in: Gepken-Jager et al. (eds.) 2005, 41–81.
Gepken-Jager, E., van Solinge, G., and Timmerman, L. (eds.), *VOC 1602–2002. 400 Years of Company Law* (Series Law of Business and Finance, Vol. 6), Deventer: Kluwer 2005.
Groot Placaet-Boek I, The Hague: H.I. van Wouw 1658.

Harris, R. "The English East India Company and the History of Company Law," in: Gepken-Jager et al. (eds.) 2005, pp. 217–247.

Israel, J.I. *De Republiek, 1477–1806,* Franeker: van Wijnen 2008.

Knuttel, W.P.C. *Catalogus van de pamfletten-verzameling berustende in de Koninklijke Bibliotheek,* The Hague 1978.

Korte Aenwysinge; Knuttel 1978, no. 3352.

Kort Onderricht; Knuttel 1978, no. 3355.

Naerder Aenwysinghe Der Bewinthebbers Regieringe; Knuttel 1978, no. 3354.

Nootwendich Discours; Knuttel 1978, no. 3348.

Placcaet Jeghens seecker Fameus Libel, in: Knuttel 1978, nr. 3349.

Roelevink, J. *Resolutiën der Staten-Generaal. Nieuwe Reeks 1610–1670. Vijfde deel, 1621–1622,* The Hague: Martinus Nijhoff 1983.

Roelevink, J. *Resolutiën der Staten-Generaal. Nieuwe Reeks 1610–1670. Zesde deel, 2 januari 1623–30 juni 1624,* The Hague: Instituut voor Nederlandse Geschiedenis 1989.

Scott, W.R. *The Constitution and Finance of English, Scottish and Irish Joint-Stock Companies to 1720, Volume II,* Cambridge: Cambridge University Press 1912.

Tegen-vertooch; Knuttel 1978, no. 3347.

Thyspf: Catalogue indication of a book or pamphlet that is included in the *Bibliotheca Tysiana,* now part of the Leiden University Library (www. library.leiden.edu)

Tweede Noot-wendiger Discours, in; Knuttel 1978, nr. 3350.

van Brakel, S. *De Hollandsche handelscompagnieën der zeventiende eeuw,* The Hague: Martinus Nijhoff 1908.

van der Heijden, E.J.J. *De ontwikkeling van de Naamlooze Vennootschap in Nederland voor de codificatie.* Amsterdam: E. van der Vecht 1908.

van Dillen, J.G. *Isaac le Maire en de handel in actiën der Oost-Indische Compagnie, Economisch Historisch Jaarboek XVI,* Den Haag: Martinus Nijhoff 1930, pp. 1–165.

van Rees, O. *Geschiedenis der Staathuishoudkunde in Nederland tot het einde der achttiende eeuw,* Volume 2, Utrecht: Kemink en Zoon 1868.

Vertooch; Knuttel 1978, no. 3345.

CHAPTER 4

THE GREAT EXPROPRIATION: INTERPRETING THE INNOVATION OF "PERMANENT CAPITAL" AT THE DUTCH EAST INDIA COMPANY

Andrew von Nordenflycht

With cross-sectional and historical evidence indicating that financial development is an essential precursor to economic development (e.g., Sylla 2002; Siegel and Roe 2009), there is much interest in understanding what supports or predicts financial development. Among other factors, financial development appears linked to strong and stable private property rights, in particular legal protection of minority investors (La Porta et al. 1997, 2000): the more investors feel that they have some level of recourse against expropriation by managers or large shareholders of corporations, the more they are willing to invest.

Identifying the need for strong investor protections is one thing, but it is quite another to actually change the level of protection in a particular jurisdiction. Existing regimes and institutions typically have vested interests who benefit from the status quo, which means that inefficient institutions can persist for some time (North 1990). In the case of financial development, the managers and/or controlling owners of large enterprises can become "entrenched" (Morck, Wolfenzon and Yeung 2005), using their substantial resources to influence government policy and action to support their ability to expropriate minority investors.

The question of financial development then becomes a historical one: to assess how financial development has occurred and how
entrenchment has been overcome in the past. In this way, historical
research into the institutional evolution of corporate governance is
essential to understanding financial development (Sylla 2002; Rajan
and Zingales 2003; Morck 2005; Musacchio 2008).

The East India companies of the seventeenth century are an important topic in this regard. Douglass North (1990) has argued that
the institutions and organizations developed to conduct long-distance
trade were the basis for the West's modern economy. And, as Oscar
Gelderblom, Abe de Jong, and Joost Jonker (2010) point out in this
same volume, the Dutch East India Company in particular has often
been viewed as the world's first diffusely held public corporation.

One of the essential features of the modern corporation that the
Dutch East India Company (Vereenigde Oost-Indische Compagnie,
or VOC) pioneered was a *permanent capital* base (Scott 1912;
Steensgaard 1974; Frentrop 2003). This describes a situation in which
the company is never required to return its full capital to investors: the
capital is permanently in the hands of the company. This contrasts with
the *terminable capital* structure traditionally employed in the late sixteenth century, in which investments were pledged for a finite period
of time, after which profit and principal were returned and the enterprise was wound up (as in modern-day private equity funds) (Scott
1912; Gelderblom and Jonker 2004).

Permanent capital facilitates long-term investments in specific assets
and is thus a key financial innovation (Blair 2004). In fact, the VOC's
establishment of permanent capital by 1622 was seen not only by
historians but also by company directors themselves as a source of
advantage that contributed to its early out-performance of its rival,
the English East India Company (EIC), which was founded at the
same time with a similar form (a terminable joint-stock with a national
monopoly) but did not establish a permanent capital base until 1664
(Scott 1912; Masselman 1963; Chaudhuri 1978; Frentrop 2003).

However, the development of permanent capital at the VOC poses
an interesting puzzle, since it was facilitated by what amounted to a
state-sponsored expropriation of minority shareholders. As described
elsewhere in this volume by Gelderblom et al. and de Jongh, as well
as in Frentrop (2003), the company was founded as a terminable
venture, with investors promised the opportunity to cash out after
ten years. But the company's directors quickly recognized a need for
long-term investments overseas (in forts, factories, and ships left in
Asia) that would be hard to wind up or transfer. They also faced poor
returns in the early years, precluding the payment of dividends that

might persuade investors to reinvest at the ten-year reckoning. So the directors petitioned the government to allow the VOC to postpone the termination and return of principal.

Minority investors (those who were not directors) protested publicly and lobbied against the postponement. In fact, they had begun to protest for other reasons as well, especially in regard to classic agency cost issues, such as directors' self-dealing at the expense of the company's profits (Steensgaard 1974; Frentrop 2003; de Jongh 2010). But the government sided with the company and postponed the termination for ten years, and, when that next termination approached, ultimately eliminated the termination altogether. So, in contrast to the hypothesis linking investor protections to financial development, the important innovation of permanent capital was facilitated not by a *strengthening* of investor protections, but by just the opposite: an *expropriation* of minority shareholders.

There are several ways we might interpret this "great expropriation." It might suggest that investor protections do not really matter—or at least do not have a straightforward relationship—to financial development. This is not inconceivable, as recent historical research suggests that correlations between the investor friendliness of legal regimes and the robustness of financial markets did not hold at the beginning of the twentieth century (Rajan and Zingales 2003; Musacchio 2008). Alternatively, it may be that the expropriation did have negative consequences on future investment and financial development in the Netherlands, but that the VOC succeeded anyway because of the initial position it established. A third interpretation is that the case of the VOC suggests that permanent capital was a financial innovation that private markets could not achieve on their own. Where investments require long-term time frames that conflict with short-term needs of investors, perhaps states need to intervene in ways that limit investor rights.

To sort through these alternative interpretations, I discuss briefly two questions. The first is whether the expropriation, by demonstrating the vulnerability of minority investments, had adverse consequences for future investment in the VOC or the Dutch Republic in general. If it did, then the expropriation-cum-innovation may not be such a contradiction of the investor protection/financial development hypothesis. If it did not, then perhaps the VOC case does add to the case against the investor protection hypothesis. The second question is whether the VOC's very similar rival, the EIC, required the same state-sponsored expropriation. If it did, then perhaps permanent capital was a type of financial innovation that private markets could not accomplish. But if it did not, it adds to Gelderblom et al.'s contention that the VOC was a mutant, off the evolutionary path toward the modern public corporation.

FINANCIAL AND POLITICAL CONSEQUENCES OF THE EXPROPRIATION

In regard to the VOC itself, the state-sponsored expropriation signaled that outside shareholders would have little voice in the company's affairs and the directors' self-dealing activities would likely continue. Did this have adverse effects on the VOC's subsequent capital market activities? In fact, the VOC never raised new equity after its initial 1602 capitalization (Frentrop 2003). For the rest of its 200-year life, it funded its operations through retained earnings and borrowing. This might suggest that the expropriation effectively barred the company from the equity market. On the other hand, it is not clear whether the company needed (or wanted) new equity, since its capital needs were met by lower-cost sources, including the returns generated by the dominant position it established with its substantial initial equity capital. While we might expect the expropriation to have signaled that the government would side with the company in any dispute with *creditors*, too, the company was clearly able to access debt markets on an ongoing basis (Frentrop 2003). Thus, the effect on the VOC's capital-raising ability is ultimately unclear.

Beyond the VOC, the expropriation did create problems for the investment-raising activity of another proposed national joint-stock monopoly, the West India Company (WIC). The WIC was intended to pursue activities in the Americas, including trade, colonization, and attacks on Spanish interests, and was modeled after the VOC, in the sense of seeking a monopoly charter from the government and organizing as a joint-stock. However, as described more fully in this volume by Matthijs de Jongh and by Gelderblom et al., the VOC's outside shareholders explicitly refused to contribute to the WIC unless not only its own charter but also that of the VOC were reformed to give more influence to and protection of outside shareholders (Frentrop 2003). This effort was partially successful in that the governance features of both the VOC and the WIC were mildly reformed in the direction of more disclosure and shareholder voice.

On the other hand, there is no obvious evidence that the state's action hindered investment in the country's economy more broadly by undermining the expectation of secure property rights. In this regard, Gelderblom et al.'s contention that the VOC was an anomaly or "mutant" is helpful. They identify that the VOC charter was quite distinct from the corporate governance and capital structure models of contemporary seaborne trading companies, in its heavy tilt toward the interests of the state. In this way the VOC was clearly intended as a distinctive instrument of the state in its war against Spain—and this may have been seen by investors as singular or unique, rather than a general policy.

In fact, historians have noted that the Dutch government generally supported free trade (Jonker and Sluyterman 2000). The majority of Dutch seaborne trade, which occurred around the North Sea and the Baltic Sea, was fairly unregulated, with lots of independent merchants. This free trade, which contrasted with the more regulated, monopolistic regimes governing Hanseatic and English merchants, has been cited as a reason that Dutch merchants grew to dominate northern European trade (Jonker and Sluyterman 2000). So the expropriation may have been seen as a one-off violation.

Consistent with this idea of the VOC as anomaly in terms of governance and state policy, it was only proposed for two other ventures in the Dutch Republic: the aforementioned WIC and the Northern Company, which organized whaling expeditions. Furthermore, neither of these follow-on monopolies was granted permanent capital and neither even retained a joint-stock form, devolving into a model of selling licenses to independent merchants (Emmer 1981).

Overall, while there were some adverse effects on the availability of investment, they were mild. Perhaps the bigger, longer-term cost of the expropriation was in contributing to the *entrenchment* of the VOC and its inefficiencies. Again, as Gelderblom et al. and de Jongh (and many other historians) detail, the VOC was intrinsically political. In particular, there were close ties between the VOC's directors and the government decision makers. VOC directors were often also representatives in the provincial and/or national governments or at least closely connected to them. And over time, the percentage of directors who were political elites increased (Frentrop 2003). Thus, the company's management had good access to the political process.

Directorships were also very lucrative, as they allowed considerable (and presumably inefficient) self-dealing. For example, as de Jongh details, directors received a commission for all the goods they procured on behalf of the company, so they could obtain both wealth and power simply by procuring as much as possible (without regard for matching supply to demand). Furthermore, the directorships were protected. They were lifetime appointments, so directors were unaccountable to anyone. And the company's monopoly meant that its position could not be challenged by competitors (at least domestically). Thus the directors began to turn into a body of government representatives who benefited immensely from the continuation of the company in its existing form, however inefficient. The expropriation, itself facilitated by this intertwining of state and company interests, enhanced the directors' power and cemented the inefficiencies. In other words, to the extent that the VOC is an exemplar of anything, it is as a classic case of managerial (or elite) entrenchment (Morck et al. 2005) and how inefficient institutions persist (North 1990).

To assess whether state intervention, (and its attendant downsides), was in fact essential to the establishment of permanent capital, it is instructive to look to the VOC's rival across the English Channel.

PERMANENT CAPITAL AT THE ENGLISH EAST INDIA COMPANY

English merchants, too, began pursuing overseas trade to East India in the late sixteenth century and organized into a single joint-stock with a state-sanctioned monopoly in 1600, two years before the founding of the VOC. Like the VOC, the EIC was a terminable joint-stock. In fact, it did not even begin with a ten-year investment horizon like the VOC but instead retained the contemporary voyage-based horizon. The first 12 voyages (1601–1613) were financed separately.

As at the VOC, the EIC directors quickly realized that longer-term investments were needed for the Asian trade (Scott 1912; Chaudhuri 1965), making the terminable structure problematic. Without even the ten-year multi-voyage horizon of the VOC, the EIC directors found it difficult to keep each voyage's accounts completely separate, especially when ships from different voyages were in service at the same time (Scott 1912). Nonetheless, the EIC continued with a voyage-based capital structure and sent 22 separate ventures to Asia between 1600 and 1657.

In 1657, the EIC got a renewed monopoly charter from the new government (Cromwell's Protectorate) and made yet another new call for capital. But the nature of the company's proposed capital base was altered in an important way. Rather than stipulating a termination of the capital base at a particular time, the company proposed that after seven years, the company would be re-valued and would buyout any investors who wished to cash out, but implied that the company would continue on regardless, replacing departing investors with new investors. This buyout opportunity was then to be offered every three years. When the seven-year buyback period arrived, very few investors availed themselves of the opportunity (Scott 1912). From this point on, directors and investors began to see the EIC's capital base as permanent. Just as the VOC ultimately silenced minority shareholder protests by paying regular dividends that kept the price of shares high and thus allowed investors to exit (Frentrop 2003), investor willingness to forego the finite terminations was likely facilitated mostly by the gradual increase in trading activity for the EIC's shares along with the establishment of more regular dividends after 1657. Although the process of establishing permanent capital took several decades longer than at the VOC, it was ultimately a consensual private process with no government coercion required.

It is also useful to note that the EIC had a more investor-friendly governance structure than the VOC from the outset. Ironically, this stemmed from the more regulated, corporatist format of the English economy of the sixteenth century. By the sixteenth century, English merchants were generally organized within guild-like structures called regulated companies. These regulated companies held a monopoly on English trade to specific regions (or in specific products). But they also had formal governance structures, with procedures for appointing the company's governor and other managers, and some had existed for decades and even centuries (Scott 1912; de Jongh 2010). When this regulated company entity was combined with the emerging concept of joint-stock financing—in which the members pooled their capital and trade was conducted as a single entity—it held the possibility for permanent capital.

And in fact, at least two early English joint-stock companies—the Russia Company and the Levant Company—adopted a permanent capital base in as early as 1553 (though neither retained either the permanent capital base or the joint-stock form) (Scott 1912). But this bestowed the EIC with a governance structure in which the company's charter stipulated that directors had finite terms and were to be elected by voting by shareholders (as opposed to lifetime tenure and government-based appointments at the VOC).

In this sense then, between the VOC and the EIC, it is the latter that was the closer, more direct ancestor of the (private) publicly traded corporation, as suggested by de Jongh (2010). And this leads one to conjecture that this more investor-friendly evolution of permanent capital and corporate governance practices at the EIC had a more positive long-term contribution than the VOC's. For example, perhaps it contributed to the English financial revolution of the late seventeenth century and England's surpassing of the Dutch Republic as the world's leading economy (Sylla 2002). This is a conjecture worth further research.

CONCLUSION

How then should we interpret the expropriation-cum-innovation that converted the VOC from terminable to permanent capital? My suggested answer has several parts. First, it seems clear that the establishment of permanent capital created an enhanced ability to make long-term investments overseas, which contributed to the VOC's dominant position in East Asian trade in the seventeenth century and led it to become one of the world's largest enterprises to that point and last for almost 200 years. In this way, the Dutch government's violation of investor property rights advanced the state's economic and political goals of capturing rents from East Asian trade at the direct expense of the Spanish empire.

But this expropriation did not come without costs. It may have led to the VOC's exclusive reliance on debt financing for the remainder of its days and it almost certainly hindered the fund-raising ability of the second such enterprise (the WIC). Its impact on the rest of the economy, though, was limited (or even nonexistent), likely because investors saw the government's interest in the East India trade as unique. Perhaps the more important cost of the expropriation was its solidification of the entrenched position of the VOC's management, which allowed the serious inefficiencies of the VOC's corporate governance system to persist. Gelderblom et al. argue that the VOC was an anomaly, rather than an exemplar of corporate governance evolution. I suggest that it was indeed an exemplar, but of the entrenchment that allows inefficient property rights regimes to persist.

Lastly, the case of the EIC suggests that the establishment of permanent capital did not necessarily require this state-sponsored great expropriation. Not only did the EIC establish permanent capital through private negotiations, but several earlier English companies also experimented with privately negotiated arrangements that established permanent capital. And while the EIC experienced its own share of abuses and corruption over its multi-century history, its corporate governance practices, specifically appointment of directors by annual votes of all (large) shareholders and more regular and open disclosure of the company's accounts, were certainly superior by contemporary standards. The EIC, then, is more of an exemplar of corporate governance innovation. The benefits of this more investor-friendly evolution are an interesting question for future research.

In the end, the way to interpret the innovation of permanent capital at the VOC via the great expropriation may be thus: financial market participants (e.g., investors and entrepreneurs) may have difficulties contracting to make long-term, risky investments. States may accelerate the attaining of such longer-term investments in ways that weaken investor influence and/or protections. But while such interventions may yield short-term advantages, they also tend to bring long-term costs, in the form of dampened future investment activity and the persistence of inefficient institutions that serve entrenched elites. Whether states can or do make the appropriate trade-offs and whether there can even be agreement on what the right trade-offs are will be subjects of ongoing debate in political economy.

REFERENCES

Blair, M.M. 2004. The Neglected Benefits of the Corporate Form: Entity Status and the Separation of Asset Ownership from Control, in A. Grandori, ed., *Corporate Governance and Firm Organization: Microfoundations and Structural Forms*. Oxford: Oxford University Press.

Chauduri, K.N. 1965. *The English East India Company: The Study of an Early Joint-Stock Company, 1600–1640*. New York: A. Kelly.

Chaudhuri, K.N. 1978. *The Trading World of Asia and the English East India Company, 1660–1760*. Cambridge, UK: Cambridge University.

de Jongh, J.M. 2010. Shareholder Activism at the Dutch East India Company in 1622, in J. Koppell, ed., *Origins of Shareholder Advocacy*. New York: Palgrave Macmillan.

Emmer, P.C. 1981. The West India Company, 1621–1791: Dutch or Atlantic? in Blusse, L. and Gaastra, F., eds, *Companies and Trade*. Leiden: Leiden University.

Frentrop, P. 2003. *A History of Corporate Governance, 1602–2002*. Amsterdam: Deminor.

Gelderblom, O. and Jonker, J. 2004. Completing a Financial Revolution: The Finance of the Dutch East India Trade and the Rise of the Amsterdam Capital Market, 1595–1612. *Journal of Economic History*, 64(3): 641–672.

Gelderblom, O., de Jong, A., and Jonker, J. 2010. Putting Le Maire into Perspective: Business Organization and the Evolution of Corporate Governance in the Dutch Republic, 1590–1610, in J. Koppell, ed., *Origins of Shareholder Advocacy*. New York: Palgrave Macmillan.

Jonker, J. and Sluyterman, K. 2000. *At Home on the World Markets: Dutch International Trading Companies from the 16th Century until the Present*. The Hague: SDU Uitgevers.

La Porta, R., Lopez-de-Silanes, F., Shleifer, A., and Vishny, R. 1997. Legal Determinants of External Finance. *Journal of Finance*, 52(3): 1131–1150.

La Porta, R., Lopez-de-Silanes, F., Shleifer, A., and Vishny, R. 2000. Investor Protections and Corporate Governance. *Journal of Financial Economics*, 58(1): 1–25.

Masselman, G. 1963. *Cradle of Colonialism*. New Haven: Yale University.

Morck, R. (ed.). 2005. *A History of Corporate Governance around the World*. Chicago: University of Chicago.

Morck, R., Wolfenzon, D., and Yeung, B. 2005. Corporate Governance, Economic Entrenchment and Growth. *Journal of Economic Literature*, XLIII (Sep 2005): 657–722.

Musacchio, A. 2008. *On the Persistency of Legal Institutions: A Look at Law and Finance c. 1900*. Boston, MA: Harvard Business School.

North, D.C. 1990. *Institutions, Institutional Change and Economic Performance*. Cambridge, UK: Cambridge University Press.

Rajan, R., and Zingales, L. 2003. The Great Reversals: The Politics of Financial Development in the 20th Century. *Journal of Financial Economics*, 69: 5–50.

Scott, W.R. 1912. *The Constitution and Finance of English, Scottish and Irish Joint-Stock Companies to 1720*. New York: Peter Smith.

Siegel, J., and Roe, M. 2009. Political Stability: Its Effects on Financial Development, Its Roots in the Severity of Economic Inequality. Working paper. Harvard University.

Steensgaard, N. 1974. *The Asian Trade Revolution of the 17th Century: East India Companies and the Decline of the Caravan Trade*. Chicago: University of Chicago.

Sylla, R. 2002. Financial Systems and Economic Modernization. *Journal of Economic History*, 62(2): 277–292.

PART II

OVERCOMING THE AGENCY CHALLENGE OF EARLY GLOBAL TRADE

CHAPTER 5

LITIGATION PLUS REGULATION: THE PROTECTION OF INVESTOR RIGHTS IN LATE-MEDIEVAL VENICE

Yadira González de Lara[‡]

> *The expense of the administration of justice may no doubt be considered as laid out for the benefit of the whole society. (Adam Smith 1776, Book V, Chapter I)*

INTRODUCTION

There is a consensus among economists, historians, and lawyers that the protection of property rights and the enforcement of contracts are among the proper functions of government. The intricacy of this consensus is that it does not tell us exactly how the state can design a functional legal system and what it takes it to effectively secure property and contract rights. In other words, this consensus tells us nothing about the desirable extent of government intervention (Glaeser and Shleifer 2002; Rodrik 2008).

A growing literature in Law and Economics postulates that when courts are expensive, unpredictable and/or corrupt, regulation by government agencies can provide an (efficient) alternative to judicial enforcement. While recognizing the overlap, this literature often views litigation and regulation as substitutes (for an overview, see Kessler and Shleifer 2010). Regulation and litigation, however, can also be complements. For example, avoiding excessive formalism can reduce the length and cost of judicial proceedings (Djankov et al. 2003). Regulations mandating disclosure and specifying liability standards for gatekeepers, by reducing verification and/or disclosure costs, can also improve enforcement efficiency by courts (Kraakman 1986; La Porta, Lopez-de-Silanes and Shleifer 2006; Hart 2009).

This chapter finds that in late-medieval Venice litigation and regulation conjointly provided investor protection. The Venetian regulations, though, extended beyond those usually associated with desirable intervention. First, judicial formalism was not a major problem that required intervention. Venetian courts ruled according to the principle of speedy, informal, and equitable procedure and enforced their judgments as court orders. However, they could not force an offending merchant to pay damages if he fled. It was therefore necessary to motivate merchants to submit themselves to the authorities. To accomplish this, Venice implemented a series of regulations that ensured them a rent as long as they kept their affiliation with the city.

Among these regulations were licensing and registration requirements that restricted foreign entry, thereby preserving per-citizen rents. Despite their static inefficiency, eliminating these barriers to entry would have undermined growth: anticipating outright embezzlement of funds, prospective investors would not have mobilized their capital to otherwise productive investments in overseas trade. The Venetian evidence thus lends support to the view that institutional reform based on first-best practices can easily do more harm than good (Rodrik 2008). Entry regulations are not only necessary to sustain relational contracting, as the literature has noted; they are also necessary to support dispute resolution in courts when courts have limited jurisdictional power.

Second, although judges were not as skilled, motivated, and impartial as the myth of Venice presumes (Queller 1986) the main reason why courts failed to enforce contracts in the absence of regulation was not their inability and/or unwillingness to verify an observable breach. The reason was that neither judges nor investors could observe merchants' behavior onboard and abroad. To protect investors against expropriation by controlling merchants, Venice instituted various public gatekeepers and placed merchants under their permanent oversight. These civil servants generated the (verifiable) information required to prosecute merchants for profit diversion, prevented excessive risk taking by merchants, and rendered profits less responsive to their lack of application.

Venetian regulation coping with asymmetric information thus went much beyond mandatory disclosure. Today's disclosure requirements were primarily introduced in the 1930s to protect investors against offerings of dubious quality securities (Zingales 2009). This adverse selection problem, however, did not prevail in late-medieval Venice. As their counterparts of the new millennium, Venetian investors needed to be protected mainly against "frauds and mistakes" committed by merchants who, in the absence of regulation, were accountable to no one (Ibid., 392). Furthermore, without the possibility to verify a merchant's reports, financial reporting would have been useless.

Like the American markets under the SEC, regulation of securities markets in Venice focused on intermediaries. But unlike today's brokers, auditors, analysts, and other private gatekeepers, most Venetian intermediaries were public officials. These public gatekeepers not only monitored trade, they enhanced the profitability of Venetian trade, inducing merchants to submit to the authorities and enhancing the social benefit of regulation relative to its cost. Each and every public gatekeeper was subject to strict independent reviews after his office came to term and was liable to prosecution for abuse of office or dereliction of duty by the State Attorneys, who had investigating powers and to whom all office holders were to notify any observed wrongdoing. Regulation and litigation thus conjointly disciplined market participants and intermediaries.

Knowing that merchants would not expropriate their rights, investors trusted merchants and securities markets, which were crucial to the city's prosperity, developed. Specifically, the Venetian regulatory and judicial system enabled the development of bond markets first and equity markets after 1220s. This finding sheds lights on the puzzling transition from the sea loan (a bond-like contract) to the commenda (an equity-like contract) and calls attention to the need of exploring the extent to which regulation and litigation conjointly provided investor protection in other historical episodes.[1] Furthermore, since there was a strong connection between trade and government in late-medieval Venice, one can see the development of the regulatory and judicial system as an early manifestation of shareowner activism, a manifestation that will place the origins of shareholder advocacy far back to the twelfth century.

This historical institutional analysis draws on the work of previous generations of scholars and especially on the archival work of Raimondo Morozzo della Rocca and Antonio Lombardo, henceforth MRL (1940, 1953). The almost 1,000 notarial acts published by them constitute all the surviving trading evidence for the period of analysis and are believed to be representative (Luzzatto 1952, 91; Lane 1966, 57–58). On the basis of them, I have constructed a database of 388 bond-like and equity-like contracts for the period 1122–1261. The data provides various proxies for regulation and litigation and enables to evaluate the extent to which they conjointly provided investor protection.

The Venetian Securities Market for Overseas Trade

The spectacular economic growth of Venice during the late medieval period (1050–1350) was based on the expansion of its trade along the Mediterranean and beyond (De Roover 1965; Lane 1973; Lopez 1976; Cipolla 1993). This trade required large amounts of capital and involved high risks. A commercial round-trip voyage from Venice to Constantinople, the Crusader States, or Alexandria took six to nine months and overlapping sailing seasons precluded financing it with retained earnings from a previous voyage (Lane 1973, 69–70, 120). Fitting costs were further increased due to the need of carrying a large armed crew, sailing in convoy with naval protection, and securing merchants' property rights abroad (Ibid., 23–49, 68–85, 124–131). These protective measures notwithstanding, the *risk of the sea and people*, as the Venetians referred to the possibility of loss through shipwreck, piracy or confiscation of merchandise by foreign rulers, remained high (Ibid., 77; De Roover 1965, 44–46). The commercial risk was also high: profits varied widely depending on the tariffs and bribes paid in customs, the transportation and storage fees, the rates of conversions applied to various weights, measures and currencies, fluctuations in prices, the conditions of the goods upon arrival, and so forth (Lane 1967, 95–111; Greif 1989, 860–861). Trade in ordinary goods within Europe or the East did not set such high capital requirements as trade in luxuries between Europe and the East but was less profitable and still involved high risks (Lopez 1976, 95).

To mobilize the required capital from savings into risky investment in overseas trade, the Venetians used bond-like sea loans and equity-like commenda contracts. The sea loan was a fixed payment loan in which the merchant was exempted from repayment in case of loss from shipwreck, piracy, or confiscation.[2]

I ... have received from you ... 100 hyperpers, with which I ought to go on voyage to do business ... and I ought to give and deliver to you 125 hyperpers. However, this credit ought to be at your risk from either sea or people, if this will be clearly apparent (Constantinople, December 1158. MRL 1940, # 134).

There were two types of commenda contracts. In the standard bilateral commenda, the merchant provided one-third of the capital, bore one-third of the capital loss, and was entitled to one-half of the net profit in return for both his work and risky investment.

I ... have received in *collegancia* from you ... 152 Venetian silver pennies and I have contributed against you 76 Venetian silver pennies in this *colligancia*...I should...give and deliver to you...all which accrues to you from the above mentioned *colligancia*..., namely, once the capital has been repaid, the profit which the Lord will grant I ought to divide and share with you by a true half without fraud or evil intent. And if, may it not happen, all of the above-mentioned merchandise should be lost by (the action of) the sea or men and it will be clearly apparent, we ought then to seek nothing from each other. If, however, anything survives, let us share just as we have contributed (Venice, July 1201. MRL 1953, # 53).

In the standard unilateral commenda, the merchant did not supply any capital, assumed no liability for a capital loss, and received one-fourth of the net profit.

I...have received from you...8 Venetian pounds and 4 pence, with which I ought to go on voyage to do business with and trade...and I ought to give and deliver to you...all your above mentioned capital with three quarters of all the profit the Lord will grant with a fair and true accounting, and I should retain to me one quarter of the profit. However, your aforementioned credit ought to be at your risk from either sea or people, if this will be clearly apparent (Venice, June 1226. MRL 1940, # 627).

Unlike in other localities where the commenda was a partnership, in Venice both the sea loan and the commenda were credit instruments (Besta and Predelli 1901, St. Enr. Dand., 30–33, St. Ran. Dand., 16, St. Tiep., 1229, 16; Cessi 1938, St. Nov., III, 1–3). Venetian merchant acquired the ownership of the capital they raised and had full control over it. Specifically, they traded on their own account, liquidated the investors with payment of the amount or share agreed upon, retaining always possession of their own part of the profit, and were never bounded to trade on specific goods or to follow an investor's instructions.

Over time equity funding replaced bond funding (see figure 5.1). According to Lane (1966, 61), "the change from the sea loan to the commenda substituted for a fixed obligation an obligation to share profits. To that extent it was like issuing common stock to finance an expansion of business, instead of selling bonds. It placed more of the risks on the investors." Lane's focus on risk sharing was motivated by the perception that financial markets were inefficient in the sense that agents were limited in their ability to diversify and hence could obtain better risk diversification by holding different assets.

In late-medieval Venice, merchants of substance could and did diversify their portfolios but could not diversify the human capital invested in the ventures they managed (González de Lara 2008, 254–255). Furthermore, about half of the merchants and over a third

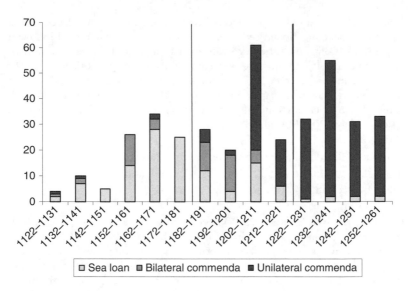

Figure 5.1 Documented sea loans and commenda contracts and their distribution over time

of the investors known for the period 1122–1261 were non-nobles. As nobility is a good proxy for wealth during this period of time, we can safely conclude that many market participants were relatively poor individuals with few diversification opportunities (Rösch 1989). Besides, significant indivisibilities and aggregate risk in overseas commerce limited the degree of risk spreading that the economy could achieve. As discussed, the length, sailing technology, and high start-up costs of trading voyages prevented the undertaking of a sufficiently large number of them and made those actually taken on subject to aggregate risk. Trading convoys, for example, presented a concentrated target at sea, exposed all merchants to the same market conditions in each port of call, and reduced the possibility to diversify across trade centers and over time, as they called only on a few locations and were organized at most twice a year (Lane 1973, 68–77). Hence, equity-like commenda contracts provided a better allocation of risk than bond-like sea loans and created an efficiency gain that could potentially be reinvested in overseas trade.[3]

INVESTOR PROTECTION

The mobilization of capital into risky investments in overseas trade was key for growth but required the development of institutions that protected creditors and shareholders from expropriation by (controlling) merchants. A merchant could expropriate from investors in various ways. First, once overseas he could flee with all the capital entrusted to him. Second, even if he returned to Venice, he could render a false account and divert part of the profit. Finally, he could take excessive risks and/or shirk during the operation of the voyage. In the absence of institutions affording investor protection, prospective creditors and shareholders, anticipating expropriation, would not have invested to begin with and, hence, mutually beneficial debt-like sea loans and equity-like commenda contracts would not have transpired. Yet, the Venetian relied extensively on debt during the twelfth century and on equity thereafter. How could investors trust merchants?

Poor Legal Protection of Investor Rights

During the late-medieval period, there was not a centralized legal system that was effective over a large geographical area, less over the whole Mediterranean (Greif 2004, 118). A Venetian court could and did force merchants within the (limited) territorial area over which it had legal jurisdiction to comply with their verifiable contractual obligations (González de Lara 2008, 269–270). Yet, it could not exercise coercion over a merchant who fled. If a merchant embezzled an investor's capital and took refugee in another jurisdiction, a Venetian court could not force him to repay. Tracking down a merchant was prohibitively costly and even if he was located, intercommunity litigation was not an option against a state in that Venice could not retaliate, for example, by interrupting trade (Greif 2004). Obviously, when considering the option to flee, a fraudulent merchant would choose a safe haven where Venice could not exert that pressure. The notorious case of Benetto Soranzo illustrates the failure of the Venetian legal system to gain extradition of *fugitives* as late as the fifteenth century. In 1455, Beneto fled Venice with all the surviving assets from his failed bank and took refuge in the lands of the duke of Modena. The Venetian authorities attempted in vain to persuade the duke to deny him asylum and when he finally intervened, Benetto merely moved to lands under the jurisdiction of the duke of Mantua (Mueller 1997, 200–211).

Leaving collateral in Venice could have mitigated the problem of outright embezzlement but most merchants left few goods behind. Over 47 percent of the Venetian merchants known for the period 1122–1261, bore non-noble family names and some had very few assets, like Dobramiro Stagnario, a manumitted slave, and Romano Mairano, whose wife received a humble dowry (Luzzatto 1952, 98–99, 108–116; Lane 1973, 52; Robbert 1999, 34). Furthermore, rich merchants typically held most of their wealth in movable goods, which they could take with them, and they had real estate holdings outside Venice and its domains (Pozza 1955). For example, at the time of his death in 1281, Lazzaro Mercadante had almost all his wealth invested in trade and owned some plots of cultivated land near Padua; in Venice, he simply kept three houses of little value (Luzzatto 1952, 61–65).

Relying on guarantors or kin to pay in place of insolvent merchants could also have mitigated the embezzlement problem. Yet, Venetian overseas trading contracts did not request naming guarantors, nor was the family held liable for a merchant's illegal actions. According to Venetian law, only sons under parental authority were liable for their father's debts (Besta and Predelli 1901, St. Enr. Dand., 68, St. Ran. Dand., 11–12; Cessi 1938, St. Nov. I.40). This is in sharp contrast with other legislations that were also devised at the time. Genoese courts, for example, held all members of a merchant's family legally responsible for the merchant's verifiable transgressions, such as outright embezzlement of an investor's capital (Greif 1994, 937–938).

A second problem with the legal system is that to enforce complex contracts, like the sea loan and even more the commenda, a court requires verifiable information. But, neither investors nor judges could provide it, among other things, because they remained in Venice and, so, could not directly monitor merchants abroad. In the absence of an institution generating and transmitting verifiable information, a merchant would have misreported a loss at sea or by the action of men in the expectation of being released from repayment, diverted part of a commenda's profits once they materialized, assumed high risks from which he was protected through limited liability and shirked.

By admitting the testimony of witnesses as evidence in judicial proceedings and conditioning repayment exceptions on the verification of losses from shipwreck, piracy, or confiscation of merchandise abroad (Besta and Predelli 1901, St. Enr. Dand., 32; St. Tiep., 1229, 16; Cessi 1938, St. Nov., III.2), the legal system facilitated the enforcement of sea loans and, to some extent, commenda contracts. The court's reliance on witnesses to verify such losses is well reflected in the available data. In 1219, for example, the captain of and various merchants traveling on the ship *Lo Carello* testified that it had wrecked close to Negroponte and that the merchant Domenico Gradenigo had lost merchandise worth 110 hyperpers (MRL 1940, # 582).

Uncovering an accounting fraud, though, was far more challenging. It required verification of the tariffs and bribes a particular merchant had paid to pass customs, the transportation and storage fees he had arranged for, the rates of conversion he got applied among a plethora of weights, measures, and currencies, the price at which he had bought and then sold his wares, whether these had been damaged on the voyage or pilfered by the crew, and so forth. Without verifiable information on such costs, prices, and events, a Venetian court could have not supported the development of equity markets.

Asymmetric information regarding a merchant's choice of action and diligence while on voyage also impaired a court's effectiveness. To punish cheaters, the court needed to know when and to what extent a contract had been violated, for example, by unduly changing route to politically unsafe but highly profitable ports, storing merchandise in a precarious but cheap warehouse, betting on exchange rates, selling on credit with lax terms but superior prices, or simply shirking.

Private Solutions' Limited Role

Economic historians have conventionally assumed that financial exchange was confined to the family when investors are offered poor legal protection (Rosenberg and Birdzell 1986, 123–124; Cipolla 1993, 164, 198). In late-medieval Venice, however, the family played a limited and declining role in financial markets. Only 11.39 percent of the sea loans and commenda contracts published by MRL for the period 1122–1261 were established among family members, thereby showing a pronounced decline from the eleventh century, when 37.50 percent of them involved kin. The data, though, might be biased, as financial relations among trustworthy relatives may have not required the services of a notary and Venetian brothers legally constituted a fraternal partnership (*fraterna*) without the need of formal contracts. Yet, notaries proved useful to trustworthy relatives for establishing legal title of their credits in potential disputes with third parties over the estate of a deceased merchant and the *fraterna* was of little importance until the mid thirteenth century (González de Lara 2008, 258–259). We thus observe notarial acts showing a loan by a widow to her granddaughter "for the needs of her home," an investment by a widowed nun in her son's voyage, and commenda contracts between brothers (MRL 1940, # 146, 356, 785).

In the absence of an effective legal system, other scholars, most notably Avner Greif (1989, 1994), have emphasized the role of reputation among or between traders. In late-medieval Venice, however, neither multilateral-reputation nor bilateral-reputation institutions prevailed. As González de Lara (2008) covers this issue in detail, a few considerations will suffice here. An informal institution based on multilateral reputation, according to which all investors in a group collectively punish a merchant who cheats any of them by interrupting their multilateral relations with him, could have theoretically supported the Venetian financial market. Yet, the Venetians' documented reliance on notaries, courts, and legal codes and the absence of any evidence regarding collective punishment suggest otherwise.

An institution based on bilateral reputation can support financial exchange if a merchant's future gains (or, more precisely, his discounted lifetime expected utility) from keeping his honest bilateral association with a particular investor is larger than the gains he can obtain by cheating. This condition seems not to have held in general. Consider the case of Rodolfo Suligo, who raised a total sum of 1071 Venetian pounds and 5 pence from 15 investors to finance a trading voyage from Venice to its colonies in 1234 (MRL 1940, 675–690 and 804). The sum was huge, about 200 times the annual rent of a profitable shop in the market place of the Rialto in the year 1238 (MRL 1940, 710; Robbert, 1999, 37). By embezzling such a large sum, he could have well established himself abroad. Furthermore, the fact that he received funds from at least 15 investors suggests quite a competitive financial market within Venice, a suggestion that is confirmed by other historical data (Luzzatto 1952, 59–115). According to Lane (1966, 62), there was an "ever-expanding volume of funds seeking investment" in Venice. But, because "there were a large number of investors eager to place funds," each investor's threat of terminating his bilateral relations with a merchant who cheated him was void. Competition among Venetian investors undermined the operation of a bilateral reputation mechanism.

When neither public nor private institutions deter outright embezzlement of funds, financial exchange does not transpire. Provided it transpires, as indeed it was the case in Venice, an appropriate contractual design can mitigate asymmetric information problems. In the absence of (symmetric) information regarding trading costs, prices, and events, a merchant would ex post render a false account and misappropriate the difference but anticipating this, an investor would ex ante refuse conditioning his payoffs on the merchant's claims. Hidden information would thus constrain the form of contracts to those with a commercial fix-repayment schedule (Radner 1968). In other words, where and when a merchant could have hidden a venture's true outcome, equity-like commenda contracts would not be implementable. Debt-like sea loans would have prevailed.

Yet, we observe many commenda contracts and indeed a time shift from bond-like sea loans to equity-like commenda contracts (figure 5.1). Furthermore, after 1230 many commenda contracts (about 30 percent) stopped invoking the merchant to render a complete, fair, and true accounting without any fraud or evil intent and the vast majority of them (about 95 percent) introduced stipulations that, in the absence of symmetric information, would have exacerbated diversion of profits from investors. Specifically, the merchant was then given a high degree of freedom "to do business by land or sea, carrying, entrusting, abandoning, and recovering all or part of the merchandise wherever it seems good to (him)" and was allowed to "dispatch" an investor's proceeds without returning in person to render accounts (e.g., MRL 1940, # 780). Theory and evidence thus suggest that formal or informal monitoring provided the required information regarding trading costs, prices, and events.[4]

Asymmetric information regarding a merchant's choice of action while on voyage could also lead to the manipulation of the voyage's risk characteristics. Both a debt-like sea loan and an equity-like commenda contract induced a merchant to assume excessive risks at sea or from the action of hostile men because his share on a profit was higher than his share on a loss (Stiglitz and Weiss 1981).

To mitigate moral hazard during the twelfth century, sea loans and commenda contracts typically specified the ship, destination, route, and sailing dates, and forbade the merchant from changing the ex ante terms of the contract, except for the explicit agreement between the majority of the merchants and the crew. By allocating control rights away from the merchant and toward a third party—the whole ship's company—with no or less conflicting interests with an investor, these stipulations restricted expropriation without severely constraining a venture's profitability. For example, in 1182, a group of merchants on a voyage to Constantinople on the ship commanded by the helmsman Simeone Istrigo came to know that the Pisans and the Genoese had been expelled from Byzantium and that their property had been seized. They then met with the helmsman and the crew and, on the basis of a majority vote, changed course to Alexandria (MRL 1940, # 331; Pryor 1983, 147–48). The ship's company as a whole (of at least 60 people if the ship was armed) also had the right to decide whether the vessel should take on additional cargo, go to the aid of a stricken ship, winter overseas, and so forth (Lane 1966). These stipulations, however, did not persist. By the turn of the century, both sea loans and commenda contracts began to confer merchants some degree of freedom to choose among various ships, routes, and destinations and after 1230 most commenda contracts allowed them to trade wherever they saw fit.

A possible reason for the adoption of the equity-like commenda contract is that it provided better incentives than the debt-like sea loan regarding the manipulation of risk toward voyages with a lower probability of safe arrival but a higher expected return if the cargo safely arrived. Indeed, the bilateral commenda, which initially substituted the sea loan, placed better incentives on the merchant by making him bear one-third of a capital loss and reducing his share on profits from one to one-half. Yet, the commenda progressed from a good incentive scheme in which the merchant shared some of the downside risk (in its bilateral form) to one in which he did not (in its unilateral form). The evolution of contractual stipulations and forms thus suggests that the severity of moral hazard declined over time (see figure 5.1).

Similarly, asymmetric information regarding a merchant's effort during the operation of the trading voyage could lead to shirking. When costly and hidden managerial effort raises the expected commercial return on investments, debt-like sea loans provide first-best incentives for the merchant to exercise effort, but at the cost of letting him bear all the commercial risk (Jensen and Meckling 1976). It might then be optimal to trade-off incentives against risk sharing through equity-like commenda contracts (Stiglitz 1974). Whether optimal or not, however, low-powered commenda contracts theoretically lead to a neo-Marshallian inefficiency. But, according to Roberto S. Lopez, the commenda "contributed greatly to the fast growth of maritime trade" (1976, 76).[5] Theory and evidence thus suggest that, by the time the commenda replaced the sea loan, the severity of moral hazard regarding managerial effort had also declined.

If the legal system, private institutions, and contractual design did not provide the foundations of Venice's financial market, how could investors trust merchants not to expropriate all or part of their capital? What institutional arrangements reduced the measurement and agency costs of using bond-like sea loans and equity-like commenda contracts? Theoretical considerations and historical evidence suggest that the observed trust and implied information reflect the combined use of regulation and litigation.

REGULATION AND LITIGATION

In late-medieval Venice, the state took the military and diplomatic initiatives required to gain exclusive trading privileges, organized protective convoys, and restricted foreign entry. These regulations generated economic rents to which only Venetian citizens had access and so motivated merchants to return to Venice, where the legal system could force solvent borrowers to repay if they failed to do so spontaneously. The state also regulated the operation of trading ventures in a manner that reduced merchants' opportunities and incentives to breach their contracts and enhanced investors' ability to verify a breach. Specifically, by 1220s colonial governors, convoy admirals, ship scribes, tax collectors, and many other public gatekeepers monitored merchants at all times, thereby preventing misconduct and generating the verifiable information required to adjudicate commercial disputes. Regulation and litigation thus conjointly provided investor protection.

Providing Incentives to Keep One's Affiliation with Venice: Naval Expansion and Barriers to Entry

The Venetian state used it naval power and skilful diplomacy to create economic rents. Specifically, it gave Venetian citizens exclusive trading rights in the Northern Adriatic, organized protective convoys, and obtained exceptional trading privileges in the Eastern Mediterranean, thereby increasing the expected profitability of its merchants beyond what they could have gained as residents of other cities (Lane 1979; González de Lara 2008, 262–65).

To preserve per-citizen rents, Venice denied foreigners access to its lucrative trade and applied tight citizenship rules. Specifically, the state passed laws and regulations prohibiting foreigners from shipping merchandise from Venice and trading in its colonies (Lane 1973, 7, 61). It also developed the administrative structures required to enforce these prohibitions. For example, during the thirteenth century merchants planning to join a trading convoy from Venice to its colonies were required to register in advance and to obtain a license (Ibid., 49). More generally, the Consuls of the Merchants in Venice and colonial governors abroad had the specific duty of ensuring that foreigners did not participate in business reserved for Venetian citizens (Sacerdoti 1899, 17, 44). The state also constrained citizenship and so access to trade by requiring immigrants to pay taxes in Venice for a long period of time, ten years during the twelfth and thirteenth centuries and up to 25 years during the fourteenth century. At various points during the fourteenth century when an overabundance of Eastern wares in Venice was eroding profits, the state also established import quotas, thereby coordinating monopolistic practices that restored high prices (Mueller 1997, 151, 265, 503, 616; González de Lara 2008, 266–267). These regulations are striking, since they were not generally applied. For example, Genoa welcomed foreigners to its colonies, granted citizenship after one year of residence in the city, without taxation, and never restricted imports (Lopez 1982, 33, 348).

Identifying these barriers to entry as essential elements of the Venetian institutional system for contract enforcement challenges the conventional view that entry regulations are an unmitigated bad. Without restrictions on entry, Venetian rents from trade would have dissipated but without these rents, merchant would have embezzled an investor's capital outright and flee to avoid legal sanctions. Anticipating expropriation, prospective investors would have not invested and mutually beneficial financial exchange would have not transpired. Entry regulations were therefore necessary for both the effective operation of the legal system and the development of financial markets. The alternative view that elite merchants captured regulation is inconsistent with the distinctiveness, timing, and nature of the Venetian regulatory process. Had this been the case, the Genoese would have introduced similar barriers to entry and the Venetians would have implemented import quotas at all times and attempted to eliminate competition from less wealthy and politically influential citizens.

Mitigating Asymmetric Information Problems: Formal Monitoring and Public Gatekeepers

The Venetian state also built up a colonial empire in the Eastern Mediterranean, organized round-trip convoys from Venice to its colonies, and implemented tight regulations and trading controls. This regulatory process, which began during the 1180s and was completed by the 1220s, both enhanced an investor's ability to verify a venture's outcome and lessened a merchant's incentives and opportunities to distort it, thereby mitigating information asymmetries and expanding the set of contracts that the legal system could enforce.

Venice obtained the right to hold permanent magistrates with administrative and judicial functions in Constantinople in 1186 and took possession of a chain of colonies with full extraterritorial rights in the former Byzantine Empire after the Fourth Crusade: a *podestà* was installed in Constantinople in 1205, a *castellano* in Coron and Modon in 1208, a *bailo* in Negroponte in 1216, and a duke in Crete in 1219. In the Crusaders States Venice had obtained large compounds with full extraterritoriality in the early twelfth century, but the Venetian population remained predominantly self-governing until about 1192, when a *bailo* was first sent to Acre. In 1208, Venice also gained consular representation in Alexandria. These colonial governors oversaw custom duties, administered warehouses and lodging facilities, enforced the use of Venetian measures, weights, and coins, kept public records of the prices the Venetians paid for cotton and pepper while Venice maintained monopsonies in Acre or Alexandria, implemented all the regulations and trading controls established in Venice, and adjudicated commercial disputes abroad (Luzzatto 1952, 62–60; Prawer 1973; Lane 1973, 17–19, 49–51, 59–62, 99–100; Lopez 1982, 374; Ferluga 1992; Jacoby 1994; Ravegnani 1995).

By 1180s the state also organized trading convoys from Venice
to its colonies. Unlike those previously planned by private individuals, these convoys were protected by state-owned galleys and "treated
as community enterprises subject to governmental approval" (Lane
1973, 49). All the vessels and merchants planning to join a particular
convoy were increasingly required to register in advance and to obtain
a license. The first trading contract mentioning such a license dates
from 1200; after 1220s the requirement prevailed and since 1266,
it was compulsory by law. Licensed convoys were operated under
admirals appointed and paid by the state and according to naval and
commercial plans formulated by its governing Councils. All decisions
regarding a convoy's sailing times, route, ports of call, and freight rates
were thus delegated to the government in Venice or to the admiral in
charge of the whole convoy overseas (Sacerdoti 1899, 43–44; Lane
1973, 68–70, 129–131, 145–146).

In addition, the Maritime Statutes of 1229 specified a ship's carrying capacity, arms, and crew, the allocation of space for freight,
equipment, and officials, and the methods for loading and unloading
cargoes. They also required that the crew swore under oath that they
would not pilfer any shipment and that the ship owners choose among
themselves a shipmaster to go with the ship. The shipmaster was held
liable for any merchandise registered with the ship scribe, excluding
losses at sea, from fire, or from the actions of hostile people. The
scribe also had the duty to register the number, weight, and owner
of any merchandise loaded and unloaded, record the contracts of all
merchants on the voyage, and report any observed fraud. He was a
semipublic official who was to be appointed by the shipmaster but
with the consent of the Consuls of the Merchant, the top magistracy
regarding trade oversight (Predelli and Sacerdoti 1902; Lane 1966).

On their arrival to Venice, ships were inspected by custom officials
to make sure they had paid the appropriate dues. By 1180 naval patrols
coerced traffic in the northern Adriatic and during the thirteenth century there were 13 control points around the lagoon. At each, half
dozen men with two or three vessels inspected all passers to make
sure that their cargoes were covered by permits to go where they were
headed and required proof that they had been cleared in Venice (Lane
1973, 17–18, 49–51, and 59–62). In about 1200, Venice minted the
silver *grosso,* which soon became an accepted medium of exchange
and unit of account for overseas trade (Stahl 2000, 204–213). Furthermore, by 1225 all commodity sales in the Rialto needed to
be registered with the *Sensali dellla Messetteria,* a group of officials
responsible for the collection of taxes and the provision of compulsory
brokerage services (Rösch 1995, 453).

Accounting for the Development of Bond and Equity Markets

The conjecture that regulation and litigation conjointly supported the Venetian financial markets for overseas trade generates various testable predictions regarding market participants and contractual forms. Empirical confirmation of these predictions lends further support to the conjecture.

First, to sustain the rents required for merchants to voluntarily submit to the authorities, Venice needed to regulate entry. Foreigners needed to be excluded from the market, as indeed they were. Over 96 percent of the contracts known for the period 1122–1261 were among Venetian citizens. The data, though, might be biased, as foreigners were less likely to use Venetian notaries than citizens. Yet, equally biased evidence from other localities, such as Genoa, shows many relations between citizens and noncitizens, thereby suggesting that the Venetians indeed contracted mainly with each other (Greif 1994, 930–935).

Second, to benefit from the system, a Venetian investor needed to be able to present evidence in support of his claims to the courts. Formal monitoring generated information, but for regulation to enhance verification, an information-transmission mechanism was needed. Access to the courts was equally needed. Living in the city of Venice itself, as opposed to any other settlement within the Venetian territory or abroad, gave traders cheap access to both information, which "flew" in the market place of the Rialto (Lane 1973, 143), and the courts, which were located downtown (Mueller 1997, 124–125). As expected, the great majority of the market participants resided in the city: 90.41 percent of the investments were undertaken by city dwellers and 96.63 percent of them were managed by city merchants.

Within the city, Venetian investors seem to have had equal access to both information and the courts, thus suggesting the operation of an impartial legal system. For example, in 1226, the nobles Tommaso Agadi and Tommaso Gradenigo respectively invested 400 and 100 Venetian pounds; the same year a women named Soria entrusted 8 pounds and 4 pence in commenda to a merchant who appears to be unrelated to her family (MRL 1940, # 638, 633, 627). Most investors in our sample bore noble family names and about half of these belonged to the ruling aristocracy, but over a third of the investors were non-nobles. Furthermore, financial relations were not driven by traders' social class: 37.30 percent of the contracts were entered among nobles and 19.94 among non-nobles but 39.37 percent were flexible contracts between nobles and non-nobles; the remaining 3.36 percent were between Venetians and non-Venetians. Regulation and litigation thus appear to have supported impersonal markets among Venetian city dwellers.

Finally, if Venetian regulations actually enhanced an investor's ability to verify a merchant's accounts while reducing the severity of moral hazard, we would expect to observe a progressive transition from debt-like sea loans to equity-like commenda contracts. Indeed, we observe such a transition. As shown in figure 5.1, the sea loan prevailed until about 1180, when the state did not yet monitor trade. In the absence of (verifiable) information regarding a venture's true outcome, market participants were constrained to rely on debt-like sea loans, despite the implied inefficient risk allocation and perverse incentives on merchants to assume excessive risk from which they were protected through limited liability. As colonial governors, convoy admirals, ship scribes, custom officials, and public brokers engaged on formal monitoring, bond-like sea loans progressively gave way to equity-like commenda contracts. Yet, these public gatekeepers were initially limited in their ability to disrupt misconduct by withholding their cooperation with merchants (Kraakman 1986) and so the bilateral commenda, in which the merchant bore one-third of a capital loss and received only one-half of a profit, was initially embraced. By 1220s, when Venetian officials effectively monitored trade, the unilateral commenda prevailed. Its adoption did not impair trade expected profitability since the Venetian regulations also rendered a venture's outcome less sensitive to a merchant's effort.

Because merchants were then effectively constrained in their ability to both misreport profits and take excessive risks, it was no longer necessary to invoke them to render a true account and it was possible to confer them the flexibility they need to take advantage of unforeseeable opportunities for profit if and when they developed, so long as they joined a licensed convoy from Venice to its well-established colonies.

The association between the organization of licensed convoys and the regulation of the trade that linked Venice with its colonies, on the one hand, and the development of equity markets, on the other hand, was so strong that we have a perfect fit. All 127 observations (out of 388) in which the merchant was explicitly required to obtain a trading license are equity-like commenda contracts. Likewise, all 147 merchant who undertook a round-trip voyage from Venice to its colonies after 1220 obtained equity funding; the vast majority of them (111) joined a licensed convoy. These two proxies for formal monitoring thus predict correctly 288 out of 388 observations, that is, they explain over 74 percent of the whole sample variation. Furthermore, the probit analysis conducted in González de Lara (2010) indicates that other proxies for formal monitoring also had a high explanatory power, whereas informal monitoring by investors themselves appears to be economically and statistically insignificant.

Conclusions

In late-medieval Venice litigation and regulation conjointly provided investors protection from expropriation by (controlling) merchants. The Venetian legal system could and did force merchants within its jurisdiction to comply with their verifiable contractual obligations but could not coerce a merchant who embezzled capital and fled, nor could it enforce contracts based on limited information.

To motivate a merchant to submit to the authorities, more extensive state intervention than is usually associated with good corporate governance was required. Venice, in particular, took the military and diplomatic initiative required to gain exclusive trading privileges, organized protective convoys, and restricted entry.

Furthermore, to enlarge the set of contracts that could be legally enforced, Venice implemented tight regulations and administrative controls over trade. Specifically, colonial governors, convoy admirals, ship scribes, custom officials, and public brokers monitored merchants at all times. These public gatekeepers generated information that investors could present as evidence to the courts, prevented merchants from manipulating the risk characteristics of their voyages, and rendered a venture's outcome less sensitive to their lack of effort. As a result, equity markets developed.

With the wave of accounting frauds at the dawn of the new millennium and the financial crisis of 2008 – both perceived as manifestations of excessive risk taking by corporate managers—modern policymakers might benefit from a better understanding of how regulation and litigation mitigated such problems in the past. Although this analysis provides some insight, to fully comprehend the Venetian regulatory and legal system requires further investigation. Why did regulators, gatekeepers, and judges support the system, instead of abusing their power or shrinking? What institutional elements within the system-curtailed corruption, and to what extent? Was the system worthy of its cost? Future research concerning these questions may further enhance our knowledge both of Venetian history and of the possibilities and limits of the current financial market regulatory reform.

NOTES

‡ My deepest debt of gratitude goes to Avner Greif and Gavin Wright for their suggestions, encouragement, and support. I have also benefit from many stimulating comments of Ran Abramitzky, Tamar Frankel, Oscar Gelderblom, Jonathan Koppell, and other participants at the Origins of Shareholder Advocacy Conference. Funding for this research was made possible by the Generalitat Valenciana (GV PROMETEO/2008/106), the Spanish Ministry of Science and Technology with FEDER Funds (SEJ2007-62656/ECON) and the Millstein Center for Corporate Governance and Performance. Very special thanks are due to Andrea Drago for his patience. The usual caveats apply.

1. Most economic historians have simply averted the transition without providing any explanation for it. According to De Roover (1965, 55) and Lopez (1976, 73, 104), it can be attributed to the church's rising doctrine against usury (for a well-accepted critic, see Lane (1966). Williamson (2002) has documented a later revival of the sea loan and has associated it to disruptions in the flows of information caused by the Black Death. Since this transition was a widespread phenomena occurring under plausibly different institutional regimes, it is likely that private-order institutions played an important role in other localities (Greif 1989, 1994).

2. Note that the sea loan differed from a bond or today's standard debt contracts in that it provided limited liability to the merchant only in case of loss at sea or by the action of hostile people. If the cargo arrived safe and sound to port, the merchant had to make up for any possible shortfall. Full repayment was secured by a lien of the merchant's entire present and future property (e.g. MRL 1940, # 134) and the garnishment of one-third of his future income (Besta and Predelli 1901, St. Enr. Dand., 36). For the legal execution of these provisions, see González de Lara (2008, p. 269–71). Also, failure to pay capital plus interests by the date of due did not result in a transfer of control rights from the merchant to the investor. When bankruptcy could be declared, the voyage was over and there remained no more decisions to be taken.

3. Risk-sharing contracts can also promote the mobilization of capital into investments with a high downside risk by ensuring an investor a sufficiently high-expected return on his capital in the absence of collateral. This problem seems not to have been historically important, as indicated in footnote 2.

4. Alternatively, this change can be thought of as a movement away from costly state verification by the investor (Townsend 1979) toward costly state falsification by the merchant (Lacker and Weinberg 1989).

5. Likewise, sharecropping has been found not to be correlated with low harvest returns in environments where individuals are free to choose contractual forms and hence matching is possible (Otsuka, Chuma and Hayami 1992; see also Ackerberg and Botticini 2002).

References

Ackerberg, Daniel A. and Botticini, Maristella. "Endogenous Matching and the Empirical Determinants of Contract Form." *Journal of Political Economy* 110.3 (2002): 564–591.

Besta, Enrico and Predelli, Riccardo. (eds.) "Gli statuti civili di Venezia prima del 1242." *Nuovo archivio veneto,* n.s. 1 (1901): 5–117 and 205–300.

Cassandro, Giovanni I. "La Curia di Petizion." *Archivio veneto,* ser. 5, 19 (1936): 72–144 and 20 (1937), 1–201.

Cessi, Roberto. (ed.) "Gli statuti veneziani di Jacopo Tiepolo del 1242 e le loro glosse." *Memorie dell'Istituto veneto di scienze, lettere ed arti* 30, no. 2 (1938).

Cessi, Roberto. *Venezia ducale.* Venezia: Deputazione di Storia Patria per le Venezie, 1963 and 1965.

Cipolla, Carlo M. *Before the Industrial Revolution: European Society and Economy, 1000–1700.* London: Routledge, 1993 (Third Edition; First Edition from 1976).

De Roover, Raymond. "The Organization of Trade" in Postan, M.M, E.E. Rich and E. Miller (eds.), *Cambridge Economic History of Europe,* vol. 3, 42–118. Cambridge: Cambridge University Press, 1965.

Djankov, Simeon, Rafael La Porta, Florencio Lopez-de-Silanes, and Andrei Shleifer. "Courts." *Quarterly Journal of Economics* 118.2 (2003): 457–522.

Ferluga, Jadran. "Veneziani fuori Venezia" in Ruggini, L.C., Pavan, M., Cracco, G. and G. Ortalli, eds. *Storia di Venezia,* vol. 1, 693–722. Roma: Ist. dell'Encicl. Ital. fondata da G. Treccani, 1992.

Glaeser, Edward L. and Shleifer, Andrei. "Legal Origins." *The Quarterly Journal of Economics* 117 (2002): 1993–1229.

González de Lara, Yadira. "The Secret of Venetian Success: A Public-order, Reputation-based Institution." *European Review of Economic History* 12.3 (2008): 247–285.

González de Lara, Yadira. "The Impact of Formal Monitoring on Financial Development: From Debt to Equity in Late-Medieval Venice." WP CEU-UCH EE 2010–05, Universidad CEU-Cardenal Herrera, 2010.

Greif, Avner. "Reputation and Coalitions in Medieval Trade: Evidence on the Maghribi Traders." *The Journal of Economic History* 49 (1989): 857–882.

Greif, Avner. "Cultural Beliefs and the Organization of Society: A Historical and Theoretical Reflection on Collectivist and Individualist Societies." *Journal of Political Economy* 102, no. 5 (1994): 912–950.

Greif, Avner. "Impersonal Exchange without Impartial Law: The Community Responsibility System." *Chicago Journal of International Law* 5, no. 1 (2004): 107–136.

Hart, Oliver. "Regulation and Sarbanes-Oxley." *Journal of Accounting Research* 47.2 (2009): 437–445.

Jacoby, David. "Italian Privileges and Trade in Byzantium before the Fourth Crusade: A Reconsideration." *Annuario de estudios medievales* 24 (1994): 349–368.

Jensen, Michael C. and Meckling, William H. "Theory of the Firm: Managerial Behavior, Agency Costs and Ownership Structure." Journal of Financial Economics 3.4 (1976): 305–360.

Kessler, Daniel and Shleifer, Andrei. (eds.) *Regulation and Litigation.* Chicago: University of Chicago Press, 2010.

Kraakman, Reinier H. "Gatekeepers: The Anatomy of a Third-Party Enforcement Strategy." *Journal of Law, Economics, and Organization* 2.1 (1986): 53–104.

Lacker, Jeffrey M. and Weinberg John A. "Optimal Contracts under Costly Falsification." *Journal of Political Economy* 97.6 (1989): 1345–1363.

Lane, Frederic C. *Venice and History: The Collected Papers of Frederic C. Lane.* Baltimore: The Johns Hopkins University Press, 1966.

Lane, Frederic C. *Andrea Barbarigo, Merchant of Venice, 1418–1449.* New York: Octagon Books Inc., 1967.

Lane, Frederic C. *Venice. A Maritime Republic.* Baltimore: The Johns Hopkins University Press, 1973.

Lane, Frederic C. *Profits from Power: Readings in Protection Rent and Violence-Controlling Enterprises.* Albany: State University of New York Press, 1979.

La Porta, Rafael, Lopez-de-Silanes, Florencio, and Shleifer, Andrei."What Works in Securities Laws." *The Journal of Finance* 61.1 (2006): 1–32.

Lopez, Roberto S. *The Commercial Revolution of the Middle Ages, 959–1350.* Cambridge: Cambridge University Press, 1976.

Lopez, Roberto S. "Il commercio dell'Europa medievale: il Sud," in M.M. Postan and E.E. Rich, eds., *Storia economica Cambridge II: commercio e inustria nel Medioevo.* Torino: Giulio Einaudi editore, 1982.

Luzzatto, Gino. *Studi di storia economica veneziana.* Padova: Cedam, 1952.

Luzzatto, Gino. *Storia economica di Venezia dall'XI all'XVI secolo.* Venezia: Centro Internazionale delle Arti e del Costume, 1962.

Morozzo della Rocca, Raimondo and Antonio Lombardo. *Documenti del commercio veneziano nei secoli XI–XIII* (2 vols.). Torino: Editrice Libraria Italiana, 1940.

Morozzo della Rocca, Raimondo and Antonio Lombardo *Nuovi documenti del commercio veneziano nei secoli XI–XIII.* Treviso: Deputazione di Storia Patria per le Venezie, n.s. 7, 1953.

Mueller, Reinhold C. *The Venetian Money Market: Banks, Panics, and the Public Debt, 1200–1500.* Baltimore and London: John Hopkins University Press, 1997.

Otsuka, Keijiro, Chuma, Hiroyuki and Hayami, Yujiro. "Land and Labor Contracts in Agrarian Economies: Theories and Facts." Journal of Economic Literature 30.4 (1992): 1965–2018.

Pozza, Marco. "I propietari fondiari in terraferma" in L.C. Ruggini, M. Pavan, G. Cracco and G. Ortalli eds. *Storia di Venezia,* vol. 2, 81–130. Roma: Ist. dell'Encicl. Ital. fondata da G. Treccani, 1995.

Prawer, Joshua. "I veneziani e le colonie veneziane nel Regno di Gerusalemme" in Pertusi, A. (ed.) *Venezia e il Levante fino al secolo XV.* Olschki: Firenze, 1973.

Predelli, Riccardo and Sacerdoti, Adolfo. (eds.) "Gli statuti maritimi veneziani fino al 1255." *Nuovo archivio veneto*, n.s. 2 (1902–3): vol. 4 and vol. 5.

Pryor, John. H. "Mediterranean Commerce in the Middle Ages: A voyage under Commenda." *Viator. Medieval and Renaissance Studies* 14 (1983): 132–194.

Queller, Donald E. *The Venetian Patriciate: Reality versus Myth.* Urbana: University of Illinois Press, 1986.

Radner, Roy. "Competitive Equilibrium under Uncertainty." *Econometrica* 36 (1968): 31–58.

Ravegnani, Giorgio. "La Romania veneziana" in Ruggini, L.C., Pavan, M., Cracco, G. and G. Ortalli, eds. *Storia di Venezia*, vol. 2, 183–232. Roma: Ist. dell'Encicl. Ital. fondata da G. Treccani, 1995.

Robbert, Louise B. "Domenico Gradenigo: A Thirteenth-Century Venetian Merchant" in Kittel, E.E. and T.F. Madden, eds. *Medieval and Renaissance Venice.* Urbana: University of Illinois Press, 1999.

Rodrik, Dani. "Second-Best Institutions." *American Economic Review P&P* 98.2 (2008): 100–104.

Rösch, Gerhard. *Der Venezianische Adel bis zur Schließung des Großen Rats. Zur Genese einer Führungsschicht* (Kieler Historische Studien, 33). Sigmaringen: Thorbecke, 1989.

Rösch, Gerhard. "Le strutture commerciali" in Ruggini, L.C., Pavan, M., Cracco, G. and G. Ortalli, eds. *Storia di Venezia*, vol. 2, 437–460. Roma: Ist. dell'Encicl. Ital. fondata da G. Treccani, 1995.

Rosenberg, Nathan and L.E. Birdzell Jr. *How the West Grew Rich: The Economic Transformation of the Industrial World.* New York: Basic Books, 1986.

Sacerdoti, Adolfo. "Le colleganze nella pratica degli affari e nella legislazione veneta." *Atti del Reale Istituto Veneto di scienze, lettere ed arti* 59 (1899–1900): 1–45.

Stahl, Alan M. *Zecca: The Min of Venice in the Middle Ages.* Baltimore: The John Hopkins University Press, 2000.

Stiglitz, Joseph E. "Incentives and Risk Sharing in Sharecropping." *Review of Economic Studies* 41.2 (1974): 219–255.

Stiglitz, Joseph E. and Weiss, Andrew. "Credit Rationing in Markets with Imperfect Information." *American Economic Review* 71.3 (1981): 393–410.

Townsend, Robert M. "Optimal Contracts and Competitive Markets with Costly State Verification." *Journal of Economic Theory* 21.2 (1979): 265–293.

Williamson, Dean V. "Transparency and Contract Selection: Evidence from the Financing of Trade in Venetian Crete, 1303–1351," Mimeo, 2002.

Zingales, Luigi. "The Future of Securities Regulation." *Journal of Accounting Research* 47.2 (2009): 391–425.

CHAPTER 6

SHAREHOLDER ACTIVISM IN THE VIRGINIA COMPANY OF LONDON, 1606–1624

Thomas Hall

INTRODUCTION

The Virginia Company of London (VCL) was founded in 1606 under charter of James I of England. Although successful in terms of founding the longest-lasting, continuously settled English colony in North America at Jamestown, the firm was an abysmal failure for its shareholders, employees, settlers, and managers. Our key finding is that two issues—shareholder activism and the role of the state—each had ambiguous impacts on the firm's performance, with sometimes positive and sometimes negative consequences.

The VCL (its seal is indicated in figure 6.1) was not an outgrowth of long-lasting, well-established governance practices, but was a work in progress. Its institutional structure, which in any event changed over time, had similarities to those of other companies from the early seventeenth century (in England and elsewhere). The firm's innovative purpose was different from its predecessors, however, in that it was chartered to establish a permanent colony, and not simply to generate revenues from mercantile activity. The role of shareholder advocacy in this context was ambiguous. On the one hand, activism led to large numbers of patriotic, interested, and active shareholders who facilitated the firm's access to the necessary financial means to found and support a colony. Advocacy also served to correct managerial practices of shirking and diversion.[1] On the other hand, peculiar institutional

Figure 6.1   Seal of the London Company of Virginia

forms (e.g., the rule leading to one share*holder* one vote) led to perverse outcomes, such that entrenched *minority* shareholders under the
sway of an influential CEO were able to maintain a disastrous status
quo that led to unnecessary human tragedies, the firm's bankruptcy,
and its eventual dissolution.

The state played a similarly ambiguous role. On the one hand, royal
charters granted the firm an extensive monopoly to extract resources
from a vast territory that encompassed much of the eastern seaboard
of North America; most importantly, this included wholesale production of tobacco in Virginia. On the other hand, the state prevented
shareholders from fully realizing the profit potential granted by their
ostensible geographic monopoly. A competing royal monopoly for
retail tobacco sales within England, along with price setting at the
wholesale level, diverted profits from the VCL's shareholders. Regulations concerning resupply missions led to fixed, inflated prices for tools
and other finished goods sent from England, and also meant that ship
captains faced incentives to offload colonists but did not ensure such
new arrivals were properly provisioned for the harsh colonial winters.
Finally, the ambivalence of James I regarding the adverse health effects
of smoking, and subsequent difficulties in portraying a positive image
of the company that marketed a socially undesirable product, made it
difficult to attract additional investors.

The chapter proceeds as follows. *First,* it outlines the initial development of the VCL, describing its institutional structure, governance,
and early history. That section provides context for, *second,* detailed
accounts of the successful effort led by Sir Edwin Sandys to remove
the firm's chief executive, Sir Thomas Smith, during 1618–1619. That
initial episode of shareholder activism resulted in a reorientation of the
firm in a potentially positive direction. Unfortunately, the opportunity
provided to Sandys was squandered, and gross mismanagement

discussed in the *third* section ultimately led to the dissolution of the firm in 1624. *Fourth,* we conclude by examining lessons from the VCL's failures. Specifically, we focus on the implications of the separation of control and cash-flow rights, the joint public/private management of firms and markets, and the ambiguous nature of shareholder activism; all of these are relevant to current research and practice.

CONTEXT OF SHAREHOLDER ACTIVISM: THE ORIGINS AND DEVELOPMENT OF THE COMPANY

The VCL is best known for founding in 1607 the Jamestown colony, the oldest continuously inhabited settlement in North America established by the English. Their geopolitical rivals, the Spanish, were accumulating substantial gold and silver specie from the New World each year.[2] England in the early seventeenth century had no possessions in the Americas from which to further its imperial aspirations, and the monarch faced political (parliamentary) limitations on borrowing. The king solved this resource constraint in the late 1500s and early 1600s by granting royal monopolies (exclusive rights to activities that are meant to generate revenue) to joint-stock companies (i.e., firms in which shares of ownership were issued to the public), including the East India Company, the Muscovy Company (with which Captain John Smith had been associated), the Bermuda (Somers Island) Company, and the Virginia Company (of London, as well as one of Plymouth[3]). This form of organization allowed the king's resources for the English imperial project to be supplemented by any politically allied gentry as well as by successful merchants, either individually or collectively in the form of trade associations and guilds. Wealthy investors purchased shares in the companies, which then used the funds to further the English imperial mission, as well as (potentially) to generate profits that would be distributed to shareholders in the form of a "division" of the accumulated stock of the firm—in modern terms, dividend payments. (See figure 6.2 for a correspondence of English Stuart-era terminology with modern equivalents.)

Formation and Initial Disappointments, 1606–1609

The VCL received a royal charter in 1606. The firm was created for at least two major purposes: to provide a profit for its shareholders and to further the cause of England in its imperial and religious rivalry with Spain. These divergent motivations would have deleterious consequences on the management and poor outcomes that beset the firm. Early investors included merchants who had provided

Stuart-era Term	Modern Equivalent	Notes/Implications for VCL
Privy Council	Regulatory (royal) oversight committee	
Adventurers	Shareholders	Term also referred to early colonists who landed at Jamestown in 1607 as well as some subsequent colonists, many of whom where granted land on account of their service, not due to purchase of shares
Garbling	Inspection of imports for quality control	Especially important regarding tobacco imports
Hundred or Plantation or Grant	Private settlement, not officially part of VCL	
Tonnage and Poundage; Impost	Import tariffs	Fees went to royal treasury; important for determining fixed price of tobacco imports
Straggling	Dispersed placement of colonial settlements	An example of mismanagement of VCL—straggling made it more difficult to mount a consolidated defense against Native American aggression, as indicated in the Massacre of 1622
Sole Importation Contract	Retailing monopoly	Another aspect of the tobacco trade in Stuart-era England; royal charter granted to provide a retailing monopoly
Somers Island Company	Bermuda Company	A sister company with many common shareholders with the VCL; shareholder meetings would frequently switch from one firm to the other; CEO was Sir Thomas Smith even after his tenure at the VCL ended

Figure 6.2 Correspondence of modern and Stuart-era English terms and concepts

Stuart-era Term	Modern Equivalent	Notes/Implications for VCL
Court Assembly and Quarter Court	Shareholder meetings	See Figure 1 for organizational scheme of the VCL and the role of the Court Assembly (which required a quorum of 5+ councilors, the treasurer and his deputy, as well as the 2 princapal officers of the company in addition to 15 members of the "Generality", meaning shareholders) and Quarter Courts (selection of councilors for both company and colony; managed distribution of land; enacted laws for the colony)
Publique	Common land held by VCL	Depreciation and deterioration of the common land was one of the original factors leading to the first wave of shareholder discontent in the 1614–1618 period
Treasurer	CEO	Also, the director of the VCL. Note that Sandys, although officially removed as treasurer, more or less directed the company from 1618 until its dissolution in 1624
Division	Payment of dividends	Originally, cash dividends were foreseen as a result of profitable activity of the VCL; eventually, the only items of value that was distributed to shareholders were grants of land in Virginia, which led in turn to the large number of private plantations in the colony
Subscription	IPO or SEO	In addition to selling shares, the VCL raised funds by offering various lotteries until these were suspended by royal edict
Magazine	Carve out for the resupply of and transport of exports from the colony	The prices which the Magazine was permitted to charge for exports of tobacco from the colony, and the exemption from royal duties and tariffs became important aspects of the initial shareholder activism of the 1618 period

Figure 6.2 (Continued)

equity finance to other joint-stock companies; they believed that several major sources of income could provide substantial dividends: extraction of gold, copper, and iron; commercial activity if a maritime passage to Asia could be found; and agriculture, both in the form of crops and of fish. Other investors, including some wealthy members of the gentry, purchased shares as well, but did so more out of a sense of nationalism (vis-à-vis Spain) and less so out of a concern for generating profits. A third group of investors of lesser means each purchased only a single share, motivated also for non-pecuniary, nationalistic reasons related to the imperial mission of the colony. Some colonists were too poor to purchase stock in the company initially, but were granted a share (eventually convertible into land) as an incentive to join the expeditions to Virginia (McCusker and Menard 1985; Heinemann et al. 2007).

Initial attempts to derive income from the company's royal monopoly on the vast Virginia territory, defined eventually as the continent between the thirty-fourth parallel (Cape Fear in present-day North Carolina) north and the forty-first parallel (Long Island Sound), met with failure. Shipments of "ore" sent back to England for analysis proved to contain neither gold nor silver. The American Indians, seen initially as potential agricultural laborers, did not respond favorably to the offers of employment. Cultural attitudes among the Powhatan—the paramount chiefdom that dominated the Chesapeake Bay region at the time—meant that for the most part, a women's labor, such as farm work (and digging Tuckahoe root for making bread), was focused on her own community, and men were too involved in hunting, raiding, and other masculine pursuits (Roundtree 1998, 3–4).[4] Despite exploration of the local waterways, including up the James River as far as the cataracts in modern Richmond, no passage to the East had been found. This mounting evidence supported American Indian arguments that a sizable mountain range (the Alleghenies) prevented passage to the Pacific Ocean. Although some shipments of timber were sent back to England, the methods by which to achieve the desires of the shareholders for substantial dividend payments were becoming increasingly unclear.

During this early period, settler mortality was atrocious, especially during the "starving time" when only 60 colonists survived the winter of 1609–1610 (over 400 had disembarked by then). Figure 6.3 presents information based on accounts from John Smith, who reported partial data[5] on settlers and their backgrounds. For purposes of the graph, settlers are grouped into four categories: gentlemen, laborers, craftsmen, and others.[6] The overrepresentation of "gentlemen" clearly suggests a very top-heavy organization, and the consequent lack of food is not surprising, especially when coupled

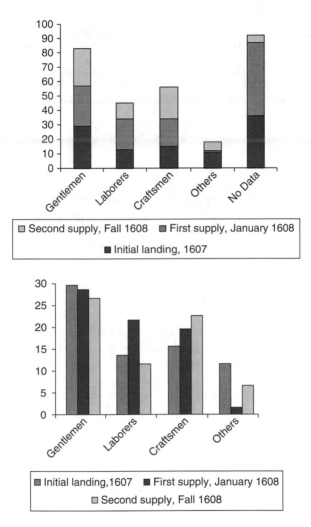

Figure 6.3 Settler categories to Jamestown, based on data from John Smith

with mismanagement of labor resources (including deploying men in activities like digging for gold (without success) along the banks of the James River (Heinemann et al. 2007).

The Second Charter and the Tobacco Export Industry, 1609–1618

The ambiguous role of the state is underscored by the fact that the VCL's dual private and public characters were repeatedly reconsidered and changed. Even quite early in the firm's history, a reorganization

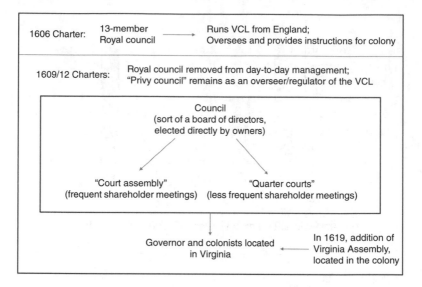

Figure 6.4 Reorganization of the Virginia Company, 1609

of its governance was undertaken. It had become clear by 1609 that less heavy intervention by the king's council would allow more flexibility in the management of the firm. In February of that year, the company had completed negotiations for the second charter (the document from the king that gave permission for the firm to exist and formalized its geographic monopoly), and began taking subscriptions to a new joint-stock fund.[7] Figure 6.4 indicates how the firm was re-organized under its second charter (based on information from Craven, 1964).

The amended charter gave the selection of the Board of Directors (Council) to "the voice of the greater part of the said Company of Adventurers, in their Assembly for that purpose."[8] The king retained veto authority, because he could deny a nominated council member the opportunity to be given a necessary oath; failure to take the oath would disqualify an applicant from membership. The Privy Council, a group of important policymakers reporting to the king, facilitated royal regulation and oversight. The new organization as a joint-stock company in the charter of 1609 attracted a wide variety of investors ("adventurers"). Each share cost 12£ 10s. (or 12.5 pounds), an amount that allowed a large number of wealthy English investors to participate in the initial public offering (known at the time as a "subscription"). At this point in time, shareholder activism clearly played a positive role—an extensive pool of shareholders contributed funds that were needed to rejuvenate the failing colony.

In the wake of this corporate reorganization, the colonists were now able to act flexibly and on their own initiative, avoiding the lengthy process of getting Royal Council approval for each proposed course of action. Yet, in the years following, renewed hopes waned in turn as each new source of potential profits yielded disappointing results. In the hopes of increasing the colony's revenues, skilled workers from Europe (Italy and Poland) were sent to Jamestown, but achieved only limited successes in growing grapes for wine and creating iron tools (Kelso and Straub 2004). Silk worms—a special interest of James I—died in transit. How would the colony generate a profit for its investors?

Hindsight indicates that 1611 was when the fundamental value proposition of the Virginia colony emerged. In that year, John Rolfe successfully bred a strain of tobacco palatable to European tastes (although still inferior to the Spanish crop from Cuba) that was raised in Virginia; it was first exported in 1612 (Heinemann et al. 2007). From this meager beginning, annual exports of tobacco from Virginia to England reached almost 50,000 pounds by 1618 (see figure 6.5). The potential ability of tobacco to finally yield a good return for shareholders, however, did not substantially improve the morale of the investors located in London, and their pessimism was in the end vindicated, for a number of reasons.

Following the discovery of a profitable export crop, why didn't the fate of the colony and the company turn around? Here we see again the ambiguous role of the state in the VCL's fortunes. This was a complex issue, with sensitive political overtones for the owners of the firm, because although King James did not like tobacco (in part due to its obvious deleterious consequences on the health of his subjects), his inclination to make its consumption illegal would have dashed his

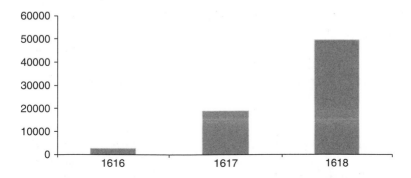

Figure 6.5   Tobacco exports from Virginia (000 pounds per year)

imperial ambitions for an independently funded colony. The Virginia enterprise needed a source of revenue to avoid bankruptcy, and the royal monopoly on wholesale production seemed the only reasonable possibility for generating earnings. The king, however, made no secret that he opposed the practice of smoking, as did many of the leading moral authorities in England—it was seen as dirty and unhealthy even as early as the late 1500s when Sir Francis Drake was a famous proponent of the leaf. To make matters worse, tobacco consumption took place primarily in "bawdy" and "tippling" houses; these were not venues with which investors wanted to be associated. Public disapproval, encouraged by the king's own personal views, also hurt the firm's ability to obtain legislation that would have helped its bottom line. For example, a separate royal monopoly to *retail* tobacco had been sold to the highest bidder and not granted to the VCL. The disreputability of tobacco, in turn, was countered by the king's desire to see the imperial project succeed; he was dissuaded from killing the goose that laid the leaden eggs.[9] In the end, it was the geopolitical importance of the English colonial mission that allowed the firm to avoid an early dissolution (McCusker and Menard 1985), because the king was not willing to abandon Jamestown and its expanding out-settlements.

Tobacco also had a counterproductive impact on the survival of colonists. Many landowners and indentured servants in Virginia devoted time and attention to raising this difficult cash crop, but at the expense of raising food for their own consumption. To stop repeated starvations[10] that resulted, as early as 1616, Governor Dale enacted a policy that required all colonists to each plant at least two acres of "corn" (edible crops), so that subsequent hunger became less likely. This edict was reissued in the reforms of 1618 carried by Capt. George Yeardley. If settlers had complied with the first order, it would not have been repeated—clearly, too many colonists were gambling on the future benefits of tobacco revenues, and not ensuring their own survival through the planting of edible crops.

Meanwhile, back in England, the initial "division" to shareholders took place in 1616. Unfortunately for the investors, the dividend was not in the expected form of cash payments distributed to shareholders but rather consisted of grants of land in the distant colony (Craven 1964 [1932], 43). As illustrated elsewhere in this volume, shareholders of the era were compensated with "in kind" payments such as spices and commodities, but a swath of swampy territory located on the other side of the Atlantic would not satisfy most shareholders, especially those concerned with monetary gain.

THE SANDYS "PATRIOT FACTION" REMOVES SIR THOMAS SMITH, 1618–1619

There were several reasons for the shareholder revolt that eventually led to the ouster of Sir Thomas Smith. These include the land dividend, the firm's poor financial performance up to 1618, investor concern that reliance upon the disreputable crop of tobacco would drown the high-minded patriotic mission of the colony, and suspicions about insider dealing by members of the merchant faction.

Shareholder activism was a natural reaction to perceived shirking and diversion on the part of the firm's management. First, a carve-out firm known as the Magazine conveyed resupply to the colony and delivered its surplus; that entity seemed to be charging inordinate fees for its products and collecting substantial revenues for transport of tobacco back to Europe.[11] In addition, the colony's governor located in Virginia, Capt. Samuel Argall, was reported to be spending inordinate time and attention on his own plantation as opposed to the VCL's common land ("publique").[12] This was part of a larger movement of establishing private plantations, which drained scarce labor resources from the company, especially now that many of the initial seven-year contracts of indentured servitude were expiring.[13] To exacerbate matters further, the firm's chief executive, Sir Thomas Smith, spent considerable time managing the other companies he ran, the Somers Island Company (with jurisdiction over Bermuda) as well as the East India Company.

Smith, an experienced merchant with an eye to the profits of the company, was in the process of pushing through some substantial reforms in 1618. First, Argall was removed; the shareholders chose as his replacement Capt. George Yeardley, who had served ably as deputy governor between the Dale and Argall administrations. He was commissioned on November 18, 1618, and, carrying a set of vital instructions, he set sail in January 1619 to take over day-to-day management of the colony. Second, Smith attempted to placate unhappy shareholders by instituting a number of governance reforms. Court meetings of shareholders in 1618 were devoted to issues such as land tenure, abolition of martial law, and the establishment of the Virginia Assembly—the first democratic body in the English New World. These three issues were resolved as follows. Three classes of claimants to land tenure were addressed in the reforms: (a) adventurers (shareholders), who deserved "dividend" payments in the form of land ownership; (b) "ancient planters," who somehow survived the very calamitous early years and were thought to deserve some extra consideration for the tribulations they had faced; and (c) recent settlers, who were divided into new and old categories, on the basis of whether their arrival pre- or postdated the departure of Governor Dale in 1616. Additional provisions were codified for future settlers, including tradesmen.

Despite these reforms, the fortunes of the colony—and the chances for positive returns on investment to shareholders—were still in doubt, and Smith's actions were portrayed by his enemies as too little, too late. The mounting frustrations of investors and the public were successfully channeled and directed by Sir Edwin Sandys, a noted member of parliament (in the House of Commons). He has been characterized as an idealist who placed primary emphasis on the imperial possibilities of a successful colony in North America (Rabb 1998). To convince the vast number of small shareholders to allow him to run the company, Sandys stressed his intention to rejuvenate the settlement by vastly expanding the number of colonists located in Virgina, by reducing the reliance on tobacco, and by renewed efforts to develop other activities that would generate shareholder returns (including growing grapes to be used in viniculture, working of iron, and producing silk from worms imported from China).

Shareholder advocacy at this point in time had a positive impact on the VCL; it led to a change in leadership that provided an opportunity for improved profitability, and served to limit shirking and diversion that was taking place. Sandys was able to assemble a large group of allies, the "patriot party" or "patriot faction," which clearly threatened to replace the current leader, Sir Thomas Smith. The latter's supporters, primarily wealthy merchants, became known as the "court" faction. An observant leader who well understood the threat to his reputation that the shareholder revolt represented, Smith decided to save face and declined to run for reelection as treasurer, allowing Sir Edwin Sandys to take control of the firm in early January 1619 (Craven 1964 [1932], 68). Back in Virginia, Yeardley arrived with new orders. Argall's private plantation—a mile north of the Jamestown fort—was reassumed by the company.

This episode of shareholder activism rested on both fact and perception: it was demonstrably true that the firm was not performing well in terms of return on investment, but it was less clear that anyone else could have done better. Smith was an experienced CEO (treasurer) who also held key posts in the (English) East India Company and the Somers Island Company. Although he was clearly qualified to run the firm, his incentives were not perfectly aligned with those of other shareholders. Smith's enemies called attention to various legitimate problems: spending his time managing the other

companies he ran, allowing his son-in-law to manage the highly profitable carve-out firm called Magazine, and allowing Argall a personal
plantation in Virginia. Doubt about the fundamental value proposition of the firm was combined with accusations of malfeasance on the
part of Smith, and Sandys remained in *de facto* control of the firm
from 1619 until its dissolution.

MERCHANT BLOCKHOLDERS ARRANGE THE COMPANY'S DISSOLUTION, 1623–1624

Unfortunately, the skills of Sandys as a persuasive politician were
not matched by his managerial abilities. Although VCL's investors
as well as the colonists in Virginia welcomed the renewed energy
and enthusiasm accompanying the change in leadership, the execution of Sandys's grand ideas left much to be desired. As promised,
he repeatedly shipped large numbers of settlers from overcrowded
England to the new colony—but he allowed this to happen during
the autumn. Without time to grow crops for themselves, and tax-
ing the limited stores of the colony, many of them faced starvation.
This mismanaged colonizing schedule occurred year after year despite
repeated warnings and protests from Virginia. Mortality rates were
horrific.

In addition, poor provision was made for defense against the ever-
present threat of Native American resistance—colonists began to build
settlements further and further from the protection of the fort at
Jamestown in a practice condemned as "straggling." This risky settlement policy was exploited by the well-organized Powhatan Indians;
347 colonists were killed in a surprise attack of 1622. The resulting
conflict lasted eight years, and decimated the Powhatan paramount
chiefdom.[14]

To mask this "overhasty" colonization and malfeasance, and to
protect his own reputation in parliament, Sandys concealed from the
shareholders the true state of the Virginia colony. How was Sandys
able to block action for several years, despite repeated rumors of
disastrous starvation in Virginia as early as 1618? Why didn't responsible leaders of the VCL end Sandys's continued and irresponsible
off-loading of ill-prepared colonists?

One answer lies in the governance practices of the company.
In fact, each share*holder* ("adventurer") held one vote, placing minor
investors on equal terms with large blockholders. This allowed the
Sandys faction to control the shareholder meetings ("courts"), outvoting the stockholders who held multiple shares, were generally
more experienced merchants, but who each had only one vote.

Sandys shrewdly prevented his enemies from packing the shareholder meetings in return by changing the rules and only allowing his allies to participate, effectively excluding Smith and the other merchants who owned larger blocks of shares. A series of contentious shareholder meetings led external observers to discount charges of mismanagement as simple personality conflicts among the key factions.[15] This atmosphere of rancor obfuscated the true performance of the firm, prolonging the ability of Sandys to continue shipping colonists during the autumn.

In addition, it was difficult for investors and the public at large to obtain objective information on the status of the colony. A series of effective propaganda campaigns led by Sandys served to conceal the consequences of his gross mismanagement; he was a pioneer in using the relatively new technology of pamphlets directed to the public.[16] There is also some evidence that he altered written accounts from Virginia. In 1623, as part of the activities that would eventually result in the dissolution of the company, a royal investigator named Nathaniel Rich would later complain that some of the record books of the meeting minutes were "blurred" and illegible; this "suggests…that official records had been subject to no little editing" (Craven 1964 [1932], 7).

When eventually the consequences of his mismanagement became known due to the circulation of a polemical tract[17] by Nathaniel Butler, the blockholding "court" faction of merchants led by Smith precipitated the second major episode of shareholder activism in the VCL. The charges were clear: Sandys was not able to turn the firm into a profitable company, was unable to face the fact that his mismanagement had led to the needless deaths of hundreds of colonists, and, finally, was unwilling to report the true nature of the catastrophe to the public, to shareholders, and to the king. To determine the truth of numerous charges and countercharges, a royal investigation was initiated in 1623, and after the realities of Sandys's performance were independently verified, the firm's charter was revoked in 1624. In these final days, the role of the state and of shareholder activism exhibited by Smith's court faction took on a more positive role—at least the mismanaged colonization schedule would no longer be followed, saving countless future colonists. But the dissolution prevented any possibility that shareholders would receive a positive return on their investments in the VCL. Smith and the greater merchants, frustrated with being blocked from effective control of the firm, decided to bring its existence to an end; the collateral damage to Sandys's reputation was an additional incentive for their actions.

Conclusion: Aftermath and Legacy of the VCL

The VCL provides an interesting case study in the evolution of the English system of Common Law. Although any detailed history of the company would be replete with complex subtleties, our narrowly focused study resulted in the key finding that two important aspects of the firm—its shareholders' activism and its interaction with the state—each had both positive and negative impacts on the firm's chances for success.

Shareholder advocacy was essential to the firm's initial attempts to obtain capital—excitement and interest in the colonial mission helped the company raise funds for its initial voyages. Numerous investors, both private individuals and collective bodies such as guilds, became subscribers to the joint-stock company. Early disappointments—including the disastrous situation in Virginia, the dividend that took the form of 50 acres of land, as well as accusations of mismanagement by Sir Thomas Smith—provided impetus for the company's reform during the 1618–1619 time frame. Unfortunately, once he obtained control of the firm, the new executive, Sir Edwin Sandys, was able to manipulate shareholder activism to his own ends, changing the rules such that constraints on new shareholder voting led to the perverse situation, unprecedented to our knowledge, of entrenched minority shareholders. Ultimately, dissatisfaction by merchants and other large blockholders led to the dissolution of the firm. This had the beneficial result of preventing the annual starvation of autumn-arriving colonists, but also ended any potential for the firm's shareholders to ever generate a positive return on their investment.

The state was helpful in a number of ways—the royal charter provided a substantial and potentially valuable monopoly to the firm's owners. Yet the state interfered in other ways with the VCL's ability to generate profits—the Magazine benefited from fixed prices on the resupply missions. The rules provided incentives for ship captains to unload colonists, whether properly provisioned or not. Although the VCL had the monopoly on tobacco wholesale production and export, a separate monopoly sold by the king allowed others to benefit from its retail sales in England. Finally, the king's decision to dissolve the company in 1624 had an ambiguous effect—it prevented annual starvations associated with landing ill-prepared colonists, but it denied any future possibilities for the firm to become profitable.

The firm was one of the least successful joint-stock companies of its era. Unlike its sister-firm the Bermuda Company (also known as the Somers Island Company) or the English East India Company, the VCL was a dismal failure as a profit-making entity. It faced problems

unique to its colonial mission: unlike the island of Bermuda, it had no
protective ocean to cushion it from well-organized aggression from
the Powhatan Indians; the events of 1622 in which many Europeans
all along the James River died was evidence of that. The Sandys administration's over-hasty colonization provided a key lesson to future
English colonial efforts—settlers needed proper provisioning.

The separation of control and cash-flow rights that resulted from
the institution of one-share*holder*-one-vote is peculiar to contemporary observers. Notions of democracy and shared power were in their
very early stages, however, and the learning curve was steep. The modern practice whereby each *share* counts for one vote is *de rigueur*,
but it is important to note that there are still dual-class shareholding structures in a number of privately held and even publicly traded
firms, some of them quite successful (famously, Google). The story
of the VCL calls attention to this fact and to the consequences of
the relationships among cash-flow rights and control rights in modern
firms.

The VCL was not successful as a firm. Nevertheless, it indirectly
gave rise to the form of socioeconomic organization that eventually
came to dominate the Tidewater area of Virginia (and neighboring
regions) for centuries. In fact, its failure as a private firm is not unrelated to the success of the individual plantations—diversion resulted in
private gain for some settlers: "The development of the private estates
had much weakened the Company's resources" (Ripley 1970 [1893],
12). The eventual success of the Virginia colonial economy was a tes-
tament not to the management of the VCL, but rather to the tastes
of English tobacco consumers. In addition, the existence of the VCL
meant that a large number of young indentured servants who had
little stake in the mother country were available to colonial landowners, providing supply to a nascent labor market devoted in large part
to tobacco production. At the time of the demise of the company in
1624, indentured servitude was starting to be replaced by the lifelong
and pernicious "peculiar institution" of slavery, which was to become
the dominant mode of tobacco production until the Civil War.[18]

The implications for the modern world are striking. Today's headlines are replete with political "interference" in joint-stock firms: one
can cite as clear examples the backlash against bonuses for AIG executives or the politically mandated resignation of the CEO of General
Motors. If modern firms are run on the basis of one-person-one-
vote leadership through the political system of representation, will
subsequent failures be as spectacular as they were in the seventeenth
century? Or, even more cynically, should we view the VCL in broader
terms, as a success in terms of the colonial project of England in the

Tudor era, where politicians manipulated shareholders and diverted their profits for the benefit of the "greater good" associated with the English imperial mission?

NOTES

1. In modern corporate finance terms, "shirking" refers to situations in which managers, and notably the CEO, spend time doing things other than finding and successfully implementing all projects that add value to shareholders. "Diversion" refers to situations in which the firm's resources are diverted away from shareholder dividends (or capital appreciation); notable examples of diversion include lavish offices, dedicated limousine drivers, et cetera.

2. A fact that allowed the English anti-Spanish pirating adventures to flourish. Perhaps the most famous among such early privateers, Sir Francis Drake, was a key proponent of an English colony to counter those of Spain.

3. The Plymouth Company founded a colony in 1607 on the coast of modern Maine that was abandoned by 1608; it was known as Sagadahoc (Cave, 1995).

4. Roundtree argues that early English explorers identified Powhatan women as performing "support jobs for their huntin' and fishin' husbands . . . " and explores the complexities of women's labor in 1607 Virginia. She describes Powhatan men as enjoying "temporary exertions characteristic of warfare and the chase, tempered by periods of resting and politicking."

5. Because it is probable that the omitted settlers were likely to be less important, the numbers for laborers are probably underrepresented. Nevertheless, a large group of nonlaboring gentlemen would be a burden on workers who had to clear forest, establish the settlement, and grow food, as well as explore the area.

6. Smith identifies "gentlemen" and "laborers" as such. Our category of "craftsmen" includes carpenters, blacksmith, sailor, barber, bricklayers, mason, tailor, drum, surgeon, tradesmen, eight Dutch and Poles, jewelers, refiners, perfumer, gunner, tailors, apothecaries, cooper, and tobacco-pipe maker. The "other" category includes anyone else, including those indicated as Counsel or were appointed to be of the council (management), preacher, boys, Mistress Forrest and her maid. Source: Capt. John Smith accounts, http://www.preservation virginia.org/rediscovery/page.php?page_id=30.

7. Although we know details of the share price of the second charter, there was some participation by investors even as early as 1606: "It is impossible to speak with exactness regarding the financial arrangements of the first years. A provision in the first instructions directing the settlers to live, work, and trade together in a common stock through a period of five years suggests the possibility of

a five-year terminable stock, i.e., a fund that would be invested and reinvested through a term of five years before it was divided, together with earnings thereon. But other evidence indicates that there may have been a separate stock for each of Newport's voyages, as was the case with each of the early voyages of the East India Company to the Orient" (Craven 1957, 16–7).

8. Second charter of the Virginia Company of London, collected by Force, *Orders and Constitutions.*

9. "The house of Commons in 1621 came very near passing a law prohibiting the importation of all tobacco into England, and were restrained from doing so only by the plea of those interested in Virginia and Bermuda that such an act would ruin the plantation" (Craven 1964 [1932], 93).

10. One explanation for this seemingly irrational policy relates to English-Indian relations. If the settlers believed that they could simply extort food from Indians, there was no need to grow it themselves. While Pocahontas and her paramount chief father, Powhatan, remained alive, a tenuous peace remained, forestalling any major Indian attack. After their deaths in 1617 and 1618, respectively, tensions mounted, and it became more difficult for the English to obtain necessary food-stuffs, especially for the large groups of autumn-arriving colonists.

11. A later commentator found the Magazine's relationship with the company as "so fruitful of abuses, that it was abolished in 1620" (Ripley 1970 [1893], 12).

12. Argall received possibly the first land grant to a private individual from the company, "conveying... large contiguous areas of land with the privilege of farming the grant as a private plantation" (Craven 1964 [1932], 57).

13. "[Recipients of private land grants]had sought to avoid the cost of transporting their colonists from England by persuading settlers already in Virginia to take up divisions in these new plantations, which of course was a practice opposed to every interest of the company. Captain Argall seems to have been held the chief offender, and the governor was especially warned that the patent secured by him in 1616 was in no way to be respected since it had been secured by slight and cunning" (Craven 1964 [1932], 65).

14. "Attacking from Jamestown to the fall line on both sides of the river, the Indians practically wiped out the new settlements of Henricus, Bermuda Hundred, Martin's Hundred, and Berkeley Hundred, where the first Thanksgiving service had been held in 1619; after the mas-sacre, settlers did not return to these sites. Jamestown was saved by a warning from two Indian converts to Christianity. At this point [Chief] Opechancanough made the tactical error of ending his assaults, assuming the English would, in Indian fashion, withdraw from battle and return to England. He was sadly mistaken. After the Great Assault the English retaliated with a policy of 'perpetual war without peace or truce' against the Powhatans.... Before the attack the English had felt a responsibility to engage in the civilizing mission

of Christian conversion and English civility. After the attack, however, the English believed the Indians had forfeited that possibility" (Heinemann et al. 2007, 31).

15. Craven (1964 [1932], 105) characterizes the situation as follows: "There are numerous instances in which the opposition to Sandys was motivated not so much by disagreement with his policies and sincere alarm at the state of the colony as by the simple fact that Smith and Warwick disliked Sandys and were anxious to satisfy some longstanding grudge."

16. "In 1623, Sandys's enemies charged him with having led hundreds of the king's subjects to their death by the spreading of false rumors through the publication of letters, books, and 'cozening ballads' " (Craven 1964 [1932], 96).

17. "Unmasked Face of our Colony in Virginia as it was in the Winter of the year 1622." Butler, governor of Bermuda, had only remained in that office by fighting off Sandys's attempts to dislodge him. At the conclusion of his three-year term, he took a side trip to Virginia in the winter of 1622–1623. There, he witnessed the colony during its "most severe trial, and returned to England full of information and with his hatred of Sandys augmented by the affronts of colonial leaders who regarded him as something of a busybody and spy" (Craven 1964 [1932], 254).

18. The institution of slavery developed over a long time span, and the rights of blacks (free, semi-free, and slave) varied across time and space as well. At the time of the VCL's dissolution in 1624, there were only a handful of African Americans living in Virginia (Heinemann et al. 2007).

BIBLIOGRAPHY

Andrews, Kenneth R. (1984) *Trade, Plunder, and Settlement: Maritime Enterprise and the Genesis of the British Empire, 1480–1630* (Cambridge: Cambridge University Press).

Berle, Adolf, and Means, Gardiner. (1932) *The Modern Corporation and Private Property* (New York: Harcourt, Brace & World).

Billings, Warren M., Thad W. Tate, and John E. Selby (1986) *Colonial Virginia: A History* (White Plains, N.Y.: KTO Press).

British Museum: 12496, Folio 165 (industry), Folios 448–9 Virginia Company.

Cave, Alfred A. (1995) "Why Was the Sagadahoc Colony Abandoned? An Evaluation of the Evidence," *The New England Quarterly*, vol. 68, no. 4: 625–640.

Craven, Wesley Frank (1964 [1932]) *Dissolution of the Virginia Company: The Failure of a Colonial Experiment* (Glouster, Mass: Peter Smith Publishers).

Craven, Wesley Frank (1957) *The Virginia Company of London, 1606–1624* (Williamsburg, Virginia: Virginia 350th Anniversary Celebration Corporation). Ferrar Papers, Magdelene College, Cambridge.

Force, Peter, *Orders and Constitutions, Partly Collected out of his Maiesties Letters Patents, and Partly Ordained upon Mature Deliberation, by the Treasuere, Counseil and Companie of Virginia, for the Better Governing of the Actions and Afaires of the Said Companie Here in England Residing.* Tracts, Vol. III, No. 6. Washington, 1836–1846.

Gillan, Stuart and Martin, John (2007) "Corporate Governance Post-Enron: Effective Reforms, or Closing the Stable Door?" *Journal of Corporate Finance,* vol. 13, no. 5: 929–958.

Haile, Edward (ed.) (2001) *Jamestown Narratives: Eyewitness Accounts of the Virginia Colony, The First Decade: 1607–1617* (Champlain, Virginia: Roundhouse Press).

Hecht, Ann (1969) *The Virginia Colony, 1607–1640: A Study in Frontier Growth,* Ph.D. Dissertation, University of Washington.

Heinemann, Ronald, John Kolp, Anthony Parent and William Shade (2007) *Old Dominion, New Commonwealth: A History of Virginia, 1607–2007* (Charlottesville: University of Virginia Press).

Hume, Ivor Noel (1994) *The Virginia Adventure; Roanoke to James Towne: An Archaeological and Historical Odyssey* (Charlottesville: University of Virginia Press).

Jervis, Michael and van Driel (1997) Jeroen The Vingboons Chart of the James River, Virginia, circa 1617, *William and Mary Quarterly* 3rd. Series, Vol. 54, No. 2, 357–374.

Kelso, William and Straube, Beverly (2004) *Jamestown Rediscovery, 1994–2004* (Williamsburg, VA: Association for the Preservation of Virginia Antiquities).

Kingsbury, Susan M. (1906–1935) *Records of the Virginia Company of London,* four volumes (Washington, D.C.: Government Printing Office).

Lang, Robert Guy (1963) *The Greater Merchants of London in the Early Seventeenth Century.* Unpublished dissertation, University of Oxford.

McCusker, John J. and Menard, Russell R. (1985) *The Economy of British America, 1607–1789* (Published for the Institute of Early American History and Culture at Williamsburg, VA by Chapel Hill, NC: University of North Carolina Press).

Morgan, Edmund (1975) *American Slavery, American Freedom: The Ordeal of Colonial Virginia* (New York: W W Norton).

Morton, Richard Lee (1960) *Colonial Virginia* (Chapel Hill: University of North Carolina Press).

Neill, Edward D. (1968) *History of the Virginia Company of London, with Letters to and from the First Colony Never Before Printed* (New York: B. Franklin).

Public Record Office (UK): State Papers 39/8, no. 77: New Merchant Adventures—Sign Manual, James I.

Rabb, Theodore (2000) *Enterprise and Empire: Merchant and Gentry Investment in the Expansion of England, 1575–1630: The Emergence of International Business, 1200–1800, Vol. III Enterprise and Empire* (New York: Taylor and Francis).

Rabb, Theodore (1998) *Jacobean Gentleman: Sir Edwin Sandys, 1561–1629* (Princeton: Princeton University Press).

Ripley, William Z (1970 [1893]) *The Financial History of Virginia* (New York: AMS Press).

Roundtree, Helen (1998) Powhatan Indian Women: The People Captain John Smith Barely Saw, *Ethnohistory,* vol. 45, no. 1: 1–29.

Scott, W.R (1951 [1910]) *Joint Stock Companies to 1720. Volume I: The General Development of the Joint-Stock System to 1720; Volume II: Companies for Foreign Trade, Colonization, Fishing, and Mining* (New York: Peter Smith).

Smith, John (2009) Original accounts of the Jamestown early voyages, accessed online at: http://www.preservationvirginia.org/rediscovery/page.php?page_id= 30.

Southern, Ed (2004) *The Jamestown Adventure: Accounts of the Virginia Colony, 1605–1614* (Winston-Salem, NC: John F. Blair, Publisher).

CHAPTER 7

SHAREHOLDERS' RIGHTS IN THE EARLY ITALIAN COMPANIES: AGENCY PROBLEMS AND LEGAL STRATEGIES

Corrado Malberti

The roots of the modern Italian company law are in the French Code de Commerce of 1807 that shaped the basic traits of these entities, recognizing their legal personality, their capitalistic nature, and the limited liability of the shareholders (Ungari 1974, 32). Before that moment the early Italian companies established in the different states that would become the Kingdom of Italy in 1865 underwent multifaceted experiences. In part, these companies were influenced by the legal and economic situations of the pre-unitary states where they were based, but they were also inspired by the Dutch and English East India companies, and displayed significant common traits.

Examining more than 100 charters, dating from 1638 (the first known Italian company) to 1808 (Ungari 1974, 32), I explore the relationship between shareholders and directors in these early entities. First, I investigate if this relationship can be interpreted as between (a) dispersed investors and powerful managers, (b) majority and minority shareholders, (c) concentrated investors and powerful directors, or (d) small and large shareholders. Second, through the lenses of the functional approach to comparative corporate governance (Hansmann and Kraakman 2004 I, 21), I study the agency relationship between directors and shareholders. The focus of this analysis will be on the different ex ante and ex post strategies used to address agency problems. In particular, I analyze the tools of governance provided by the charters of early Italian companies like (a) directors constraints (rules and standards), (b) affiliation terms (entry and exit), (c) appointment rights (selection and removal), (d) decision rights (initiation and veto), and (e) incentives (trusteeship and reward).

This chapter shows that the balance of powers and the tools of governance adopted by early Italian companies were related to the concentration of ownership in their shareholding structure. More concentrated ownership was associated with tension between shareholders and directors while dispersed ownership saw concentrated control and dynamic emphasizing the relationship among directors, small shareholders, and large shareholders. I argue that the governance "solutions" adopted by these early companies displayed common traits with the foreign models that were transplanted in Italy (Mignoli 1960, 669), but Italian company law displayed some of its distinguishing traits even during this period.

The first section of this chapter offers a short history of the evolution of Italian companies and of their ancestors. The different strategies adopted to address agency problems in the charters of early Italian companies are then examined. Finally, I explore the lessons to be drawn from this analysis of early Italian companies and similarities to contemporary corporate governance issues, particularly those revolving around the role of shareholders.

DEVELOPMENT OF EARLY ITALIAN COMPANIES

The problem of the origin of modern companies has been widely debated by Italian and international scholars. Although some have argued that the structure of these entities derived from the Dutch and the English East India companies (Bonfante and Cottino 2001, 281; Ungari 1974, 19; Ferrarini 2005, 193; and less recently Vivante 1929, 7; and Mori 1958, 212), others suggest that they evolved from earlier Italian institutions[1] or had other origins.[2] The Italian origins hypothesis finds the roots of modern companies in the Genoese "maone" like the famous "Maona di Chio e di Focea," also known as "Maona dei Giustiniani," which operated between the fourteenth and the sixteenth century (Schmitthoff 1939, 77; Bonfante and Cottino 2001, 278; Ferrarini 2005, 192), or, in later entities like the Genoese "Banco di S. Giorgio" (Schmitthoff 1939, 77; Bonfante and

Cottino 2001, 275; Ferrarini 2005, 193). The analysis of the basic characteristics of these organizations is useful to frame the successive evolution of Italian companies.

Beginning with the "maone,"[3] since the twelfth century it became customary for cities and states in northern Italy to finance themselves by means of public loans, which usually involved a considerable number of investors. These loans (called "maone" or "montes") were divided in "loca" that were transferable inter vivos and mortis causa (Bonfante and Cottino 2001, 275; Ferrarini 2005, 192). For various reasons cities and states that issued the loans, in some cases, proved unable to reimburse the investment made by the subscribers; thus, they granted lenders the revenues generated by the collection of certain taxes as a security for these loans. These contracts, called "compere," sometimes also required lenders to create a stable organization for the collection of the taxes given as a security (Schmitthoff 1939, 76).

Among these organizations, the "Maona di Chio e di Focea" (active between 1346 and 1566) derived from a series of separate loans used to finance the construction and operation of 29 galleys built to protect the interests of the Genoese Republic against Monaco, and, later, to conquer Chios and Phocaea. Also in this case, the borrower was unable to reimburse the loan that was converted in a "compera," with Chios and Phocaea given to the lenders as a security: the debt was divided in "loca" and, while the sovereignty of these territories remained in the hands of the Republic, creditors received the dominium utile, that is the equitable property, on Chios and Phocaea as a collateral for their investment (Schmitthoff 1939, 76; Bonfante and G. Cottino 2001, 278; Ferrarini 2005, 192).

Even if the similarities between the "Maona dei Giustiniani" and later colonial companies are intriguing, the conclusion that this and similar institutions were the first modern companies is questionable. For sure the "Maona" shared significant characteristics with modern companies. For example, its shares were transferable, and, at least in certain moments of its life, the dividends distributed to the participants depended on the earnings produced by the colonial venture (Bonfante and Cottino 2001, 279; Ferrarini 2005, 193, both citing Sieveking (1905)). However, other elements that today are considered typical—limited liability, delegated governance, and legal personality—were not clearly delineated. In fact, the "Maona" remained an association of lenders and not one of shareholders: it is disputed if the institution had legal personality or limited liability (Vighi 1969, 670; Ferrarini 2005, 193, citing Sieveking 1905, 223), in addition, also its governance structure was based on a complex scheme that kept separated the financing side of the venture from the decision making and managing sides (Cessi 1919, 8; Vighi 1969, 670). Indeed, the participants in the "Maona" never wanted to establish a company, but simply entered in a financing scheme in favour of the Genoese Republic (Vighi 1969, 669; Ferrarini 2005, 193). For the purposes of this volume, however, an interesting element of the structure of the "Maona di Chio e di Focea" is represented by the internal organization of the owners of the "loca" that displayed oligarchic traits, with a "Gran Consiglio" composed by the owners of at least 10 "loca" and a "Piccolo Consiglio" composed by 40 members.[4]

Another early institution, the "Casa di San Giorgio" has been posited as an ancestor of modern companies. Created in 1407 by means of a "compera," it arose when the Genoese Republic consolidated preexisting loans in a single debt secured by a right to collect certain taxes (Schmitthoff 1939, 77; Bonfante and Cottino 2001, 275; Ferrarini 2005, 193). The Casa di San Giorgio had transferable shares (loca) with an active secondary market satisfying the ownership requirement to some extent (Ferrarini 2005, 194). Even if the yield of the "loca" was fixed, it varied according to the earnings generated by the collection of taxes (Schmitthoff 1939, 77; Bonfante and Cottino 2001, 276).

Analysing the structure of the "Casa di San Giorgio," the interests of the investors were protected using a complex and oligarchic representative structure: a "Grande General Consiglio" was elected among the owners of at least 10 "loca," and 8 "gubernatores" were appointed among the owners of at least 100 "loca." The "gubernatores" managed the interests of the owners of the "loca," and the Gran Consiglio was competent for the most significant decisions.[5] Thus, the role of small investors was limited. The Gran Consiglio, however, did not operate as a real board, but simply as a representative of the creditors (Bonfante and Cottino 2001, 276; Ferrarini 2005, 194, both citing Sieveking 1905, 225). In addition, similarly to the "Maona di Chio e di Focea," also in this case it was clear that the owners of the "loca" did not intend to create a company, and that they simply took part in a financing scheme (Bonfante and Cottino 2001, 277).

Notwithstanding these examples, there is not widespread support for the Italian origin hypothesis. After discussing the features of early Italian companies, it will become clear why the English and the Dutch East India companies are often seen as their authentic ancestors.[6] The brief investigation of these institutions does shows that Italian states, and Genoa in particular, were an interesting laboratory, where many elements of modern company law were elaborated, so, even if the northern European models were critical, the corporate institutions clearly had local flavor.

The Earliest Italian companies

The "Compagnia di Nostra Signora di Libertà" of 1638

The first known Italian company, the "Compagnia di Nostra Signora di Libertà" (hereinafter CNSL) founded in Genoa in 1638, was inspired by the Dutch experience (Ungari 1993, 8; Ferrarini 2005, 196). The company, which derived its name from the use of the so called "armamento di libertà,"[7] faced different political and operational difficulties, and lasted until the end of 1639 (Ungari 1993, 8; Ferrarini 2005, 196).

This entity was governed by five directors (deputati) appointed for two years and selected from among the persons owning at least four of the 600 shares issued. Individual shareholdings ownership was limited to a maximum of eight shares.[8] General shareholder meetings were held on a monthly basis and shareholders had the power to decide on some managerial decisions. In particular, they had the right to fit out new ships and decide new expeditions. Auditing and controlling functions were given to six "rationali" that were appointed by the shareholders, and the distribution of profits was planned to be held on a yearly basis.

Even though shareholders owning at least four shares were eligible to the directorship, the right to appoint directors was given to the general meeting where no limitations were imposed to the voting rights of small shareholders. Similar rules on voting rights also applied for the other resolutions of the general meeting. This suggests the protection of shareholders, both as individuals and as a class, was an important feature of the CNSL.

The first Italian company used interesting tools to address the problems created by the agency relationship between directors and shareholders. First, even if only shareholders owning at least four shares were eligible to the directorship, the right to appoint the directors was given to the general meeting, where no limitations were imposed to the voting rights of small shareholders. Similar rules also applied for the appointment of the "rationali" and for the other resolutions of the general meeting. Moreover, it is also interesting to underscore that the duration of the term of the directors was relatively short and lasted only two years. In brief, the CNSL gave similar powers to all shareholders, and the monthly frequency of general shareholder meetings show that probably shareholders were strictly involved in the management of the company.

The "Compagnia Marittima di S. Giorgio" of 1653

The study of the structure of the CNSL is particularly interesting if compared with that of another Genoese company: the "Compagnia

Marittima di S. Giorgio" (hereinafter CMSG) (Ferrarini 2005, 197). The organization of the CMSG was different from that of the CNSL in many aspects, and, generally, it was less attentive to the interests of the shareholders: for example, the distributions of the profits were planned every three years and half of these profits were retained in the company. Eight directors were appointed to a staggered board for two years that principally had a managerial function. The directors were selected among the owners of at least 25 shares by the "Consiglio Maggiore," which was probably an elected corporate body, and only shareholders with at least ten shares had voting rights. A controlling power was given to two elected "riveditori."

The charter of the CMSG, by distinguishing between the position of large and small shareholders, was more oligarchic.[9] It makes the CNSL appear, in many respects, more democratic.

First Conclusions on the Structure of Italian Companies in the Seventeenth Century

In general, the analysis of the six available charters of the Italian companies established in the seventeenth century[10] is suggestive regarding the protections given to the shareholders. Some trends of the governance structure of these early entities, however, were evident. The majority of the charters drew a distinction between the role of directors and that of shareholders. The problem of the conflict of interest of the directors was not central. An explicit supervision on directors' actions was frequent, and normally the duration of companies was not particularly long.[11] In addition, no reference was made to the removal of appointed directors. Finally, while agent incentives strategies based on reward and trusteeship were not particularly developed, decision rights strategies were common, and, usually, shareholders preserved important powers on at least some managerial decisions.

ANALYSIS OF THE CHARTERS OF THE EARLY ITALIAN COMPANIES, 1638–1808

Extending this analysis of early Italian companies, I examined the charters of more than 100 entities created before the enactment of the Code de Commerce and gathered by Ungari (Ungari 1974, 119; Ungari 1993). Although this collection of documents remains partial,[12] it may still be considered a reliable, though not conclusive, basis for a general description of early Italian companies (Bonfante and Cottino 2001, 299).

The shareholding structure

A Conflict between Shareholders and Directors or between Majority and Minority Shareholders?

Examining in this framework the structure of early Italian companies, it is striking that the number of shares issued was not typically high. Among the approximately 100 charters that provide the number of shares, more than 40 percent issued 100 or fewer shares, and only less than 15 percent issued 1,000 shares or more.[13] Thus, the analysis of the charters reveals that, with a few exceptions, the number of shareholders that participated in early Italian companies was probably limited. This conclusion is confirmed by examining the few charters that provide precise data on the number of shareholders. Among the 31 charters that give this information, 23 companies had less than ten shareholders and 27 less than 30.[14] From the indications provided by these documents, we can infer that in the majority of the cases probably could not have a highly dispersed shareholding structure.

Turning our attention to companies that issued more shares, about 20 of the 60 companies with more than 100 shares reserved voting rights to persons that owned a qualified number of shares.[15] These clauses were also frequent among the few companies that issued 1,000 shares or more.[16] In ten charters, however, this provision was tied to a limitation on the number of votes available to individual shareholders.[17] In other nine companies it was the individual ownership of shares that was limited.[18]

Important differences between companies with dispersed shareholding are also found with regard to the appointment of the corporate bodies: in approximately 50 percent of the cases, directors were appointed in the charter without a clear indication on the duration of their term, and, arguably, for the entire duration of the company. In companies that issued less than 100 shares the provisions that regulated the appointment of the directors during the life of the company were rare exceptions. On the other hand, clauses on the appointment of directors during the life of the company were common in entities that issued more than 200 shares.[19]

In addition, about 70 percent of the documents make reference to the fact that directors were selected among shareholders,[20] and approximately 13 percent of the charters required directors to own a qualified participation in the company.[21] Thus, in the vast majority of early Italian companies only shareholders were eligible to become directors, and frequently this position was reserved to major shareholders.

These findings show that a first difference can be traced between less dispersed companies where the principal agency relationship was between investors and managing shareholders appointed for the duration of the venture, and companies with a dispersed ownership, where the principal relationship was that between shareholders and appointed directors. The latter companies were characterized by a relationship between directors, small shareholders, and large shareholders that emphasized the power of large shareholders, but did not allow them to increase their individual power. Other constituencies did not typically play an important role in the governance of these entities.[22]

Hansmann and Kraakman offered three typical agency relationships in companies: (a) a relationship between dispersed investors and majority shareholders, (b) between dispersed investors and powerful managers, and (c) between the company itself vis-à-vis other constituencies. Based on the analysis of corporate charters, the agency relationships in early Italian companies do not seem well described by any of these. The charters examined suggest two types of relationships were most common: (a) in concentrated companies we have the few shareholders that confront powerful managing shareholders, (b) in more dispersed companies we have large shareholders, with equal voting rights, that confront small shareholders.

Agency Problems in Early Italian Companies

Following the framework provided by Hansmann and Kraakman, we can now consider the different regulatory and governance strategies adopted by early Italian companies, to address the agency problems existing in these entities. These strategies are: (a) directors constraints (rules and standards), (b) affiliation terms (entry and exit), (c) appointment rights (selection and removal), (d) decision rights (initiation and veto), and (e) incentives (trusteeship and reward).

Directors Constraints
Beginning with the regulatory strategies, which are mandatory rules imposed by the law the parties that participate in the company, we should investigate the so-called directors' constraints that may operate ex ante as rules or ex post as standards. Obviously, considering that the documents analyzed in this research are generally charters of privileged companies, it is difficult to recognize to what extent the rules examined were mandatory exclusively among the parties or had a more general scope.

A first discovery is that standards were mentioned only in a few cases. On the contrary, directors constraints based on rules that operated ex ante were more frequent. The most common provision, found in more than 50 percent of the charters, is a rule limiting the powers of the directors to enter in agreements that exceeded a specific amount of money. In particular, these clauses were frequent in the charters of early maritime insurance companies, where lists indicating the different destinations—and the relative maximum amount of money directors were allowed to insure—were frequent.[23] In other charters the limits to the powers of the directors concerned the object of the activities carried out by the companies.[24]

Examining other provisions that addressed the problems created by possible violations of the duty of loyalty, many charters tried to solve the problems created by the conflicts of interest of directors and shareholders. Among these clauses we find rules on self-dealing, provisions similar to the modern corporate opportunity doctrine,[25] rules on the appropriation of company properties and information,[26] and prohibitions on the directors and/or shareholders to carry out activities in competition with the company.[27] Finally, other charters prohibited directors to vote on behalf of the shareholders, or limited voting rights when a resolution involved the interests of relatives.

Analyzing the clauses that dealt with the problem of self-dealing, we find an interesting variety of solutions that probably should not always be considered as authentic examples of "rules strategies." A first solution adopted, was a rule that limited the voting powers of directors in resolutions in which they had an interest.[28] Another common strategy to solve the problems of the conflict of interest was to limit voting rights in resolutions that concerned relatives,[29] a strategy that probably can be considered as an extension of the limitations on voting rights in case of a direct conflict of interest.

Nevertheless, the most common strategy used to solve the problems of the conflict of interest and self-dealing, relied on a general prohibition imposed on conflicted directors to conclude transactions, requiring the involvement in the decision making process[30] of other directors,[31] corporate bodies or officials.[32]

Affiliation Terms

Affiliation terms strategies operate ex ante, facilitating the entry in the agency relationship, or ex post facilitating the exit. Ex ante strategies were exceptional among early companies,[33] and the most common were those that (a) relied on the limitation to the ownership of individual shareholdings,[34] or (b) required a minimum ownership of shares to become director,[35] a solution that was more common among companies that issued more shares.

The analysis of ex post affiliation strategies, like the right of withdrawal or the right to transfer shares, is more interesting. Among the most common exit strategies provided in the charters examined were limitations on the duration of companies, and the possibility of shareholders' withdrawal in case of relevant losses. Many companies, however, also curbed the right to exit, imposing limitations to the transfers of shares.

Starting with the clauses on the duration of the company, 81 charters provide precise indications on this point: the shortest duration was 15 months,[36] and the longest 30 years.[37] The average and the median duration were eight years circa. Thus, early business entities were planned to have a limited lifespan, although, normally, an extension of their duration was permitted.

With regard to the exit strategies that allowed shareholders to leave the company in case of losses, the mechanisms adopted were disparate. In some cases a loss of a specified part of the share capital[38] or prolonged losses[39] led to the dissolution of the company. Some charters required a decision of the shareholders on the continuation or dissolution of the company,[40] other charters gave to shareholders a simple right of withdrawal.[41]

Examining the charters that limited the right to transfer shares, the rules adopted were heterogeneous, but a general framework of these clauses is possible. Generally, these provisions are present in about 60 documents. These clauses were less common among the earliest companies. Only in companies that issued more than 1,000 shares, in proportion, fewer charters limited the exit.[42]

In general, these limitations can be divided in three categories: (a) clauses that excluded the transferability of the shares[43] (usually more frequent in companies that issued less than 50 shares or with five shareholders or less), (b) clauses that required the approval of the shareholders or of the directors for the transfer,[44] and (c) clauses that granted to the company, to shareholders, or to other persons a right of preemption, which was the most common limitations to the right to exit. Generally this right of preemption was given "to the company,"[45] and only in a few cases to directors[46] or to shareholders.[47]

In the end, exit strategies were not widespread among early Italian companies. With the exception of clauses that granted a right to exit in case of relevant losses, rights of withdrawal were sporadic. In addition, the right to transfer shares was expressly limited in more than 50 percent of the documents examined. Thus, the most important affiliation terms strategies adopted in these entities probably relied on the limited planned duration of these companies.

Appointment Rights

Ex ante, appointment rights strategies regulate how directors are selected, ex post, they consider under what conditions directors may be removed. While removal strategies were exceptional in early Italian companies,[48] appointment procedures give useful hints to understand the structure of these entities.

In about 40 cases directors were appointed in the charter indicating their tenure coincided with the duration of the company.[49] A small number of companies had clauses that directly gave to shareholders the power to manage the company.[50] This particular governance structure, however, existed only in closely held companies.[51]

In about 20 percent of the charters the duration of the terms of the directors is limited, usually not to exceed one or two years.[52] Another interesting finding is the diffusion of staggered boards, which were adopted by about the 50 percent of the companies that regulated the duration of the terms of directors.

Normally directors were appointed by the shareholders,[53] but sometimes, we also find exceptions to this rule. We can divide these exceptions in three categories: (a) directors appointed by shareholders only indirectly,[54] (b) directors appointed by directors,[55] or (c) involvement of other constituencies in director appointment.[56]

Decision Rights

Decision rights strategies may operate ex ante by means of an initiation power given to the shareholders or ex post by means of a veto. It is worth noting that some charters gave an interesting initiation power to shareholders who, even when not allowed to vote because of minimum ownership requirement, kept the ability to make propositions at the general meeting.[57]

Analyzing the problem of the majorities required to approve resolutions, the most common rule was that of simple majority, but many companies also adopted supermajority rules.[58] About 30 charters provide information on how frequently shareholders' meetings were supposed to be held; half of the cases the general meeting was to be held at least yearly.[59] In many companies shareholders had the power to decide the most significant corporate decisions like (a) the approval of the balance sheet,[60] (b) the amendments to the charter,[61] (c) the distribution of dividends,[62] or (d) some managerial decisions of particular importance.[63] The study of the decision rights strategies suggests that in many early companies the shareholders were frequently involved in managerial decision making. In addition, many charters regulated the organization of the general meeting in detail. Beyond these general considerations, however, and without considering the appointment of the directors and the approval of the balance sheet, it is difficult to find uniform trends; the powers given to the shareholders were heterogeneous.

Incentives

Incentive strategies may operate ex ante relying on trusteeship or, ex post, rewarding successful agents. Ex ante incentive strategies were not common. With the exception of some companies that allowed disinterested directors to authorize conflicted transactions, and thus play a role similar to that of modern nonexecutive directors,[64] most charters mention two categories of "supervisors" different from both directors and shareholders: the "revisori" (10–15 cases) and the "deputati" (10–15 cases).[65] Generally, the role of the "revisori" concerned accounting procedures,[66] while the "deputati"[67] had more multifaceted controlling functions, and in some companies they also influenced managerial decision making.[68]

Examining the reward strategies, we should consider the different schemes adopted to reward directors. About 80 of the charters analyzed provide indications on this issue. The most common form of compensation (about 50 companies) consisted in a share of the earnings generated by the company, usually the 10 percent.[69] Approximately ten charters adopted a fixed compensation for the directors,[70] and about ten documents adopted a mixed strategy, with a part of the compensation based on the performance of the company and a part given as a fixed salary.[71] This brief analysis shows that pay-for-performance schemes were diffused among the first Italian companies.

Distribution of profits to shareholders offers another possible reward strategy. While the provisions on the remuneration of directors are more focused on the resolution of the agency problems between shareholders and directors, those on the distribution of profits provide information on the solutions to the problems created by the relationship between majorities and minorities.

About 100 documents provide some indications on how profits were divided among shareholders. In the vast majority of the companies, we find provisions on the periodic distributions of profits, which in general were planned to be automatic and held on a yearly basis.[72] Other companies (about 10–15) adopted another approach and paid a 4–8 percent yield on the capital invested.[73]

SHAREHOLDERS' RIGHTS IN EARLY ITALIAN COMPANIES: SOME LESSONS FROM HISTORY

Determinants of shareholders powers in early companies

This study on the regulatory and governance strategies adopted by early companies offers insight into the determinants of their corporate governance. Before the enactment of the Code de Commerce, the solutions adopted were diverse. The majority of the companies were small, their structure was simple, and the personal element played an important role. Half of the 100 companies that provided data on the number of their shareholders, or at least on the number of shares issued, had a concentrated structure. In these companies limitations to the transfers of shares were common and directors were frequently appointed for life. On the other hand, in a smaller but highly significant group of larger companies, governance structures and rules on the organization of the general meetings were well defined. These companies also were more likely to have corporate monitoring bodies like "revisori" and "deputati," directors were appointed for limited periods of time, and limitations on the right to transfer shares were less common. Limitations on shareholder voting rights were more common than in smaller companies, however.

Focusing our attention on the different agency problems that existed in early companies, we can say that the framework provided by Hansmann and Kraakman is not completely appropriate to analyze the situation of these entities. The focus of the charters examined was not on the agency problems created by a conflict between shareholders with a majority or a controlling interest in the company and minorities, or on the agency problems created by the relationship between directors and dispersed shareholders. In fact, the problems addressed and the solutions found were different.

In closely held companies, directors were appointed for life and the powers of the shareholders were limited. The principal conflicts arose between not dispersed shareholders and directors, and the typical solutions were based on provisions that reduced the powers of directors, facilitated the distribution of profits, prohibited directors to engage in competing activities, and limited the duration of the company.

On the contrary, in more dispersed companies we frequently find limitations on the voting powers of small shareholders. Once combined with voting caps, these limitations were probably functional to the creation of an oligarchic structure. Thus, the typical conflict was between dispersed shareholders, on the one side, and groups of large shareholders and directors on the other.

In these companies the most frequent protections granted to minority shareholders were based on the usually short duration of companies, on rules that facilitated the distribution of profits, on less frequent limitations to the right to transfer shares, on restrictions of the managing powers of directors, and on the recognition of voice powers in general meetings.

In conclusion, the rules governing early Italian companies did not address the agency problems created by the typical relationships (a) between directors and dispersed shareholders or (b) between majorities and minorities. The provisions of the charters reflected the concentrated ownership structure in closely held companies and, the oligarchic structure in more dispersed companies. In both types of entities, however, common trends can be found in the adoption of several tools of governance based on exit strategies, like the limited duration of the company, and the frequent distributions of profits to shareholders.

Legal transplants of foreign experiences in early Italian companies

This research also suggests that early Italian companies were one of the first examples of legal transplant in company law. The similarities between the Italian "maone" and the first companies based in England and in the Netherlands are important. The CNSL was a business entity established "all'olandese" that is, translated in English, in the Dutch manner. Even the word "azioni," which is still used to identify shares, was imported from the Dutch and adopted by some early companies (Vighi 1969, 672; Ungari 1993, 26).[74]

Still the models created in England and in the Netherlands were not simply replicated by early Italian companies, even if the similarities are striking and relevant (Bonfante and Cottino 2001, 299). The investigation of the charters here examined, however, also shows that several Italian distinguishing features characterized the implementation of these foreign models. Many companies were quite different from their sources of inspiration, although they generally played a marginal role in the Italian economy of that period (Ungari 1974, 26; Ferrarini 2005, 201). The reasons for deviation from international models are difficult to ascertain but this study does show the limits of legal transplantation and demonstrate that, even at the earliest stages, Italian company law presented some distinguishing traits.

CONCLUSION

This chapter examined the governance structure of the Italian companies before the enactment of the Code de Commerce. Using a functional approach to comparative corporate law, I have presented the different strategies adopted in early companies to face the problems created by the different agency relationships based on an empirical analysis of more than 100 charters of entities founded between 1638 and 1808.

This research also shows vividly that many of the problems currently being debated by Italian scholars, and some of the distinctive features of contemporary Italian companies, characterized these early entities:

(a) the majority of the companies examined were probably closely held, as the majority of modern "società per azioni" are today;

(b) in the majority of companies we find pervasive limitations to the right to transfer shares, as are those that today we find in many bylaws;

(c) the problem of the involvement of the general meeting in the decision making process, which is still discussed;

(d) the ambiguities on the role of the monitoring corporate body, which evoke the recent evolution of Italian corporate law with regard to the distinction of functions between the "sindaci" and the "revisori";

(e) the troubling relationship between the monitoring corporate bodies, on one side, and the shareholders' meeting and the board of directors on the other sides;

(f) the central role of major shareholders in large companies that, however, are placed on the same or on similar steps, a situation that brings to mind that of modern companies governed by groups of shareholders bound by shareholders agreements.

The early Italian companies examined in this chapter may be divided in two groups: a group of companies characterized by an agency relationship between concentrated shareholders and directors, and a group of companies characterized by an agency relationship between large shareholders and small shareholders. In light of these particular agency problems, it is not surprising that frequently these entities relied on solutions that were distant from those that today are generally adopted by modern "società per azioni." In addition, certain governance tools that are common among contemporary companies were unknown at the beginning of Italian company law. Even if today the Dutch and the English East India companies are considered the authentic ancestors of Italian companies, these models were adapted to the specific needs of these early Italian entities and displayed some distinctive traits that in part still characterise Italian company law.

Appendix

Appendix Table 7.1   Documents Examined*

Year	Company	Place	Co.
1638	Compagnia di Nostra Signora di Libertà	Genoa	1
1653	Compagnia Marittima di S. Giorgio	Genoa	2
1670	Compagnia Generale per le miniere del vicentino	Venice	3
1681	Compagnia di Negozio per il commercio con il Portogallo ed il Brasile	Turin	4
1681	Compagnia d'Assicuratori†	Venice	II
1695	Compagnia per la compra de' grani forestieri	Turin	5
1709	Compagnia della Camera imperiale di Comacchio	Comacchio	6
1715	Compagnia per il Commercio del Levante	Genoa	7
1715	Compagnia delle manifatture forestiere e del paese	Florence	8
1719	Imperiale Privilegiata Compagnia Orientale	Wien	9
1719	Casa di S. Giuseppe	Milan	10
1720	Compagnia di Nova institutione	Venice	11
1720	Compagnia di manifatture†	Venice	VII
1738	Compagnie Anglaise des Mines et Minières en Savoie	Chambéry	12
1739	Compagnia di Commercio per le Indie Orientali	Naples	13
1740	Compagnia d'Assicurazione Marittima	Genoa	14
1741	Compagnia Generale di Assicurazioni Marittime	Genoa	15
1747	Compagnia mineraria della Baronessa De Warens	Chambéry	16
1750	Compagnia Privilegiata di Trieste e Fiume	Trieste-Fiume	17
1750	Impresa del Seminario	Genoa	18
1751	Real Compagnia delle Assicurazioni Marittime	Naples	19
1752	Compagnia Reale del Piemonte per le Opere e Negozi in seta	Turin	20
1753	Nuova Compagnia di Commercio	Messina	21
1756	Società Minerale di Livorno	Livorno	22
1756	Nuova Compagnia Pietro Agostino Viviani della stamperia all'Insegna di Giano	Florence	23
1756	Casa di Commercio di Mantova	Mantua	24
1760	Società della Miniera di Rame in Garfagnana	Genoa	25
1760	Grande Compagnie Savojarde	Chambéry	26
1761	Società e compagnia di- Cavalieri per far rappresentare le opere in musica nel nobile teatro di Torre Argentina	Rome	27
1761	Compagnia delle Sicuità Marittime nella Piazza d'Ancona	Ancona	28
1764	Compagnia d'assicurazioni†	Trieste	XII
1766	Compagnia d'Assicurazione	Trieste	29
1767	Compagnia per la Nuova Fabbrica di Cotonine e Mussoline bianche e stampate all'uso di Germania	Pisa	30
1768	Compagnia Lagomarsino per la fabbricazione di tele con colla	Genoa	31
1768	Società per l'esercizio della Stamperia Reale	Turin	32
1769	Società dei Signori Cavalieri e Dame o Compagnia Pignatelli	Naples	33

1769	Società della Fabbrica e Negozio di lanaiuolo «Leonardo Biadi e Compagni»	Florence	34
1771	Compagnia del Partito Generale del Tabacco	Bergamo	35
1777	Sonnaz et Compagnie	Savoy	36
1778	Caisse d'Assurances Générales pour le cas d'incendies	Turin	37
1779	Camera d'Assicurazione Mercantile Marittima in Trieste	Trieste	38
1780	Compagnia del Commercio per le Assicurazioni Marittime	Genoa	39
1781	Imperiale Società per il Commercio Asiatico di Trieste ed Anversa	Trieste-Antwep	40
1782	Associazione per il Commercio Marittimo	Nice	41
1782	Società Triestina delle nave nominata Cobenzell da Trieste per l'indie Orientali, e per la China	Trieste	42
1782	Compagnia della Fabbrica di Setarje e Tintoria	Venice	43
1784	Compagnia del Dazio Pelli del Ponente	Venice	44
1785	Compagnia Austriaco-Americana	Trieste	45
1785	Banca di Sconto di Genova	Genoa	46
1785	Compagnia d'Assicurazioni Marittime	Genoa	47
1786	Banco di Assicurazione e Cambj Marittimi	Trieste	48
1786	Compagnia di Commercio Toscana	Livorno	49
1786	Società Nobile Patriotica per la Manifattura delle Tele	Turin	50
1787	Impresa del Partito Generale dei Sali di quà dal Mincio	Venice	51
1787	Camera di Assicurazioni e Cambi Marittimi	Trieste	52
1787	Approvata Compagnia di Assicurazioni Marittime	Livorno	53
1788	Compagnia Nicolò Campeis & C. per la vendita dei legnami	Venice	54
1788	Compagnia Veneta di Sicurtà	Venice	55
1788	Veneta Società di Assicuratori	Venice	56
1789	Societé en commandite pour le commerce des Indes Orientales sous pavillon Savoyarde [Societé de la Mer Rouge et de l'Inde]	Nice-Bruxelles	57
1789	Società Greca di Assicurazioni	Trieste	58
1789	Compagnie des Messageries de Savoie	Carouge	59
1789	Società per il negozio di telerie e cristalli	Livorno	60
1790	Compagnia Marittima	Genoa	61
1790	Compagnia Nuova	Genoa	62
1790	Compagnia Nazionale per le Assicurazioni Marittime	Genoa	63
1790	Nuova Compagnia particolare di Assicurazioni Marittime	Genoa	64
1790	Real Compagnia del Corallo	Naples	65
1790	Compagnia d'Assicurazioni Marittime	Livorno	66
1791	Società Montefiore, Tedesco e Compagni	Florence	67
1791	Società mercantile G.B. Biliotti e Compagni	Livorno	68
1791	Società per la spedizione alle Indie Orientali del vascello «Il Granduca Ferdinando III di Toscana»	Livorno	69
1792	Compagnia di Mercanti e Tiraoro per finare e partire l'argento e l'oro	Venice	70
1793	Associazione Reale per le Manifatture di seta	Turin	71
1793	Camera Veneta d'Assicurazioni	Venice	72

162

Appendix Table 7.1   (Continued)

Year	Company	Place	Co.
1794	Banco d'Assicurazioni	Venice	73
1794	Compagnia d'assicurazioni Marittime	Livorno	74
1795	Veneto-Illirica Società di Assicurazione	Venice	75
1795	Società Generale Fraissinet, Van Arp & Compagni	Livorno	76
1795	Società Poggiali e Compagni per la Fabbricazione e Vendita del Sapone	Livorno	77
1797	Compagnia Genovese delle Assicurazioni Marittime la Genovese	Genoa	78
1797	Compagnia Novissima d'Assicurazioni Marittime	Genoa	79
1797	Nuova Compagnia di Assicurazioni	Livorno	80
1798	Società di Negoziazione in Cambi e Monete Ferdinando Chelli	Florence	81
1799	Banco Patriotico	Turin	82
1801	Compagnia del Commercio per le Assicurazioni Marittime	Genoa	83
1801	Società «Li Amici Assicuratori»	Trieste	84
1801	Scancello Sicurtà e Cambi	Trieste	85
1801	Compagnia Vincenzo Gheno & Compagni	Venice	86
1802	L'Amica società di Assicurazioni	Venice	87
1802	Compagnia Francesco Gueze & Compagni	Livorno	88
1802	Casa di Commercio Ulivi & C.	Livorno	89
1802	Società di Negozio Ventura, Dell'Aquila e Compagni	Livorno	90
1803	Casa di Commercio Carlo Carassali & Compagni	Livorno	91
1803	Scancello Sicurtà e Cambi	Trieste	92
1804	Scancello di Sicurtà Marittime, Vedovili e Pupillari	Trieste	93
1804	Società di Negoziazione in drappi di lana e tela Sapiti & Compagni	Florence	94
1804	Casa di Commercio Giorgio Velludo & Compagni	Trieste-Venice	95
1804	Casa di Commercio Rob. Otto Franck & Compagni	Livorno	96
1805	Società Greca di Assicurazioni in Venezia	Venice	97
1805	Caisse de Crédit	Turin	98
1805	Camera di Assicurazioni Marittime	Trieste	99
1805	Banco di Sicurtà	Venice	100
1805	Scancello Veneto di Sicurtà	Venice	101
1806	Compagnia d'Assicuratori	Trieste-Smyrna	102
1806	Società Illirica d'Assicurazioni	Trieste	103
1806	Società d'Assicurazioni Marittime Bassi e Ziegler	Livorno	104
1807	Società dei Nuovi Assicuratori	Trieste	105
1807	Compagnia d'Assicuratori Marittimi	Trieste	106
1807	Casa di Commercio L.R. Buccellato & Compagni	Livorno	107
1807	Casa di Commercio Giacomo Jaume & Compagni	Livorno	108
1807	Società degli Assicuratori Marittimi	Livorno	109
1808	Società Francesco Marchi & Compagni per la fabbricazione di pane pasta e vendita di detto genere	Sesto Fiorentino	110

*Unless otherwise indicated, the charter is available in Ungari (1993).
† In the version available in Ungari (1974).

NOTES

1. For a well-known formulation of the Italian origin hypothesis see Goldschmidt (1913, 227) and Schmitthoff (1939, 74), who, investigating the problem of the origin of joint-stock companies in 1939 wrote that "[i]t is still the leading doctrine that the joint-stock principle originated in Italy." For a detailed criticism of the theory proposed by Goldschmidt (Vighi 1969, 665).

2. For other historiographic hypothesis see Vighi (1969, 665) and Mori (1958, 211), who both argue that Gierke suggested that the first examples of companies should be find in the ancient German mining companies (Gerverkschaften) (but see also Schmitthoff (1939, 74), who argues that Gierke supported the Italian origin hypothesis), and Sicard 1953, in support of the French origin hypothesis (De Maddalena 1956, 263).

3. To examine the structure of these early entities according to a modern framework, it may be useful to highlight that, according to comparative corporate law scholarship, companies generally display the following characteristics: (a) legal personality, (b) limited liability, (c) transferable shares, (d) delegated management with a board structure, and (e) investor ownership, in particular see Hansmann and Kraakman (2004 II, 1).

4. Bonfante and Cottino (2001, 279), who, citing Sieveking (1905, 217), lay stress on the fact that the organization of the "Maona" was subject to significant changes during its life.

5. Bonfante and Cottino (2001, 276) and Ferrarini (2005, 194), who says that the "Grande General Consiglio" "was made up of 480 stockholders."

6. Ironically, this conclusion was popular in Italy even at the beginning of the twentieth century (in particular see Mori 1958, 213; Vighi 1969, 668), while it seems that the Italian origin hypothesis remained prevalent in other countries (Schmitthoff 1939, 74). Interestingly, in support of their arguments both Vighi and Schmitthoff make reference to Lehmann (1895).

7. Meaning that the rowers were free men and not slaves or convicts (Ungari 1993, 8; Ferrarini 2005, 196).

8. See the charter of Co. 1 (all companies are indicated by the abbreviation Co. followed by a number, for the correspondence between the number and the name of the company see the Appendix).

9. See Co. 2.

10. Co. 1, Co. 2, Co. 3, Co. 4, Co. II, Co. 5.

11. In the available cases respectively 6, 10 and 15 years.

12. For example, more than a half of the companies examined were based in Venice, Genoa or Livorno, and, due to the destruction in the WWII of the archives of Milan, Naples and Messina, only a few documents on companies based in important states like the Kingdom of Naples, Austrian Lombardy and the Papal States are

available. Another problem is that of the temporal distribution of the charters: while there are only six charters that go back to the seventeenth century and 14 that can be dated between 1700 and 1750, 65 documents date back to the second half of the eighteenth century, and 28 charters date back between 1800 and 1808.

13. For example, Co. 17; Co. 40; Co. 41; Co. 49; Co. 98.

14. Among the companies with less than ten shareholders, see Co. 43; Co. 44; Co. 67; Co. 87.

15. For example, Co. 15; Co. 93.

16. Co. 17; Co. 38; Co. 40; Co. 45; Co. 52; Co. 65; Co. 71; Co. 98; these limitations to voting rights were almost inexistent in companies with a concentrated ownership structure.

17. Normally, shareholders were not allowed to cast more than four votes: Co. 73; Co. 97; Co. 99; in some cases, however, this number was higher: for example, Co. 38 (12 votes); Co. 45 (20 votes).

18. For example, Co. 14; Co. 61.

19. For example, Co. 49; Co. 65.

20. In about 20 percent of the charters there was no reference to this problem, while in the remaining 10 percent of the cases only a part of the directors were explicitly required to be shareholders (e.g., Co. 8; Co. 48).

21. For example, Co. 14; Co. 19; Co. 24; Co. 37; Co. 38; Co. 39.

22. Even without considering the normally privileged nature of early companies, the external constituency that played the most important role was the government. In some cases, for example, all or part of the directors were appointed by public authorities: Co. 20; Co. 65; cf. Co. 3.

23. Among the earliest: Co. 14; Co. 15.

24. Co. 71; Co. 89; Co. 91; Co. 107; Co. 108; Co. 37; Co. 60.

25. Co. 26; Co. 105; Co. 28; Co. 42.

26. Co. 17; Co. 38; Co. 48; Co. 52; Co. 94; Co. 99; Co. 103.

27. Co. 4; Co. 15; Co. 4; Co. 15; Co. 21; Co. 34; Co. 45; Co. 48; Co. 52; Co. 58; Co. 67; Co. 73; Co. 91; Co. 97; Co. 99; Co. 20; Co. 28; Co. 36; Co. 76; Co. 90; Co. 110; Co. 75; Co. 102; Co. 103.

28. Co. 24; Co. 46; Co. 39.

29. Co. 1; Co. 2; Co. 24; Co. 65.

30. Solutions of this type probably should be better framed as examples of "trusteeship strategies" and not of "rules strategies."

31. Co. 78; Co. 101.

32. Co. 56; Co. 62; Co. 63; Co. 64; Co. 72; Co. 79; Co. 83; Co. 87.

33. See, for example, Co. 42; Co. 5; Co. 8; Co. 27; Co. 33; Co. 50; Co. 24; Co. 18; Co. 58; Co. 70; Co. 99.

34. About ten charters adopted this clause, see supra 18.

35. Co. 1; Co. 2; Co. 14; Co. 19; Co. 24; Co. 37; Co. 38; Co. 39; Co. 45; Co. 48; Co. 52; Co. 58.

36. Co. 74.

37. Co. 21.

38. A half of the share capital in Co. 52; Co. 58; Co. 99; one fifth in Co. 90. Other charters imposed the dissolution only in case of loss of the entire capital (Co. 85; Co. 92). In one case any loss, upon request of any shareholder, may have caused the dissolution of the company: see Co. 67.
39. See Co. 77.
40. Co. 102; Co. 103; Co. 105; Co. 89; Co. 107; Co. 52; Co. 58; Co. 99.
41. For example, Co. 66; Co. 81; Co. 110.
42. However, also among these companies, we find charters that limited the right to transfer shares: see Co. 38; Co. 52; Co. 65.
43. A clause adopted in about ten charters: see, for example, Co. 51; Co. 100; Co. 51; Co. 100; Co. 43; Co. 44.
44. For example, Co. 46; Co. 79; Co. 85; Co. 106.
45. For example, Co. 58.
46. For example, Co. 80.
47. For example, Co. 36.
48. Three documents mention the removal of the directors: Co. 25; Co. 37; and cf. Co. 17.
49. This conclusion is probably also supported by the fact that approximately 25 documents had provisions that regulated the substitution of the directors indicated in the charter only in exceptional circumstances (e.g., in case of death or resignation): see, for example, Co. 68; Co. 96; Co. 75; Co. 78.
50. Co. 84; Co. 85; Co. 87; Co. 102; Co. 103.
51. More precisely, five shareholders in Co. 87 and Co. 102, eight in Co. 103, and four in Co. 85.
52. In some cases the duration was longer: three-year terms were not rare, for example, Co. 71, and cf. Co. 8. Longer terms were exceptional: see Co. 22, where the duration of the terms was five years.
53. As already said, in many charters only major shareholders had voting rights, and frequently only these shareholders were allowed to sit on the board.
54. Co. 7; Co. 39.
55. In particular, some charter gives to directors the power to substitute their colleagues in case of resignation or impediment: Co. 79; Co. 83; and see also Co. 65.
56. In particular public authorities: see, for example, Co. 20 and, at least with regard to the first directors, Co. 65.
57. Co. 48; Co. 52; Co. 58.
58. For example, many charters required majorities of 2/3, for example, Co. 14; Co. 15; Co. 70.
59. In other companies the meeting was supposed to be held every six month (Co. 22; Co. 46), every three months (Co. 38, and Co. XII), or even more frequently (Co. 1; Co. 49; Co. 33).
60. Co. 16; Co. 26; Co. 45; cf. Co. 38.
61. For example, Co. 25; Co. 46; Co. 63.
62. Co. 4; Co. 12; Co. 22; Co. 29; Co. 46; Co. 47; Co. 57.

63. Co. 31; Co. 5; Co. 68; Co. 110; Co. 25; Co. 43; Co. 44.
64. Cf. supra 31.
65. As predictable, these supervisors were relatively more frequent in large companies: Co. 38; Co. 52.
66. Co. 20; Co. 38; Co. 48; Co. 52; Co. 97.
67. "Deputati" is a word that in other companies was also used to indicate the directors, for example, Co. 60; Co. 72; Co. 87.
68. Co. 9; Co. 19; Co. 21; Co. 66.
69. For example, Co. 29; Co. 38; Co. 97; Co. 99; Co. 101. For higher shares see, for example, Co. 31 (20 percent); Co. 68 (25 percent); Co. 98 (33.33 percent); Co. 95; and Co. 96 (50 percent); for lower shares see, for example, Co. 41 and Co. 45 (2 percent).
70. Co. 4; Co. 17; Co. 19; Co. 51; Co. 65; Co. 67; Co. 79.
71. For example, Co. 30; Co. 35; Co. 80; Co. 104.
72. For example, Co. 3; Co. 11; Co. 19. For longer periods see, for example, Co. 2, and Co. 49 (three years) or Co. 67 and Co. 90 (two years). For shorter periods see, for example, Co. 37 and Co. 46 (six months).
73. For example, Co. 5; Co. 67, and cf. Co. 10; Co. 22; Co. 43; Co. 90; Co. 34; Co. 43.
74. See Co. 7; Co. 8.

REFERENCES

Bonfante, G. and Cottino, G. *L'imprenditore* (Padova: Cedam 2001).

Cessi, R. Studi sulle Maone medievali, *Archivio storico italiano*, LXXVII (1919), I, 8ff.

De Maddalena, A. I mulini di Tolosa (Alle origini delle società anomine), *Rivista delle società* (1956), 263ff.

Ferrarini, G.A. Origins of Limited Liability Companies and Company Law Modernisation in Italy. A Historical Outline, in Ella Gepken-Jager et al. eds., *VOC 1602-2002 400 Years of Company Law* (Deventer: Kluwer Law International 2005), 187ff.

Goldschmidt, L. *Storia universale del diritto commerciale* (Torino: Utet 1913).

Hansmann, H. and Kraakman, R. Agency Problems and Legal Strategies, in Reinier Kraakman et al. eds., *The Anatomy of Corporate Law. A Comparative and Functional Approach* (Oxford: Oxford University Press 2004), 21ff.

Hansmann, H. and Kraakman, R. What is Corporate Law, in Reinier Kraakman et al. eds., *The Anatomy of Corporate Law. A Comparative and Functional Approach* (Oxford: Oxford University Press 2004), 1ff.

Lehmann, C. *Die geschichtliche Entwicklung des Aktienrechts bis zum Code de Commerce* (1895).

Mignoli, A. Idee e problemi nell'evoluzione della « company inglese », *Rivista delle società* (1960), 633ff.

Mori, G. Alle origini delle società per azioni in Italia; la "Società Minerale" di Livorno *(1756)*, *Rivista delle società* (1958), 209ff.

Schmitthoff, M. The Origin of the Joint-Stock Company, *University of Toronto Law Journal*, 3 (1939), 74ff.

Sicard, G. *Aux origines des sociétés anonymes: Les Moulins de Toulouse au Moyen Age*, in (Paris: Armand Colin 1953).

Sieveking, H. Studio sulle finanze genovesi nel Medioevo e in particolare sulla Casa di S. Giorgio, *Atti della Società Ligure di Storia Patria*, XXXV (1905), 1st part.

Ungari, P. *Profilo storico del diritto delle società anonime in Italia*, in (Roma: Bulzoni 1974).

Ungari, P. *Statuti di compagnie e società azionarie italiane, 1638-1808*, in (Milano: Giuffrè 1993).

Vighi, A. [Notizie storiche sugli amministratori ed i sindaci delle società per azioni anteriori al codice di commercio francese (contributo alla storia delle società per azioni)], *Rivisita delle società*, (1969), 663ff.

Vivante, C. *Trattato di diritto commerciale, II, Le società commerciali* 5th ed. in (Milano: Vallardi 1929).

CHAPTER 8

COMPAGNIE DES INDES: GOVERNANCE AND BAILOUT

Reza Dibadj

The French Company of the Indies (*Compagnie française des Indes*) has been not been well studied by historians, lawyers, or economists (Weber 1904, xxi). Part of the reason for this lacuna is that the "archives of the successive Companies, the whole of which constitutes the French Company of the Indies, have almost totally disappeared" (Weber 1904, xxvii). This is regrettable, since the story of the company, whose trading privilege was granted by Colbert in 1664 only to be suspended in 1769 after a polemical battle for survival, presents both a fascinating human saga and a window onto the intersection of business and politics in seventeenth- and eighteenth-century France (Montagne 1899, 1). One could focus on the colorful characters involved, such as Necker (Lavaquery 1933, Harris 1979, Lüthy 1961) or Dupleix (Martineau 1929), or the macroeconomic imbalances engendered by mercantilist policies (Lüthy 1960, 858). In this analysis, however, the focus is squarely on the corporate governance challenges encountered by the company, in particular the struggle by shareholders to resist the state's control of the company. There are striking parallels between the powerlessness of the *Compagnie's* shareholders and those of today's large corporations, along with a similar ambivalence about the role government should play vis-à-vis troubled enterprises. Above all, the *Compagnie's* story demonstrates the risk of weak corporate governance.

This chapter is structured into four parts. First, the tumultuous history of the *Compagnie française des Indes* is recounted with attention to issues involving shareholder participation. The second section draws governance lessons from this tortured history. Third, I explore shareholder powerlessness as the root cause of the *Compagnie*'s woes. The fourth section explains the role of government in this enterprise. I argue that the *Compagnie*'s ultimate fate reflects intellectual fashions of the time, varying skill in public relations, and hidden agendas of the key players. Recognizing the bargains made by the company with the state since its inception, its demise is not altogether surprising.

GOVERNANCE AND THE TORTUOUS HISTORY OF THE FRENCH EAST INDIA COMPANY

The French were latecomers to trade in the East Indies (Sottas 1905, 1). Louis XIV's minister, Colbert, however, sought to enhance France's role in international trade. As a mercantilist, he believed that corporations should be instruments of the state—a means to organized self-improvement and competition with other nations (Bègue 1936, 22–25). As part of a broader effort to enhance France's role as a maritime power, including the development of a merchant marine (Weber 1904, 100), and "persuaded by the example of Holland that large commercial enterprises on foreign lands could only succeed via powerful companies granted exclusive monopolies"(Sottas 1905, 5), Colbert provided the impetus for the founding of the *Compagnie des Indes orientales* to which Louis XIV gave the exclusive privilege to trade east of the Cape of Good Hope (Grange 1974, 18; Margerison 2006, 26). As a consequence, the "Declaration of the King establishing a Company to carry out commerce in the East Indies, was given at Vincennes during the month of August 1664 and was registered in Parliament the 1st of September" (Sottas 1905, 5).

Initially, the company's organization was quite decentralized, with nine out of 21 directors being designated from outside Paris in France's regions:

Admirer of the commercial success of the Dutch, here as in other domains, Colbert wanted to organize the company along the model of the V.O.C. [*Vereenigde Oost-Indische Compagnie*], with five regional chambers established at Lyon, Rouen, Le Havre, Nantes and Bordeaux. Each one would have an autonomous budget, and would have the right to arm ships, buy or sell merchandise, and nominate one to three of its members, depending on the number of shares, to integrate itself into a general chamber in Paris. The preeminence of the latter would be assured, as it was in Amsterdam, by the designation of twelve directors on a total of twenty-one.

(Haudrère 2006, 71)

Directors were chosen from among major shareholders: for the Parisian directors those with more than 20,000 livres in shares, and those with 6,000–10,000 livres in shares for the regional directors (Bègue 1936, 51), with shareholders owning at least 6,000 livres in shares being eligible to vote (Sottas 1905, 10). This structure implicitly put the control of the firm in the hands of wealthy investors, and left smaller shareholders out of the governance structure. The "directors were to serve for periods of seven years, thereafter for staggered terms during the next five years so that eventually two would be replaced each year. A director could be reelected" (Wellington 2006, 20). According to the statutes of the company, the first shareholder meeting was to be held on December 1, 1664 (Sottas 1905, 20), with annual meetings purportedly to be held on May 2 every year thereafter (Sottas 1905, 10–11).

After the death of Colbert in 1683, a reorganization ensued in 1684: the regional chambers ceased to exist (Bègue 1936, 52–53), the size of the board of directors increased, as "[t]welve new directors were substituted for nine older ones" (Bègue 1936, 52), and "[e]ight years later were added eight other new directors" (Bègue 1936, 52). Perhaps most interestingly "the king named without subterfuge the directors" (Bègue 1936, 58), without so much as the formality of shareholder vote.

Despite a 50-year monopoly on trade east of the Cape of Good Hope and attempts to expand in India, by the second decade of the eighteenth century, the *Compagnie* had not succeeded in capturing a significant portion of the East Indies trade for France. In 1718, it sent only two ships on voyages, in contrast to the 39 and 16 voyages embarked upon that year by the Dutch and British East India companies, respectively (Haudrère 2005, 845). Its nominal capital was at almost 5 million livres, down significantly from Colbert's initial capitalization of 15 million livres; indeed, all but a few merchants from Saint-Malo had apparently given up (Haudrère 2005, 25–28). Siba Pada Sen attributes this malaise to "the rigid control of the State, depriving the shareholders of any independence or initiative; the Protectionist policy of the government . . . ; the lack of capital necessary for sustained commercial activity; and the European policy of Louis XIV, involving continuous wars for nearly half the period of the Company's existence" (Sen, 38–39).

John Law, the Scottish-born Minister of Finance appointed by the regency of the Duc D'Orléans to revive the French economy following the costly War of Spanish Succession, took Colbert as a role model, and sought to use the French corporate structure developed by his predecessor to relieve France of her massive debts. Law created a bank, issued bank notes to increase the money supply, and began to build a vast commercial enterprise by merging various French corporations with roots in the late seventeenth century and early eighteenth century. In 1719 he merged the *Compagnie des Indes orientales* into the *Compagnie d'Occident* to form the *Compagnie des Indes* (Sen 1958, 38). The new company held a monopoly over French foreign trade—including with India, Louisiana, Senegal, and Guinea (Wellington 2006, 51).

The new governance structure of the company reflected royal privilege. By the royal proclamation of August 29, 1720, the number of directors was reduced to 24 men selected by the king, but whose successors were to be elected by shareholders (Bègue 1936, 53; Wellington 2006, 55). The popular name of the company was the Mississippi Company, and from November 1719 to early February 1720 its shares rose by a factor of eight, only to falter and collapse beginning in late February 1720 as Law's inflationary policies ultimately caused a loss of faith in the French monetary system in general, and Law's company in particular (Haudrère 2005, 60–68). Law himself ultimately fled France for Holland, and the French government restructured and recapitalized the company through, among other things, the issue of life annuities (Weber 1904, 323–326).

The firm's governance structure would continue to evolve after the great bubble and crash. In March 1723, a 20-member Council of the Indies (*Conseil des Indes*) was established, "with members selected by the King from among the officers of his Council and of the Navy and also prominent merchants" (Sen 1958, 40). Then,

a new proclamation on August 30, 1723 reduced the directorate to twelve men selected by the Crown from shareholders holding at least fifty shares. Two new bodies of overseers were created. They were four inspectors, chosen by the Crown from the Council of the Indies, and eight syndics who were elected each year at shareholders' meetings. The inspectors were supposed to oversee the interests of the Crown, while the syndics were to represent the shareholders. The inspectorship was abandoned in 1731 when the controller-general took over sole overall control, albeit through a commissioner that he appointed.

(Wellington 2006, 56)

The role of the syndics, like those of the inspectors, was "to supervise the management of the Directors" (Weber 1904, 431). The directors, whose number was reduced to six by 1731 (Bègue 1936, 55), "were designated by the king and the duration of their mandate was not specified; the shareholders' assembly was to fill vacancies and to discharge and replace directors" (Bègue 1936, 55). No shareholder meeting was called until a shareholder revolt in 1745 (Lüthy 1960, 861–862)—perhaps motivated by the fact that the majority of shareholders had changed from court nobility at the company's inception to bankers by the 1740s (Haudrère and Le Bouëdec 1999, 9; Haudrère 2006, 75). The financiers whom John Law had earlier challenged eventually regained their shareholdings (Weber 1904, 311, 324; Murphy 1997, 131, 334), and were now manifesting their displeasure with the *Compagnie's* direction. As a consequence of the revolt, the shareholders were given the right "of electing twelve persons from whom the King would choose six Syndics. But this concession was not maintained in practice" (Sen 1958, 40). Even the number of syndics was in a perpetual state of flux, exacerbating the confusion (Bègue 1936, 56).

The directors and the syndics, unlike modern boards of directors, were principally concerned with day-to-day management:

Every day an administrative assembly brought together at company headquarters directors and syndics; all business was discussed: correspondence, expeditions, nominations and revocations. The form of these assemblies was meticulously regulated; recording of the deliberations, signing of minutes, memos, and correspondence. Once a week, the royal commissioners participated in the assembly to keep current on business; the most important were decided in their presence. Once a month, the assembly was presided over by the Controller General [Minister of Finance].

(Bègue 1936, 57)

Some observers even suggest bluntly that the directors "were also reduced to the status of simple clerks and the real management of the Company lay in the hands of the King's agents" (Sen 1958, 41).

There is some evidence that the political responsibilities of the company took precedence over commercial considerations. With increasing amounts of company resources being devoted to fund the colonial wars of Dupleix, France's governor in India (Montagne 1899, 180 n.1; Weber 1904, 683), the company once again found itself in trouble in the 1740s (Sen 1958, 29; Lüthy 1960, 860; Subramanian 1999, iii; Wellington 2006, 81). This prompted yet another reorganization in 1748, as the number of directors and syndics was set to eight and six, respectively (Wellington 2006, 56). A director would be chosen by the Crown from a list of three candidates proposed by the administrative assembly; with regard to the selection of a syndic, the administrative assembly would propose four names; shareholders would select two, and the Crown would choose one (Wellington

2006, 56). This did nothing to diminish the power of the state, though, which went well beyond the selection of directors and syndics:

> The controller-general could have the final say in any matter, as well as exerting a continuing direction and influence through his royal commissioners whom he could appoint at will and whose numbers could be changed at will. They attended meetings of the administrative assembly and reported the company's business to him at weekly meetings. He could command the assembly to reconsider any decision at its next meeting.
>
> (Wellington 2006, 56)

Put succinctly, "[t]here was no doubt that the government considered the company its own agent, and that the interests of the state were paramount to all else in the conduct of its affairs" (Harris 1979, 17).

The Seven Years' War, lasting from 1756 to 1763, devastated the French colonial project in general (Wellington 2006, 84), and the company in particular (Lüthy 1960, 861; Harris 1979, 18; Margerison 2006, 27). As one French historian summarizes it: "[A]rose, in 1763, the Treaty of Paris which reduced our colonies so little that the *Compagnie des Indes* no longer had, as it were, any reason to exist" (Montagne 1899, 146). True to form, yet another reorganization ensued (Weber 1904, 449).

A provisional structure was established through a royal edict of August 1764: "[A] new board of nine syndics was chosen, presumably by stockholders. The new syndicate then appointed five new directors. The *Royal Almanach* for 1765 dropped the names and office of the royal commissioners, which had been listed in the 1764 *Almanach*. Evidently the company was in entirely new hands" (Harris 1979, 22). Ostensibly, the idea was to reduce the role of the state and concomitantly provide for greater shareholder power (Sen 1958, 45). Historians give the Genevan banker and shareholder Jacques Necker credit for this attempt (Grange 1974, 19; Harris 1979, 20; Margerison 2006, 28)—though, as we shall see, his motives may not have been altruistic.

Even though the state was apparently willing to concede somewhat on organization, it was unwilling to provide the company with much financial assistance (Harris 1979, 21)—something that was needed despite the company's recovery in trade (Harris 1979, 22). By 1767, the company was in serious crisis and a series of agitated shareholder meetings ensued. On April 4, 1767, the company's administration finally proposed an organizational structure, nearly three years after the edict of August 1764, but one that gave limited power to shareholders:

The regulations called for the assembly of shareholders to elect six syndics for six-year terms and ten directors to serve for life. The regulations did not require that those currently serving as syndics or directors be re-elected to the assembly in order to retain their positions. The Controller-General, whose role was not established in the temporary regulations ... was authorized to meet on a weekly basis with the company administration, an indication that the government had no intention of leaving the *Compagnie des Indes* to its own devices.

(Margerison 2006, 29)

The shareholders were to meet twice a year, in January and July (Wellington 2006, 52). While there were no royal commissioners, the king retained the power to choose the directors and syndics from a list of five to six candidates elected by the general assembly (Harris 1979, 26). Overall, the new statutes were disappointing to those who wished to reform the company's governance (Harris 1979, 26).

A committee of shareholders was appointed to study this organizational structure and to report back to the shareholders at the next meeting, scheduled for July 3, 1767. At this meeting, however, there was an open shareholder revolt, with shareholders upset over a company that was financially weak and essentially governed by the state (Harris 1979, 24–25). The fracas was dramatic and brief:

The tumultuous assembly of July 3 was presided over by a syndic, Marion, who soon lost control of the proceedings, as everyone began shouting at once.... The insurgents succeeded in electing a new slate of administrators. But the arrival of the controller general Laverdy, brought an end to the revolt. After scolding the delegates for 'behaving as if they were living under the laws of England,' Laverdy set aside the act of the assembly and confiscated the minutes of the meeting. This was the end of the revolt.

(Harris 1979, 25)

Laverdy presided over the next meeting, on March 12, 1768, in which the statutes were finally adopted (Harris 1979, 25; Margerison 2006, 35). This reorganization was registered on June 28, 1768 (Wellington 2006, 91). During the latter half of 1768, shareholder dissatisfaction mounted once again (Harris 1979, 26). Problems were exacerbated with the arrival of Étienne Maynon d'Invault—who wished to end the company's monopoly and liquidate its assets—as the new Controller-General in September 1768 (Margerison 2006, 25). When the state limited its financial assistance (Harris 1979, 23; Wellington 2006, 92), the situation grew increasingly dire and a committee of shareholder deputies was designated to study the company's options (Weber 1904, 590 n.2; Harris 1979, 27). Reporting back at the March 29, 1769, shareholders' meeting, the shareholder

Duval d'Epremesnil presented the conclusions of a majority of deputies: commerce in Asia would become profitable, but an urgent loan would be needed....[I]n the name of a minority of three deputies....[Another large shareholder,] Panchaud presented his project to transform the company, after it had abandoned commerce in the Indies, into a *caisse d'escompte* [savings bank]....Le Count of Lauraguais, one of the large personalities of the social chronicles of the day, amateur in political economy as in agronomy, came to defend Panchaud's project. [Finally] Necker pronounced himself against the savings bank project, and in favor of a new loan.

(Haudrère 2005, 785–786)

At the meeting, the majority of shareholders voted to continue the company's operations; unfortunately, however, they "made no decision on how to finance this trade" (Margerison 2006, 38).

As a consequence yet another committee—this time composed of shareholders, directors, and syndics—was formed to make recommendations (Harris 1979, 27–28). At the next shareholder meeting on April 3, 1769, the committee proposed a short-term loan to finance the company's operations until the fall (Harris 1979, 28). Maynon d'Invault, however, was not in agreement and insisted at the meeting

that the shareholders agree to mortgage their only remaining asset, the annual *rente* from the tobacco monopoly, which funded the shareholders' dividend....[But if] the shareholders agreed to end the commercial operations of the *Compagnie des Indes*, the Controller-General made it clear that the King would be amenable to Panchaud's plan to establish a *caisse d'escompte*. Having devised the most unpleasant choice possible for the shareholders, Maynon d'Invault insisted that the King, seemingly acknowledging the authority of the assembly, wished to provide 'the greatest liberty to the shareholders' in making this decision.

(Margerison 2006, 38)

The shareholders rejected Maynon d'Invault's proposal and approved the short-term loan; on April 6, 1769, the king reversed himself and approved the loan (Harris 1979, 28). The shareholders' victory was short lived, however. Unwilling to let the shareholders win, Maynon d'Invault hired the publicist André Morellet to publish a treatise as part of a campaign to put an end to the company, providing him with details of the company's finances (Bègue 1936, 74). Morellet's treatise was published in June 1769 (Harris 1979, 30; Margerison 2006, 41); yet, rather than accede to the government's wishes and approve suspension of the company, the committee called a shareholders' meeting on August 8, 1769 (Harris 1979, 29).

At the meeting, Jacques Necker famously rose to defend the company. While Necker did advocate for greater shareholder power (Harris 1979, 33), he argued that the company's performance could only be understood by acknowledging its mission as a state enterprise. For example, in "pursuit of the Indies commerce, the company had expended funds on the construction of ports and fortifications, roads, arsenals, churches, hospitals, and other public buildings and had supplied troops to defend these structures" (Margerison 2006, 45–46). The core of Necker's contention, thus, was that "[w]ith respect to the help asked for from the state…the question cannot be posed only in terms of duties and assets. The company, political instrument of the monarchy, has a right to compensations for the losses suffered in such service" (Grange 1974, 20). The impact of Necker's effort on the meeting was dramatic:

> In the course of his [Necker's] oration, the gloomy mood of the shareholders lifted; optimism regarding the company's future returned; and the assembly, once again emboldened and defiant, stood between the ministry and its goal of suspending the company's privilege…. Unsure of his next move, Maynon d'Invault tried to prevent further deliberation, but the marquis de Sancé, a former syndic, reminded the Controller-General that the King had granted them "the complete liberty to vote" on their fate. The assembly then authorized a committee of shareholders to investigate Necker's financial suggestions.
>
> (Margerison 2006, 48)

But before the committee could meet, and without consulting either shareholders or administrators, the Crown simply suspended the company's monopoly on August 13, 1769 (Harris 1979, 31; Margerison 2006, 48).

GOVERNANCE LESSONS FROM THE FRENCH EAST INDIA COMPANY

To the extent the company's story is one of failure, it provides a cautionary tale in terms of organization, financing, and agency. Like the Dutch East India Company, lack of shareholder power is an important explanation for many of the abuses and failures experienced by the firm. But in both cases, the deprivation of shareholder influence might properly be seen as a by-product of the company's relationship with the state. Indeed, given the company's origins—with its very existence and purpose derived directly from the Crown—the impotence of shareholders might be seen as inevitable.

Organizational Stability

First, and perhaps most obviously, an unstable structure is unlikely to be conducive to good corporate governance. One of the most surprising and challenging aspects of studying the company is simply trying to keep up with a dizzying number of reorganizations. In the 106 years of the company's existence, governance was changed at least seven times: after Colbert's death in 1684; with the rise and fall of John Law in 1720, 1723, and 1731; in the face of Dupleix's failing colonial adventures in 1748; and in the final scramble to salvage the company in 1764 and 1768. This point is perhaps so apparent that it is not worth dwelling on.

Adequate Financing

Second, adequate financing—including basic working capital—is a necessity. Throughout its existence the company was weakly and hap-hazardly financed. Even before it began operations, the company was in financial trouble: its initial share offering received a lukewarm reception from investors (Sen 1958, 46; Haudrère and Le Bouëdec 1999, 137). At least one historian suggests that the initial desire to create regional chambers is reflective of Paris' lack of financial clout in 1664, foreshadowing the company's recurring financial problems (Haudrère 2006, 71). This problem was exacerbated by the payment of fixed dividends to shareholders regardless of company performance (Sen 1958, 41)—either in return for forcing the shareholders to invest more money (Wellington 2006, 46) or simply to maintain a false illusion of prosperity (Bègue 1936, 68).

As a result, the company "always lacked adequate working capital to permit itself healthy administration, instead living hand to mouth, from one expedition to another" (Lüthy 1960, 862). Calls to share-holders for short-term financing became even more desperate toward the end of the company's life (Harris 1979, 23). As one historian aptly sums the history of the company and its lack of financing:

The dependence of the French state with respect to the government is accentuated by the absence of a significant independent financial organization, such as a bank analogue to that of Amsterdam or that of London. It has practically no working capital, and its capital resulting from the liquidation of the debt of the state at the time of the System, is more nominal than real. When it needs advances, it must solicit them from the royal treasury. Some finance ministers agree to lend these funds, others refuse. In the latter case, the company must borrow money which becomes harder and harder to find as loans multiply and which require paying interest to the detriment of the general budget.

(Haudrère 2005, 822–823)

Or put very succinctly, the "weak link . . . in the company's visions were its finances" (Wellington 2006, 22).

Agents Who Serve Shareholders

Third, a successful company must employ responsible agents. A basic problem at the top of the corporate hierarchy was the inexperience of both directors (Bègue 1936, 58–59) and the king's commissioners (Bègue 1936, 111). Sadly, lack of managerial skill was not the only issue as Daniel Bègue found that "[i]n general the directors were mostly attached to their personal interests and the shareholders often had vehement complaints against them" (Bègue 1936, 59). In foreign lands, "[t]he most perceptive and clever governors enriched themselves by all means, even if it meant defrauding the company" (Bègue 1936, 79). Up and down the corporate hierarchy, fraud was apparently rampant—"practiced by all, employees of the *Compagnie,* fiscal agents, directors, sometimes even the king's commissioners" (Bègue 1936, 89). Particularly toward the end of the company's life, "[t]he internal enemies were none other than the servants of the *Compagnie,* enriched by its spoils, and no longer having anything to gain in the state in which it found its affairs" (Montagne, 185–186). Simply put, the experience of the *Compagnie* illustrates the need for the shareholder protection measures discussed in the chapters on China and early Venice. Left to their own devices, those entrusted with the interests of shareholders repeatedly disregarded their responsibilities, legal and moral.

Root Cause: Weak Shareholders?

One might therefore point to the lack of shareholder power and oversight as the root cause of the governance failures and the company's ultimate demise. As the historical overview suggests, from the beginning the shareholders played only a token role in the company as state influence was dominant. The irregularity of shareholder meetings—a chronic problem that haunted the company from its inception (Sottas 1905, 20; Bègue 1936, 60–62) well into the eighteenth century—offers the most vivid illustration of the problem (Bègue 1936, 63; Wellington 2006, 56). To the extent shareholders did protest during meetings, they were often overridden by the Crown, perhaps most dramatically during the meeting of July 3, 1767 (Margerison 2006, 41).

Two caveats, however, complicate the story of shareholder oppression. One is simply that the shareholders were participating in an enterprise that depended on government monopoly; as a consequence, an expectation of state participation in corporate affairs seems more than reasonable. The same is true, of course, in the cases of the

Dutch East India Company and the Virginia Company of London, both of which are discussed in this volume. Indeed, the *"Compagnie* did not result from a spontaneous association of private interests; it was the state that linked these individuals for an enterprise of general use. Its origin and *raison d'être* are not the enrichment of some, but the necessity of founding an establishment useful to the state" (Bègue 1936, 107–108). What did the government give the shareholders in return? In addition to exclusive trading privileges, "the company gains multiple and immediate advantages; it obtains the right to commission sailors, supplies of wood reserved for the royal navy, reductions in customs duties and taxes" (Haudrère 2005, 822). The price was state control over the company throughout its history:

> The French company, created by the will of the minister Colbert, modified by the dispositions of the minister Law, belongs to the king and his administration, which governs it through a high ranking government official or "commissioner," leaving to the directors a reduced scope attributed to bureau chiefs, and to representatives of shareholders mediocre means of control, though slightly increased after 1745.
>
> (Haudrère 2005, 822)

In the words of one historian, the company was effectively "an appendix of the Finance Ministry for its financial administration and the Ministry of the Navy for its fleet, shipbuilding, and commercial enterprises. The shareholders were consulted, to consent to sacrifices, only at the most difficult moments which coincided with wars" (Lüthy 1960, 861).

The second caveat is that the shareholders—by requesting fixed interest payments rather than dividends (Bègue 1936, 68–69; Harris 1979, 20)—perhaps unwittingly transformed themselves into de facto creditors (Weber 1904, 686). Creditors, of course, do not have the same rights as shareholders, so it should be less surprising to find the company's pseudo-creditors with less say in the company's governance (Lüthy 1960, 871), and less concern regarding the company's success (Sen 1958, 42). This ironic twist might be explained by the fact that the shareholders wanted more security in the face of repeated state requests for additional investment. But it does complicate the narrative, especially since shareholders only complained when their their capital was at risk (Bègue 1936, 63)—behavior one typically associates with creditors.

Might the company serve as an examplar in any positive sense? To be sure, it evinced some surprising features such as staggered boards (Weber 1904, 94), the right to buy shares on credit (Bègue 1936, 65–66), the ability to resolve disputes by arbitration (Weber

1904, 198; Bègue 1936, 52), hybrid securities that combine features of debt and equity (Weber 1904, 549; Bègue 1936, 68), and a position to supervise directors on behalf of shareholders in the form of syndics. But staggered boards and private arbitration can hardly be considered positive for investors. Hybrid securities and purchasing equity on credit may present financial innovations, but have precious little to do with increasing shareholder value. Perhaps only the notion of a syndic is worth some debate, though in modern corporate governance it is precisely the directors who represent shareholder interests. It is unclear that adding another layer will solve much—not to mention the disagreement in the literature as to how fruitful the company's syndics actually were (Bègue 1936, 59; Haudrère and Le Bouëdec 1999, 13). It is interesting to note, however, that such a two-tiered governance system has echoes in French history; for example, local government in thirteenth-century Toulouse used both consuls and a general assembly (Mundy 1997, 233–238), and there is more broadly a long-standing French tradition of governance by committee, made especially visible during the French Revolution (Cobban 1943, 19). Overall, though, the picture of governance that emerges is bleak. To be sure, there was certainly "friction between the stockholders and the royal appointees who governed the company" (Harris 1979, 17)— especially at times of crisis. But "[n]otwithstanding the many changes in its organization, the company remained essentially a Crown corporation with private ownership of the company shares" (Wellington 2006, 57). As such, the shareholders had precious little voice. The saga of the company's governance thus serves as a cautionary tale of what not to do.

EXPLAINING GOVERNMENT PARTICIPATION IN THE FRENCH EAST INDIA COMPANY

In 1769 the company was allowed to fail even as it pleaded for a bailout from the government to stay afloat. One might explain this outcome simply, as Daniel Bègue summarized: "[T]he publication of the financial situation of the *Compagnie,* accompanied by unfavorable comments from abbé Morellet, delivered the fatal blow to the *Compagnie*" (Bègue 1936, 132). But this simplification obscures the issues raised by the debate throughout the 1760s regarding the fate of the company. A closer look offers insight into the dynamics of government participation in privately owned corporations, an issue that resonates today and with many of the cases discussed in these pages. A review of the events leading to the collapse of the *Compagnie* reveals four factors contributing to the outcome.

Ideas Matter

The French monarchy, espousing mercantilism, had a tradition of intervening in economic affairs (Grange 1974, 17). Perhaps surprisingly, however, "[b]eginning in the second half of the eighteenth century, we witness in commercial circles an increase in the hostility felt toward privileged commercial companies" (Haudrère 2005, 789). An important explanation for this change lies in the rise of the Physiocrats, then called "economists" (Wellington 2006, 91–92). Their ideas "extolled the virtues of freedom of enterprise, freedom of trade, and condemned the vices of government regulation of the economy and state-supported monopolies" (Harris 1979, 18). Eventually, the "hostility of the economists won over the government, who hindered the efforts of the *Compagnie* to emerge from the ruins of war" (Bègue 1936, 132).

The Physiocrats had two prominent intellectual leaders: Jean-Claude Vincent de Gournay, who is credited with popularizing the term *laissez-faire, laissez-passer* (Weber 1904, 584) and became Intendant of Commerce in 1747, and François Quesnay, who in 1758 published his *Tableau économique* (Harris 1979, 18). In 1755, Gournay even wrote a report to his superior, Controller-General Moreau de Séchelles, advocating a plan to liquidate the company (Grange 1974, 19; Wellington 2006, 92). Gournay argued that with "free trade among private shippers and merchants . . . instead of twelve ships making the annual voyage to the East there would be a hundred" (Harris 1979, 23–24). But Gournay's attempt was unsuccessful, as the Crown was willing to help the company through the Seven Years' War (Harris 1979, 24). Similarly, in 1759, a royal commissioner, Charles-Robert Boutin, also argued for the dissolution of the company—also to no avail (Haudrère 2005, 784; Margerison 2006, 27).

The Physiocrats, however, were willing to be patient. Their moment finally came in September 1768 when Maynon d'Invault, a follower of Gournay (Haudrère 2005, 784) and an "adversary of the company" (Grange 1974, 19), was named Controller-General. One historian even goes so far as to suggest that "[m]ore than the collapse of its colonies, more than the enormous debt accumulated by two wars sustained back-to-back, more than the inanities, the clumsiness and even the vices of its administration, physiocratic theories triumphed over the grandiose conception of Colbert" (Weber 1904, 584). This may be a bit melodramatic but physiocratic theory certainly helped create the conditions for the company's demise.

Effective Advocacy

The Physiocrats' victory might be explained not just by the power of their ideas but by the effectiveness of their chief advocate, Morellet, "one of the foremost publicists for the *économistes*" (Harris 1979, 29), who seemed to understand contemporary media better that his adversary Necker (Lüthy 1960, 878; Grange 1974, 20). Recognizing that any debate over a government bailout of the *Compagnie* necessarily involved swaying public opinion, he "shaped a language of patriotism emphasizing the sacrifices shareholders had made in the interest of the state" (Margerison 2006, 37).

Maynon d'Invault, in response, hired his close friend, André Morellet, and gave him all of the company's "records and accounts that could be useful" (Harris 1979, 30). The numbers he employed in argumentation were "impossible to critique since they were sourced from documents provided by the company itself" (Haudrère 2005, 795–796). In his physiocratic argument against a government bailout (Wellington 2006, 92), Morellet "sought to destroy the republican concept of patriotism as the virtuous self-sacrifice of the individual undertaken in the interest of the entire community of citizens and to replace it with the glorification of the individual's pursuit of his own self-interest" (Margerison 2006, 43). In doing so, he "injected the discourse of commercial liberty into the contest between the ministry and the shareholders" (Margerison 2006, 42).

Perhaps what made Morellet successful was that he understood that the battle he was engaged in was not just one over ideas, but also a broad public relations campaign. Morellet tried to reshape public perception regarding their patriotic responsibilities:

Morellet, however, was not content simply to challenge the shareholders' understanding of patriotism; he also hoped to persuade general public opinion that the shareholders' defence of the company was unpatriotic in itself. Instead of viewing the company as an agent of the state involved in defending French interests in the arena of international affairs, Morellet portrayed it as a vast sinkhole consuming the valuable resources of the monarchy.

(Margerison 2006, 43)

To the extent the battle over the bailout of the company was a contest between lobbyists, Morellet clearly bested Necker and was the eventual victor (Haudrère 2005, 796).

Hidden Agendas

Some have suggested that the contest between Morellet and Necker was essentially theatrical. Morellet was "the recruiter and faithful support of Necker's salon" (Lüthy 1961, 387) even at the time of their public battle, so some historians "suspect that the famous debate was staged like a bogus wrestling match" (Harris 1979, 30)—apparently "to the great satisfaction of both protagonists" (Haudrère 2005, 797). This is evidence of the most circumstantial sort but clearly many of the key players in this tale were conflicted. Most obviously, Morellet was a paid advocate for the finance ministry, much to the dismay of shareholders such as the Comte de Lauraguais (Margerison 2006, 44). And Panchaud, the significant shareholder who advocated turning the company into a savings bank, attempted to turn the company's misfortunes into his own benefit (Margerison 2006, 30)—not to mention his "obvious collusion with the ministry" (Margerison 2006, 39) in arguing for suspension of the company's commercial privilege.

Jacques Necker is perhaps the most complex protagonist of all. Like the Physiocrats he extolled the motivation of profit and freedom from government intervention while still arguing for a government-granted monopoly, making him either a pragmatist or a hypocrite, depending on one's sympathies (Harris 1979, 43). Beyond this inconsistency, Necker was not only motivated by his bank's shareholdings in the company, but also wanted to profit by providing expensive credit to the company through an English bank with which he was affiliated, Bourdieu & Chollet (Lüthy 1960, 864; Margerison 2006, 39). This is not even to mention that the debate staged with Morellet "is for the future minister [Necker] admirable publicity, especially given that he gives himself the fine role of being the last defender of an heroic company, dead for the glory of the king" (Haudrère 2005, 797).

Conclusion

In many ways, the *Compagnie des Indes* provides an unfortunate checklist of things to avoid in corporate governance. The company exhibited an unstable organization, anemic and unreliable financing, weak leadership, and corrupt insiders. One might argue that these unfortunate attributes are all symptoms of shareholders powerlessness in the face of a greedy state. And that it is precisely the interference of the state that ruined the company (Weber 1904, 686; Sottas 1905, 5; Wellington 2006, 23). But the story proves more nuanced. The enterprise enjoyed a state monopoly and served public purposes from its inception. This may have set a trap in which the company got more and more ensnared over time. The quid pro quo between government and the shareholders always posed the risk that when the company no longer served the government's political goals, it would lose state support. This is precisely what happened in France by the late 1760s when "commercial expansion is sacrificed to needs judges more urgent by the government" (Haudrère 2005, 822).

It is therefore too simplistic to say that government intervention ruined the company; shareholders entered into a particular bargain with the state from the outset (Sottas 1905, 5). Rather the story of the company presents another early example that resonates with the story of the Dutch East India Company and other mercantilist enterprises: the intersection of corporate governance with government ownership, state policy, and politics is treacherous place. Summing up the fate of the *Compagnie des Indes,* one observer succinctly noted in terms that are strikingly contemporary that "[a]s long as the shareholders received their dividends and the Directors their emoluments, nobody worried about the future" (Sen 1958, 42). Sadly, the lesson learned by the shareholders then and now is that reliable corporate governance is most valuable when times are tough but it must be nurtured even when they are not.

REFERENCES

A Messieurs les défendeurs des actionnaires et des administrateurs de la Compagnie des Indes. Paris: Didot Jeune (1790).

Bègue, Daniel (1936). *L'Organisation Juridique de la Compagnie des Indes.* Paris: Éditions Domat-Montchrestien.

Cobban, Alfred (1943). *Local Government During the French Revolution.* English Historical Review 50: 13–31.

Doutes d'un Actionnaire sur le Mémoire de M. l'Abbé Morellet contre la Compagnie des Indes (1769).

Éclaircissements sur le Mémoire de M. l'Abbé Morellet, concernant la partie historique de la Compagnie des Indes, et l'origine du bien des actionnaires (1769).

Grange, H. (1974). *Les Idées de Necker.* Paris: C. Klincksieck.

Harris, Robert D. (1979). *Necker: Reform Statesman of the Ancien Regime.* Berkeley: University of California Press.

Haudrère, Philippe (2005). *La Compagnie Française des Indes au XVIIIe Siècle.* Paris: Indes Savantes.

Haudrère, Philippe (2006). *Les Compagnies des Indes orientales: Trois siècles de rencontre entre Orientaux et Occidentaux (1600–1858).* Paris: Éditions Desjonqueres.

Haudrère, Philippe and Le Bouëdec, Gerard (1999). *Les Compagnies des Indes.* Rennes: Ouest-France.

Lavaquery, E. (1933). *Necker: Fourrier de la Revolution 1732–1804.* Paris: Plon.

Lüthy, H. (1960). *Necker et la Compagnie des Indes.* Annales: Économies, Sociétés, Civilisations. Vol. 31, pp. 852–881.

Lüthy, H. (1961). *La Banque Protestante en France.* Paris: S.E.V.P.E.N.

Margerison, K. (2006). *The Shareholders' Revolt at the Compagnie des Indes: Commerce and Political Culture in Old Regime France.* French History 20: 25–51.

Martineau, A. (1929). *Les Dernières Années de Dupleix.* Paris: Société d'Éditions Géographiques, Maritimes et Coloniales.

Mémoire pour la Compagnie des Indes contre le Sieur Dupleix (1763).

Mémoire pour les Actionnaires de la Compagnie des Indes (1790). Paris: Lottin.

Montagne, Charles (1899). *Histoire de la Compagnie des Indes.* Paris: Émile Bouillon.

Morellet, A. (1769). *Mémoire sur la situation actuelle de la Compagnie des Indes.* Paris: Chez Desaint.

Morellet, A. (1769). *Examen de la Réponse de M. N** au mémoire de M. l'Abbé Morellet, sur la Compagnie des Indes.* Paris: Chez Desaint.

Morellet, A. (1787). *Réponse précise au Précis, pour les actionnaires de la nouvelle Compagnie des Indes.* Paris: Chez Demonville.

Morellet, A. (1787). *Mémoires Relatifs à la Discussion du Privilège de la Nouvelle Compagnie des Indes.* Paris: Chez Demonville.

Morellet, A. (1821–1822). *Mémoires de l'abbé Morellet de l'Academie française sur le dix-huitième siècle et sur la révolution française.* Paris: Librairie Française de l'Advocat.

Mundy, John H. (1997). *Society and Government at Toulouse in the Age of the Cathars.* Toronto: Pontifical Institute of Mediaeval Studies.

Murphy, Antoin E. (1997). *John Law: Economic Theorist and Policy-Maker.* Oxford: Clarendon Press.

Le Pour et le Contre, ou Réflexions sur la Compagnie des Indes (1788). Paris: Marchands de Nouveautés.

Sen, S.P. (1958). *The French in India, 1763–1816.* Calcutta: Firma K.L. Mukhopadhyay.

Sottas, Jules (1905). *Histoire de la Compagnie Royale des Indes orientales.* Paris: Plon.

Subramanian, Lakshmi (ed.) (1999). *The French East India Company and the Trade of the Indian Ocean: A Collection of Essays by Indrani Ray.* Delhi: Munshiram Manoharlal Publishers.

Weber, H. (1904). *La Compagnie Française des Indes.* Paris: Librairie Nouvelle de Droit et de Jurisprudence.

Wellington, Donald C. (2006). *French East India Companies: A Historical Account and Record of Trade.* New York: Hamilton Books.

CHAPTER 9

THE RISE AND FALL OF THE RISHENGCHANG BANK MODEL: LIMITING SHAREHOLDER INFLUENCE TO ATTRACT CAPITAL

Randall Morck and Fan Yang

INTRODUCTION

In the early 1800s, an era of profound isolation, the remote northern inland province of Shanxi hosted China's premier financial center. Shanxi banks offered empire-wide branch networks and a full array of services markedly resembling those of Western banks. While most accounts suggest a purely Chinese origin, and thus a remarkable case of parallel economic evolution, a strong case can be made that Western banking diffused into Shanxi via Russia.

Nonetheless, the Shanxi banks were distinct Chinese innovations. Their unique dual class equity, managerial incentives, and contracting arrangements ensured confidence in their bank drafts, which sustained trade, and even public finances, amid the mounting chaos of the late Qing dynasty. To illustrate, we describe the Sunrise Provident Bank, capitalized in 1823 with dual share classes. To discourage entrenchment, managers' shares carried nonbinding votes in management meetings only; while owners' shares carried votes only on grand assessment days—held after each fiscal cycle (typically three or four years) to fire or retain managers and reallocate their shares. This precisely inverts modern dual class structures, which grant insiders overwhelming voting control. To further align managers' and owners' interests, both classes paid identical dividends. To motivate long-term thinking, but keep their heirs out of decision making, upon their death or retirement managers' shares were converted into a third entirely nonvoting class that paid dividends for a fixed term and then expired. Managers' good faith was guaranteed by their relatives' service as hostages.

Adopted with variations by other Shanxi banks, these structures mitigate very modern governance problems. While infuriated modern shareholders might pine to hold CEOs' relatives hostages, they might seriously consider paying managers with finitely lived nonvoting shares and inverting voting rights in dual class equity structures to mitigate, rather than magnify, agency problems.

THE BANKS

In 1823, Li Daquan founded the Rishengchang [日昇昌] Bank in Pingyao county, Shanxi Province.[1] The name combines *ri* [日, *lit. sun*], *sheng* [昇, *lit. rise*], and *chang* [昌, *lit. prosperity*], so we render it *Sunrise Provident Bank*. Li owned Xiyucheng, a dyed goods operation that bought raw materials in Sichuan and ran stores in Beijing, Shenyang, Tianjin, and other centers. Lei Lutai, a Tianjin (or Beijing) manager, observed expensive silver shipments often passed each other, going in opposite directions on this "long and arduous route" (Yang Lien-sheng 1952, 82) and perceived a business opportunity: replacing expensive private security, wagons, and pack animals with a clearing house.[2]

Initially offered in Tianjin, Wuhan, and Pingyao, the service was unexpectedly lucrative. Probably in 1823, Lei persuaded Xiyucheng's owner, Li Daquan, to focus on branch banking, rather than dyed goods by offering interregional accounts settlement, deposit accounts, loans, and currency exchange services. Li capitalized the bank, based in Pingyao, his home county, with 300,000 *tael*—about 450,000 silver dollars (Liu Shangxue 1937)—and Lei perhaps added 20,000 *tael* (Fan Chunnian 1935; Lu Guoxiang 1936).[3] Top management included Lei as General Manager and two assistant managers: Mao Hongsui and Cheng Dapei.

A few years later, Mao resigned, apparently over strategy disagreements with Lei. Within a few years, Mao organized five more banks, and soon their managers were leaving to found yet others. Generally similarly capitalized, the proliferating banks [*Shanxi piaohao*] were, despite China's long economic history, the first institutions to offer a full range of banking services—making Pingyao and the nearby Qixian and Taigu counties into financial centers.

From 1823 to the early 1840s, the Shanxi banks grew rapidly by providing bank drafts for traveling merchants—the business opportunity Lei Lutai discovered. A buyer could deposit cash at his local branch and obtain a bank draft [*huipiao*]. This was ripped in half, with one half sent to the seller as a promise of payment and the other sent to the seller's branch of the bank. When the buyer confirmed receipt of the goods, the seller could claim the missing half of the bank draft at his branch and effect the transfer of funds into his account there. Figures 9.1 and 9.2 displays two forms of bank draft in common use—the former for ordinary clients and the latter for long-standing clients with large balances.

The banks also exchanged currencies. Twenty forms of bulk silver circulated in this era, each with a different weight or purity. Thus, a note on figure 9.1 tells the cashing branch to use a specific unit without informing the client; figure 9.2 defines the unit explicitly.

In their formative years, the banks paid depositors 0.2 to 0.3 percent per month and lent at 0.6 to 0.7 percent per month.[4] Their biggest clients were merchants and wealthy individuals, especially nobility with whom the banks had connections. The banks also recorded loans from one party to another, as in figure 9.3. These certificates may have traded at a discount, but we have no evidence of this. Figure 9.4 records a recurring transfer from one account to another. Figure 9.5 is a simple deposit record.

HARMONY IN EQUITY

In stable times, Confucian hierarchical principles and imperial edicts could enforce agreements, usually without resort to actual courts. But seemingly incomprehensible foreign victories from 1842 on undermined both traditions and imperial authority, and resort to formal courts was not only shameful but multiply ineffective. First, the law was an insiders' game of ritual formalism (Simeon Djankov, La Porta, Florencio López de Silanes, and Andrei Shleifer. 2003; Rafael La Porta, Florencio Lopez-de-Silanes, and Andrei Shleifer. 2008). Second, merchants' (including bankers') descendents were barred from civil service exams for three generations, so local magistrates (judge-prosecutors) were mainly from landholding classes and under social pressure to protect their own. Third, unrestrained by juries, or even defense attorneys, magistrates charged for verdicts. Finally, merchants filled the cellar of the Confucian caste hierarchy—below peasants and tradesmen—so their bribes likely seemed dirtier.

The banks therefore needed their own contract enforcement system, one robust enough to inspire trustworthy behavior in branch

Panel A. Photograph

Panel B. Transcription[1]

豐裕慶	Feng Yu Qing Bank
王孝唐當日取	Withdraw on same date
憑帖來取	By presenting this draft to withdraw
庚字肆佰伍x號x錢	[internal note][2]
一千文	1,000 cents
咸豐十一年二月十六日帖	Emperor Xianfeng's 11th year [1861] 2nd month 16th day

Panel C. Translation

By presenting this bank draft to the Feng Yu Qing Bank, Mr. Wang Xiaotang may withdraw cash in the amount of 1,000 cents after Feb. 16th 1861.

Notes

1. The smaller characters in the background are anti-fraud print.
2. The characters 庚字 represent the number 7 in the Chinese decimal counting system. 庚字肆佰伍x號x錢 indicates the form and purity of the cash, and that this may not to be disclosed to the client.

Figure 9.1 A bank draft on the Feng Yu Qing bank payable to Wang Xiaotang
This bank draft is the form the Shanxi banks issued for ordinary clients. Although the depositor's name appears in the draft, it is payable to the bearer. (See Chen 1937).

Panel A. Photograph

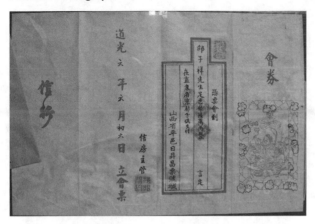

Panel B. Transliteration

會券	Draft
憑票會到	by presenting this draft
邵子祥先生足色銀陸萬兩整	Mr. Shao Zixiang 24 carat[1] silver 60 thousand tael
言定	promises to
在直隸省京都分號交付	withdraw at the Beijing Branch of the Sunrise Prudent Bank
山西省平邑日昇昌票號緘	sent by Shanxi, Pingyao, Sunrise Prudential Bank headquarters
信房主管（印）	by the Chief of the Letter Office
道光六年六月初六日立會票	Emperor Daoguang's 6th year [1826] 6th month and 6th day completed this bank draft
信行	by mail

Panel C. Translation

Mr. Shao Zixiang deposited 60 thousand Tael of 24 carat[1] silver in Shanxi, Pingyao at the Sunrise Prudent Bank Pingyao headquarters and would withdraw this amount at the Beijing Branch of the Sunrise Prudent Bank by presenting this bank draft. This draft is prepared by the Chief of the Letter Office at June 6th, 1826, and will be sent by mail.

Note: Anti-fraud marks include the green stamp and smaller red stamps superimposed.
1. The Chinese 足色 means 100%, however this is technologically infeasible. Twenty-four carat is 99.99% purity.

Figure 9.2 A bank draft on the Sunrise Prudent bank payable to Shao Zixiang
This bank draft is the form issued for highly trusted long-term clients with large balances. Panel A. Photograph.

Panel A. Photograph

Panel B. Transliteration

錢業公會公製借券	Finance guild public loan sample
今借到 [creditor]	Today obtained loan from [creditor]
現銀圓 [amount] 圓整	Cash silver [amount] Yuan exactly.
言明	Agreed to
行息期限 [rate & maturity] 依照原借款現銀圓本李一並歸還	
	interest and term[rate & maturity]based on principal and interest completely repaid
不得以他項代替以招信用此據	
	There to be no substitution of alternate forms of cash for repayment. This form serves as evidence.
經手人[banker]	Prepared by[debtor]
民國　年　月　日	Date [year, month, day]

Panel C. Translation

Today I obtained from [creditor's name] silver yuans in the amount of [amount of loan]. I agree to an interest rate of [interest rate] and to the payment in full on [date] of both principal and all interest and not to substitute any other medium of exchange. This form is evidence of agreement to the loan on these terms. Prepared by the debtor [debtor's name] on [date].

Figure 9.3 Note of loan—Blank form
The bank used this form to record loans by one party to another. The "form of cash" here is the local yuan, and the contract specifies that no other form of cash be substituted for repayment.

managers throughout China. The management at each branch consisted entirely of professionals: a general manager made all major decisions, assisted by various vice presidents, who supervised clerks and other employees. For brevity, we call these insiders. The banks

Panel A. Photograph

Panel B. Transliteration

同治八九十十一年十月十七日
Emperor Tongzhi's 8th, 9th, 10th and 11th years, the 10th month and 17th day
來往暫記帳
Interim record of account transfer

Panel C. Translation

Interim record of account transfer as of 1869, 1870, 1871 and 1872, on October 17th of each year.

Figure 9.4   Record of a recurring account transfer

were not widely held: each had relatively few large shareholders—wealthy Shanxi merchants, whose role in governance was carefully constrained, and actually quite limited.

Share ownership normally confers cash flow rights, which give shareholders dividends, and voting rights, which let shareholders choose the firm's top managers. Michael Jensen and William Meckling (1976), considering cash flow rights only, argue that insiders with too few shares have insufficient incentive to maximize shareholder value—a *divergence of interests* problem. This reasoning argues that higher insider stakes improve governance, and underpins Michael Jensen and Kevin Murphy (1990) and others, who would compensate managers with stock or stock options.

A major downside of large insider equity ownership is *entrenchment*—the attendant voting rights. If insiders, or their heirs, control enough votes, they cannot be displaced even if they no longer provide able management (Randall Morck, Andrei Shliefer, and Robert Vishny. 1988; René Stulz 1988). This argues for insider stakes sufficiently low that other shareholders can outvote them. More generally, insider stakes then ought to be medial, balancing divergence of interest problems against entrenchment problems.

Panel A. Photograph

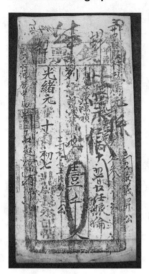

Panel B. Transliteration

錢票	Money draft
收張萬禎	Received from Zhang Wanzhen
捌佰參肆號錢一千文	[Type of cash][1] 1,000 coins
光緒元年十月初七	Emperor Guangxu's 1st year, 10th month, and 7th day

Panel C. Translation

On October 7th 1875, the bank received from Zhang Wanzhen 1000 unites [of a specific type of cash].

Notes

1. In this era, China lacked a uniform system of cash. Payments were in silver, bronze, or copper coins, valued by their weight and purity. The "type of cash" here refers to the standards of weight and purity of the 1,000 silver, copper or bronze.

Figure 9.5   Record of a deposit

The Sunrise Provident and its fellow Shanxi banks developed a more thoroughgoing solution to this balance with dual class shares that separated cash flow rights from voting rights. In modern corporations, dual class shares generally give insiders magnified voting power and scant cash flow rights and outsiders primarily cash flow rights, worsening divergence of inters and entrenchment problems simultaneously (Tatiana Nenova 2003; Paul Gompers, Joy Ishi, and Andrew Metrick 2010). The Shanxi banks also used dual class shares, but with the exact opposite configuration: insiders held large equity blocks, but of nonvoting shares only—maximizing their cash flow rights to counter divergence of interests problems while bestowing no voting rights at all, thus precluding entrenchment.

The Shanxi banks had two classes of equity—capital shares [*yingu*], and expertise shares [*ding shen gu*]—generally equal in number.[5] These were not precisely the same as voting and nonvoting shares in a modern corporation, so a short explanation is in order.

Capital shares, which represented fractional ownership of the bank's assets, were initially owned by the founding shareholders and passed to their heirs. The capital shareholders collectively owned all of the bank's assets, and had a price equal to the bank's assets divided by the number of capital shares. Thus, if the Sunrise Provident was capitalized at 300,000 *taels* and had 30 capital shares outstanding, each was worth 10,000 *tael* or 150,000 silver dollars. The capital shares were not, as far as we can tell, traded. However capital shareholders could redeem their capital shares recover their initial contributions to the bank's capital in silver. Capital shares were entitled to dividends, paid out at the end of each fiscal cycle—either three or four years long.[6]

At each fiscal cycle end, the bank declared a *grand assessment day* [*da zhang qi*], on which the profits of the last fiscal cycle were reported to the capital shareholders, who then decided the dividend. At the same meeting, the capital shareholders evaluated the performance of the management team and employees, and adjusted the insiders' expertise shareholdings appropriately. Expertise shares that were unassigned to any manager or employee continued to pay dividends, but into a fund that added to the bank's assets. Also on the grand assessment day, the capital shareholder decided whether to replace the general manager or renew his appointment for another fiscal cycle and, based on the general manager's reports to capital shareholders, whether to replace or renew the other insiders.

Capital shareholders had no control over the bank's daily operations, and could not influence its business decisions directly. Yet they had unlimited liability for the bank's debts, for limited liability would not be an option until the 1904 Civil Code (Yang H.K. 1937; William Kirby 1995; William Goetzmann and Elisabeth Köll 2005). This open-ended liability meant that the insiders, the professional managers and employees who actually operating the bank, had to be very carefully incentivized.

Managers and employees made no monetary investment in the bank—their investment was their expertise—but their expertise share paid the same dividend per share as the capital shares. The typical general manager or vice president was granted one expertise share, though some got as much as 1.3 shares (Fan 1935). Clerks were typically granted from 0.2 to 0.3 expertise shares (Chen Qitian 1937). Expertise shareholder had no claim on the bank's assets.

In the most profitable fiscal cycles, dividends averaged 12,000 *tael*, roughly 18,000 silver dollars[7], per share. Insiders received salaries too—but even the general managers made no more than 1,500–2,000 *tael* per fiscal cycle (Lu 1936; Jie Zunsan 1944). Insiders' prosperity thus primarily depended on the dividend and the next expertise shareholdings allocation, so their compensation was even more dependent on their performance than was capital shareholders' income.

The expertise shareholders could influence the day-to-day operation of the firm, each having a voice proportional to his expertise shareholdings. This voice bestowed the right to make and vote on suggestions to the general manager, who might act on them or not. Final control over all business decisions was entirely in the hands of the general manager.

In modern dual class firms, voting shares pass to heirs, who may be less able and prone to entrenchment (Brian Smith and Ben Amoako-Adu 1999; Randall Morck, David Stangeland, and Bernard Yeung, 2000; Belen Villalonga and Raphael Amit 2006; Francisco Pérez-González 2006). If an expertise shareholder retired in good standing, or died on the job, his expertise shares turned into a third equity class, *dead share*s [*gugu*], which continued paying dividends to him or his designated heir for a period defined in his employment contract.[8] Dead shareholders, unlike expertise shareholders, had no voice in business decision making. If an expertise shareholder quit or was fired for cause, his expertise shares evaporated instantly. For example, Mao's expertise shares in Sunrise Provident ceased to exist when he resigned to found a rival bank. Capital shares passed from generation to generation, but their voting rights only came alive on grand assessment days, when they could vote on the hiring, firing, and compensation of managers.

In short, the banks used carefully tuned equity ownership structures to make professional managers' wealth primarily dependent on their expert shares' future dividends, and on their individual performance assessments, which determined the quantity of shares they owned. This minimized the divergence of interest problems highlighted by Jensen and Meckling (1976). By giving expertise shareholders no vote in decisions regarding their hiring, firing, and compensation, this arrangement precluded entrenchment problems (Morck et al. 1988; Stulz 1988). Moreover, the conversion of expertise shares into dead shares first removed retirees and heirs from involvement in business decisions, and the dead shares' sunset provisions later removed them from the shareholder list entirely. Since capital shareholders had no voice in day-to-day business decisions, controlling shareholders could not dictate bank lending policy, again precluding entrenchment.

Of course, this could all unravel in various ways. We shall see how the capital shareholders in the following sections, by manipulating their powers to reward or fire general managers on grand assessment days, subsequently nonetheless found ways to bias bank lending policies.

Incentive Compatibility

Qing China was a society in which people mistrusted outsiders, and generally trusted only family or people with whom they had long-standing ties. In such societies, large businesses run by professionals are disfavored (Rafael La Porta, Florencio Lopez-de-Silanes, Andrei Shleifer and Robert Vishny. 1997). Monopolistic merchant guilds circumvented these problems by vouching for traveling merchants, who paid association fees. While some guilds took members from many regions, "the Shanxi Dyed Goods Guild was restricted to families that originated in Pingyao county" (Peter Golas 1977), and the Shanxi banks adopted similar restrictions.

The banks hired only from Shanxi, and some even kept to only one county. This was a powerful governance mechanism, for managers' expertise share dividends were paid to their families in Shanxi. The social and economic status of their families depended on their performance, and any malfeasance endangered not just their families' economic and social status, but their families' freedom and lives.[9]

The banks checked prospective hires' backgrounds back three generations. This was relatively straightforward because families seldom moved far, and old neighbors intimately knew each others' families and family histories. A candidate with clean background presented a personal guarantee letter from an eminent personage in his county. The background check and guarantor ensured the loyalty and honesty of the employees, but also protected them. If a dispute arose, the guarantor undertook negotiations with the bank to ensure the manager was not impugned unjustly.

The contracts employees signed also contained clauses to spread the capital shareholders' unlimited liability around. Employees also agreed to unlimited liability, pledging their property, and that of their families for their performance, with capital shareholders even "taking their wives and children as hostage" (Dong Hai 1917; Chen 1937).

Self-dealing by insiders at remote branches was prevented by an assortment of rules (Jie 1944). To keep branch employees from developing side interests, they were forbidden from any other business activities, including lending their own savings to anyone. They were granted no leave, save for their parents' funerals, were accompanied by no family, and could not marry while on branch duty. They were allowed to write one letter home each month, but the letter was reviewed by the head office in Shanxi before being forwarded to the family.

This arrangement offends modern sensibilities, but it was a realistic response to conditions in the late Qing dynasty, especially given the capital shareholders' unlimited liability. The arrangement motivated both hard work and honesty in an economy of endemic corruption. Throughout the bank's century-long history, we find no hint of fraud or deceit by any professional manager.

Jade Parachutes

The Shanxi banks also devised a complicated pension system to ensure that those who worked hard for the shareholders were handsomely rewarded. This pension scheme was called either a *pension account* [*gong ji jin*] or a *god of wealth account* [*caishen zhang*], and consisted of three funds.

One fund was bad state-of-the-world insurance.[10] At the end of each fiscal cycle, the capital and expertise shareholders negotiated the fraction of retained earnings that would go into this fund. The money in it could be used to top up a future dividend if an act of God harmed the bank's earnings.

A second fund paid interest to the capital shareholders, and contained their deposits—for capital shareholders were free to reinvest any fraction of their dividends. This fund provided a capital base for financing the development and expansion of the bank. Chen (1937) states that drawing it down required the capital shareholders' approval.

The third fund paid dividends to dead shareholders—retired expertise shareholders and their heirs (for a time). Thus, Jie (1944) describes as typical a general manager formerly having one expertise share getting one dead share lasting for eight years and a lesser insider with one expertise share getting a dead share lasting seven years. Insiders with fractional expertise shareholders were granted identical fractions of a dead share, but expiring sooner for smaller fractions. Thus, dead shares arising from 0.8 or 0.9 of an expertise share terminated after six years, those arising from 0.6 or 0.7 of an expertise share terminated after five years, and so on.

This gave retiring managers strong incentives to look to the long-term profitability of the bank, and to choose and train their successors well, for their incomes in retirement and the prosperity of their heirs would depend on the performance of their successors. According to some reports, the first general manager of the Sunrise Provident nominated a candidate other than his own son as the next general manager on these grounds (Wang Yidian 1998, 2001).[11]

Opportunity in Crises

Bureaucrats and the feudal nobility were de facto above the law, and could confiscate wealth with impunity because their ability to manipulate the legal system made redress impossible. As the Shanxi banks grew more prominent, they presented a more attractive target for such predation. Consequently, the Shanxi banks, like other Shanxi merchants, sought to ingratiate themselves with important officials.

To this end, the banks directly financed the government, as when the Qing court fled to Xi'an in 1900, after the Dowager Empress Cixi's declaration of war on the major Western powers precipitated their occupation of Beijing. The banks also did a brisk business handling "donations" to the dynasty that bought honorary titles for their clients (Li Hongling 1917) and capital shareholders (Wei Juxian 1937/38).[12] The banks also invested in future civil servants by, for example, lending them funds or financing their travel to Beijing to take Confucian civil service examinations.

The banks' Beijing branches, especially, spent heavily entertaining officials and nobles. This provided returns in several ways. It attracted as deposits not only the wealth of courted officials and nobles, but whole ministries' budgets—the latter often paying no interest (Wei Juxian 1944). As their private and official business grew, the banks widened their branch networks throughout the empire.[13]

The nineteenth century saw a sequence of disasters for the Qing and China, but the Shanxi banks turned each into a lucrative opportunity. The Treaty of Nanking, ending the First Opium War (1839–1842), required China to pay Britain a $21 million indemnity in silver. To raise this, the dynasty ordered each provincial government to transfer a levy of silver to British agents in the new treaty enclaves. Inland provincial governments, unable to transport huge amounts of silver securely to the treaty ports, faced a crisis—in which Lei Lutai, still General Manager of the Sunrise Provident, saw an opportunity. Lei instructed branch managers in inland provinces offer their provincial governments bank drafts to transfer the silver to the designated ports before the deadline. In preparation, Lei moved silver to its port branches, so when the provincial representatives arrived, sufficient silver awaited them. This worked flawlessly, and averted impending disaster. The impressed emperor dubbed Lei's bank the Clearance Everywhere Under Heaven Bank, echoing his traditional mandate "everywhere under heaven."[14] A plate so inscribed thenceforth surmounted the door to its Beijing branch.

The Taiping Rebellion (1851–1864), led by the bizarre "little brother of Jesus" Hong Xiuquan, deprived the dynasty of taxpayers in a swath of east central provinces, and cut loyal southeastern provinces off from the capital. To transfer government revenues through rebel territory, the dynasty again turned to bank drafts. Thereafter, the military budget [*junxiang*], poll tax [*dingliang*], sale tax [*lijin*], and provincial indemnity levies [*gesheng ding'e tanpai waizhai*] all moved about China through interest-free accounts at the Shanxi banks, which lent at 7 to 8 *li* (Wei 1944).

When British opium traders provoked a Second Opium War (1856–1860), the Qing turned defeat into disaster by reneging on an 1858 peace treaty and arresting, torturing, and executing British diplomats. The infuriated Western powers occupied Beijing and added an 8 million *tael* ($12 million) war indemnity to the 1860 treaty, which legalized Christianity and opium, pried open more ports, and established more enclaves of foreign law.[15] Again, the banks profited transferring silver to the ports.

The 1900 Boxer Rebellion brought another foreign invasion that drove the Qing court from Beijing to Xi'an—its flight financed by the Shanxi banks. The dynasty's failure to protect diplomats and Christians during the rebellion triggered yet another indemnity in the 1901 Boxer Protocol, again in silver, which Shanxi banks again helped transfer from inland provinces to foreign agents on the coast.

During their best years, from 1880 to 1900, the Shanxi banks' dividends averaged 12,000 *tael*, or 18,000 silver dollars, per fiscal cycle. These were huge fortunes: for comparison, a county administrator [*zhixian*] earned an annual salary of 45 *tael* or $67.50 in silver dollars. Shanxi's best and brightest were well advised to forsake the Confucian civil service for careers in banking.

The Setting of the Sunrise Provident

Lei Lutai died at his desk in 1849. Though his son was an employee, Lei named another his successor. Cheng Qingpan and two subsequent general managers loaned prudently, and the bank prospered. In 1880, the capital shareholders, at Li's request, created a new class of *nonvoting capital share* [*fugu*] for managers.[16] These let managers reinvest their dividends in the bank without gaining votes.[17] The new securities did not expire, passed to heirs, and paid interest rather than dividends. This may well have sharpened incentives, but it also showed that the voting rules could change.

Li Wudian, Li Zhenshi's nephew and adopted son inherited his father's capital shares in 1891. Wudian continued selecting highly capable managers, but also sought to influence lending—a course his father avoided. In the 1910 grand assessment day, Wudian created yet another share class, awarding himself 1.7 *empty shares* [*konggu*], with full voting rights in grand assessment days but without the investment in silver associated with a capital share. Thus outvoting all other capital shareholders, Li made himself a vice president and awarded himself one expertise share—making his voice equal to the general managers in expertise shareholder meetings.[18] The bank now had a controlling shareholder who was also a top insider. The other managers dared not oppose Li's lending decisions, for he controlled their jobs, expertise share allotment, and retirement benefits. When the general manager dared oppose Li, contradictory orders only added to a general confusion.

The bank's performance deteriorated—it lost money in 1911 and again in 1912—and the other capital shareholders, Li's brothers, exercised their rights to withdraw their capital in silver. In desperation, Li ordered the bank to borrow from sources other than depositors.

In 1914, the bank's Beijing manager was unable to make good his guarantee of a debt of the failed Heshengyuan Bank, and fled to Shanxi. A warrant was issued for the arrest of the Sunrise Provident's capital shareholders, who still carried unlimited liability. In 1915, under the new civil code, the creditors became the banks' new common shareholders and withdrew the charges against the Li brothers. As an act of charity, the new owners granted the Li brothers a thousand silver dollars per year. The reorganized Sunrise Provident Bank, with a single equity class, lasted until 1932, when it closed at the height of the Great Depression.

The Financial Center

This saga of financial entrepreneurship leaves the odd placement in time and space of this financial center unexplained. The 1820s, when the banks took root, lie in the middle of a long era of isolation from the outside world, and Shanxi lies in China's remote northern interior.

Splendid Isolation

In 1823, when the Sunrise Provident was founded, the Silk Road, a caravan route from China to the Middle East, had long ago dried up. The Little Ice Age, an abnormally cold global climate from the sixteenth to the nineteenth century, desiccated northwest China and Central Asia, reducing populations already bled by the Golden Hoard and commerce already drained by banditry. By the late 1700, the Silk Road was all but impassable. Thus, Shanxi merchants did business in Xingjiang, the route's former entrepôt in western China, but none along the route itself. Western relic hunters of the eighteenth and nineteenth centuries describe ruins along the once magnificent trade route.

Maritime trade was also slowed to a drip. The Ming criminalized overseas trade, save from 1405 to 1433 when Admiral Zheng He charted the African coast. After Zheng's death, the next emperor destroyed the ships, burned his records, and banned ocean trade. In 1661, the Qing army sterilized a 50 *li* (16km.) wide band along China's coast—levelling all buildings and marching all residents inland in three days—all to isolate rebels on Taiwan.[19] The band, thrice widened and marked by signs warning "Anyone found over this line shall be beheaded instantly," was patrolled by soldiers dispensing instant death to transgressors (Gu Cheng 2003). Coastal areas were resettled in 1683, and limited maritime trade resumed in 1685 in four ports—Guangzhou, Zhangzhou, Ningpo and Songjiang. In 1757, the Emperor Qianlong closed them all—precipitating the uninvited arrival of British ships in 1759 and Guangzhou's restricted reopening in 1760. Under the restrictions, the *cohong* system, select merchant groups [*kung hung*, hence *cohong*] bought quotas for trade with pre-screened unarmed male foreigners on a riverbank outside the city wall during a limited "trading season" only.[20] Under constant observation and harassment by bribe-seeking officials, foreigners risked unpredictable fines, enthusiastic torture, arbitrary imprisonment, and instant death until 1842, when British victory in the First Opium War opened four more ports and established Common Law enclaves in all five.[21] Given this xenophobia, chronicles of the Shanxi banks understandably presume a purely Chinese provenance.

Original Sins

The most colorful, and least plausible, explanation capitalizes the banks with gold and silver stolen from Ming treasury as that dynasty collapsed in the 1640s (Dong 1917; Chen 1937; Wei 1944), though a 1.5 ton (pre-Ming) coin hoard discovered at a Shanxi construction site in 2007 lends the notion unexpected credence.[22] Another argument has defecting 1640s Ming soldiers reappearing in Shanxi as private security to the region's merchants—a distinct edge under waning rule of law (Han Yefang 1921; Lu 1936; Wei 1944). Yet another blacklists locals from top civil service positions for Northern Song (960–1127) dissent or hiding 1640s Ming soldiers (Wei Juxian 1935), redirecting talent to commerce. While Shanxi locals are oddly absent from Qing top rank exam records (Xiao Yuanjin 2004), the dynasty's nineteenth-century enthusiasm for the banks' services asperses this thesis somewhat (Fan 1935; Chen 1937; Li Weiqing 1937).[23]

The most plausible explanation of Shanxi's financial prominence has its salt works at Lake Xiechi fostering mercantile activity that ultimately needed banks (Jun Shi 1917; Miyazaki Ichisada 1993). A state salt monopoly persisted, with minor interruptions, from the Han (206–220 B.C.E./C.E. until 1370).[24] That year, the army began using salt rights [*yan yin*], initially redeemable only at Lake Xiechi, to pay for transporting provisions to troops on the Great Wall (Wang Hongxu 1789, cited in Zhang Zhengming 1992). Shanxi merchants, handling this business from its outset, thus got a piece of the State's monopoly and the State quite likely netted more revenues because of higher overall efficiency. This policy remained in effect long enough for Shanxi merchants to accumulate substantial wealth.[25] It also accords with evidence that Shanxi was not an important commercial center until the Ming dynasty (Liang Xiaomin 2007).

Every study posits the banks' Chinese roots (Dong 1917; Han 1921; Fan 1935; Hou Zhaolin 1936; Lu 1936; Chen 1937; Wei 1944). This is plausible, for China has a long financial history. At least as early as the Southern Qi (420–589), pawnshops [*dangpu*] made secured loans (Peng Xinwei 1954, trans. p. 244). These needed independent managers, fully responsible for their decisions, and appraisers, skilled at valuing collateral; and paid both with profit sharing, a practice Yang (1952, 73) argues the Shanxi banks copied.

Silver shops [*yinpu*] or exchange shops [*duifang*] long changed money: trading lengths of silk; bulk weights of gold, silver, and copper; standard quantities of wheat, rice, silk, and salt; and (in some periods) coins and paper money (Peng 1954). Difference currencies predominated in different eras. Coins and silk both served in the Tang (618–907), even as local governments' offices in the capital issued certificates of deposit [*fei qian* or *flying cash*] to merchants conducting long-distance trade.[26] The Song (960–1279) invention of paper money apparently replaced *flying cash*, but hyperinflation in the 1160s, and again under the Ming in the 1440s so undermined confidence in fiat money that China abandoned the innovation around 1445. Thus, the latter Ming and Qing regressed to commodity money. Grand Secretary Zhang Juzheng's 1581 *single whip* tax reform, mandating payment in bulk silver only, reenergized the exchange shop business.

Counting houses [*guifang*, lit. *cupboard houses for saving*] and apothecaries offered savings accounts (Peng 1954, trans. p. 324), but without interest. The Tang Penal Code "made it a crime for a person to put to profitable use funds entrusted to him" (Peng 1954, trans. p. 326)—suggesting a black market in interest.

Foreign Contamination

Each of these institutions did something akin to banking, but none were banks. The sudden appearance of genuine banks in the late Qing may thus be a remarkable example of parallel evolution: perhaps similar economic conditions shaped similar contractual and organizational forms in China and the West. However, Shanxi merchants' trading patterns suggest their banks may derive from Western models after all. The Silk Road was choked off, and the ports were all but hermetically sealed; but across the Gobi desert from Shanxi, Tsarist Russia was wide open and "every year, Shanxi merchants transport countless silk, cloth, tea, sugar, cigarettes, and china to Lanzhou and Xinjiang; or, though Kyakhta to Russia; to their branches as far as Moscow...and St. Petersburg" (Liu Jiansheng, Zhang Peng, and Zhang Xinlong 2007, quoting Sui Yuan Tong Zhi Gao).

In fact, virtually all of the trade went through Kyakhta, a trading post created by the 1727 Kyakhta Treaty on Russia's border with Outer Mongolia, then part of China.[27] A Russian state monopoly and Qing requirements for the prior preclearance of all exports in Beijing initially kept trade to a trickle. But in 1755, the Qing dispensed with preclearance; and in 1762, Catherine the Great opened Kyakhta to private merchants, and the Tea Road soon boomed. By the mid-nineteenth century long Boyar caravans, laden with Chinese tea for resale to Europe and America, snaked toward St. Petersburg; and the "merchants in Kyakhta were all Shanxi merchants" (Liu et al. 2007, quoting Sui Yuan Tong Zhi Gao) and "most of the merchants are Shanxi merchants" (Liu et al. 2007, quoting He Qiutao 1860). The Tea Road made fortunes for Russian and Shanxi merchants until China's Opium War defeats reopened maritime trade.

Banks in tsarist Russian, though pressured to lend to court favorites and chronically unstable, took deposits, made loans (primarily to favored nobles), exchanged currencies and let merchants transfer funds to each other. But St. Petersburg, the site of the westernmost known Shanxi merchant operation, was also Russia's doorway to Europe, and hosted branches of major Western European banks, with British bankers especially important. Thus, Swart Thompstone (2004) writes "For two centuries after the foundation of St. Petersburg in 1703, the British merchant community exercised a remarkable influence over the city's economic relations with the wider world. This community operated as a 'City of London' in miniature. . . . " He reports British merchant families in St. Petersburg numbering about 1,000 in the 1790s, rising to some 2,500 in the 1820s.

It seems plausible that Shanxi merchant in St. Petersburg might notice these banks. Li Daquan, running Xiyucheng dyed goods operations, organized silver shipments between Tianjin and Shanxi. These would have gone through Kalgan, where Kyakhta caravans passed beneath the Great Wall. Perhaps Li heard of banking from Shanxi merchants who had travelled to European Russia—and decided to try his hand at it. Amid Qing xenophobia, he would wisely omit mentioning a foreign model.

Ignoble Ends

After a string of humiliating military defeats and rebellions, the Qing launched genuine reforms as the new century opened: elected assemblies, railroad nationalizations, and civil service and army reform. The army, backed by provincial governors and railroad owners, revolted. Provinces seceded, and the rule of law fell away. Sun Yatsen returned in 1911 to declare a republic. His Kuomintang won a constitutional assembly election, but reactionaries seized power. Provinces again seceded, warlords carved out petty kingdoms, and for the next two decades China was a mere geographic region (Michael Spence 1991). Over the next few years, the Shanxi banks either liquidated voluntarily or limped into bankruptcy.

Several factors worked to their demise: foreign banks in treaty enclaves benefited from relative rule of law and legal innovations such as limited liability. Rival Chinese banks gained similar flexibility under a 1901 German Civil Code (Kirby 1995; Goetzmann and Köll 2005), Railroads and telegraph lines let all such entrants establish rival account clearing operations. Their lower costs let these upstarts pay more interest and charge less for loans than the Shanxi banks (Li 1917; Wei 1944). Meanwhile, the Shanxi banks' cash cows—interest-free government deposits and intergovernmental transfers—evaporated, there being no government to speak of. The only institutional improvement that stuck, the standardized the currency, merely ended their domestic currency exchange business. As rising chaos overwhelmed the country, the Shanxi banks' borrowers defaulted. Lacking collateral—reputation had always been enough—and unprotected by limited liability, the banks' capital shareholders and managers, by dint of the indemnification clauses in their employment contracts, faced the full losses.

LEARNING FROM HISTORY

The Shanxi banks present two intriguing puzzles. One is geographic: why did a banking center arise in a remote northern inland province—akin to America's financial center being in Fargo, North Dakota, rather than Manhattan. The other is temporal: how did such a close parallel to contemporary Western banks arise in this era of xenophobia, isolation, and relative institutional decay? While the second puzzle leads most to posit purely Chinese solutions to the first, we offer an alternative explanation.

China's traditional trade routes—the Silk Road and its maritime ports—were indeed largely sealed off against foreign influence; but Shanxi merchants ran a booming tea trade across the Gobi desert, through Siberia, to St. Petersburg. They alone could leave and reenter China freely, and while in the Russian capital, they surely observed both Russian banks and the large colony of British banks located there. Were America's only access to the outside world a North Dakota border crossing, its financial capital might well have developed in Fargo. We thus posit that the Shanxi banks exemplify institutional diffusion, not parallel evolution.

Nonetheless, the Shanxi banks were uniquely Chinese models of corporate governance. To illustrate, we describe the dual class equity of the Sunrise Provident Bank, the first and largest Shanxi banks. Its managers (expertise shareholders) voted in more frequent meetings advising the general manger on lending and strategy. Its owners (capital shareholders) voted only on top managers' retention and expertise share allotment at the end of each three or four-year fiscal cycle. Since both share classes paid the same dividend, and insiders' compensation was primarily dividends from expertise shares, managers' incentives were well aligned with owners' wealth maximization. Since capital shareholders could not influence lending, their social obligations could not skew lending.

This neatly inverts modern dual class equity, which magnify the voting power of insiders and disfranchise other shareholders. Modern lawmakers, regulators, and firms might consider the Shanxi bank's approach: firms might pay insiders expertise shares, with no votes at shareholder meetings. Controlling shareholders might augment their wealth by adopting corporate charter amendments that bar them from influencing business decisions, and let them only hire and fire top executives and set formulas that determine their pay.

Another potentially imitable Shanxi practice is a fiscal cycle three or four years long: tax and accounting rules mandate quarterly and annual disclosure, but longer fiscal cycles for managerial compensation purposes merit consideration. Yet another is dead shares for top executives who retire in good standing—or expire at their desks. These pay dividends for a set number of years and then expire, commending the executive's attention toward long-term profits and providing his retirement and immediate heirs, yet not bequeathing voting rights. Top managers might merit votes at lending and strategy meetings, but these need not persist after retirement nor pass to heirs.

Finally, in the aftermath of the 2008 banking crisis, our readers' attention may linger on the banks' capital shareholders holding top managers' wives and children hostage. While these governance safeguards might displease civil libertarians, we find no instances of fraud by managers in any Shanxi bank at any time.

NOTES

1. Alternative founding dates are 1797 (Fan Chunnian 1935; Lu Guoxiang 1936), 1815 (Jie Zunsan 1944), 1831 (Chen Qitian 1937), and 1824 (Wei Juxian 1944). Wang Yidian (1998) argues for 1823 on the grounds that the first fiscal cycle was six years and the first grand assessment day was in 1829.

2. Yang Lien-sheng (1952, 82) puts Li in Tianjin; Lu (1936) has him in Beijing. He was perhaps reassigned, or ran both simultaneously.

3. By the nineteenth century, paper money was long abandoned and commodities such as bulk silver, measured in *tael*, served as currency. The *tael* had different values in different cities: a *Canton tael* was 37.5g, a *Shanghai tael* was 33.9g, and a *customs* or *haiguan* [海关] *tael* was 37.8g. The conversion rates between common *tael* were well known, and local units took precedence unless a particular weight or purity was specified. Historians generally take one *tael* as 37.5g during this era. The silver dollar (piece of eight), then used in both China and the United States, contained 25.56g of pure silver, making one *tael* roughly 1.5 silver dollars. One *tael* is now 50g on the mainland and 37.8g in Hong Kong.

4. Chen (1937) describes interest rates of 2–3 *li* monthly for deposits and 6–7 *li* monthly for loans. Monthly rates in *li* (厘) are in units per thousand, while annual rates in *li* are in percent.

5. Capital shares, or *yingu*, with *yin*, meaning *silver*, and *gu* meaning *share* are literally *silver shares*. Expertise shares, or *ding shen gu*, with *ding* meaning *represent* and *shen* meaning *body* or *labor*, are literally *representing labor shares, or shares representing labor.*

6. The banks used fiscal cycle several years long, not fiscal years, for updating their balance sheets.

7. Lu (1936) lists the most profitable years as 1880–1900, during which the best performing bank distributed 20,000 *tael* per share per cycle and the worst distributed 5,000–6,000 *tael*. The Sunrise Prudent paid 12,000 *tael* per share per cycle.

8. *Gugu,* with the first *gu* meaning *dead* and the second *gu share,* are lit. *dead share. Gu* also means *alumnus,* so these might alt. be *alumni shares.*

9. Chen (1937) quotes Negishi Tadashi (1907) on bank policy re. employee fraud: "if the employer finds an employee to have defrauded him, the employer can seize the employee's private property, or enslave his wife and children if he has insufficient property."

10. Jie (1944) calls this fund *a bei huang kuan,* lit an *account preparing for a bad state.*

11. Confirmed by a telephone interview with Wang Yidian, a local historian involved in the restoration of the China Piaohao Museum on the site of Sunrise Provident Bank in 1990s.

12. Wei Juxian (1937/38) records the Sunrise Provident buying its second generation owner the title *zhifuwei jia siji shangdai hualing.*

13. The next revision of this paper will contain a map of the Shanxi banks' branch operations.

14. *Huitong tianxia* [匯通天下, lit. *draft everywhere under heaven*] (telephone interview with Wang Yidian confirmed this to be a well-known part of the Sunrise Provident Bank's history, and that its Beijing branch had a large plate [竖匾] inscribed with these words above its main entrance for many years.

15. The 1858 Treaty of Tianjing, which the Chinese government failed to honor until 1860, opened eleven more ports: Niuzhuang (currently Yingkou), Dengzhou, Taiwan (Tainan), Danshui, Chaozhou, Qiongzhou (Haikou), Nanjing, Zhenjiang, Hankou, and Jiujiang.

16. *Fugu,* with *fu* meaning *attached* and *gu* meaning *share,* are literally *attached shares.*

17. In a telephone interview, the local historian Wang Yidian described these as more like debt than equity.

18. Some authors diplomatically dub *konggu* [lit. *empty share*] *privilege shares.*

19. A *li* (里) currently equals 500 meters. From the Tang until the late Qing, a *li* was 323 meters.

20. Foreigners could reside year-round in Macau which, though on mainland China, was *de facto* a lonely Portuguese island.

21. The 1842 Treaty of Nanking opened four more ports—Xiamen, Shanghai, Ningpo, and Fuzhou—and removed the onerous restrictions on foreigners in Guangzhou. The ports so opened were called *treaty ports.*

22. See, for example, "1.5 Tons of Ancient Coins Discovered in North China" *People's Daily,* August 30, 2007, pp. 20–21.

23. Qing ties to the banks raised concerns: for example, an 1864 petition to the Emperor warning "The Shanxi banks, after becoming familiar

with the system, may start to undermine local officials and corrupt our system" (Chen 1937, citing Xie Yanxi 1864).

24. *The Theory of Salt and Iron,* a Western Han (206–220) treatise by Huan Kuan, discusses state monopolies on salt and iron in terms of demand inelasticity; and Ye Shichang (2002) dates both monopolies to 119 B.C. Ji Chengming (1996) describes a section entitled "Treatise on Food and Money" in the Tang dynasty (618–907) chronicle *New Tang History* stating that local governments, not the imperial government, controlled salt production from 618 to 758, and taxed it rather than producing it directly. In 758, an official named Liu Yan persuaded the imperial government to reclaim its salt monopoly

25. In 1492, the *kaizhong* policy was superseded by a new *zhees* policy, which paid merchants in salt certificates for supplying the troops directly, rather than merely transporting government provisions to them (Liang Xiaomin 2007).

26. Peng (1954), citing "Treatise on Food and Money" in the *New Tang History* 54 (Oyang Xiu and Song Qi 1060), explains *that* "during emperor Xianzong's reign, because cash was scarce, the use of bronze utensils was again prohibited. At that time, when merchants came to the capital, they would entrust their cash to the local governments' representative offices, and to the various armies, commissioners and rich families, so as to lighten their burdens as they hurried away in all directions. When the tallies were matched, they could withdraw their money. This was called flying cash."

27. Two other land portals, Zuluhaitu and Nerchinsk, were also officially opened to trade between Russia and China. However, they were both remote, inaccessible, and saw no significant trade activity.

References

Chen, Qitian (Gideon); 陈其田. 1937. 山西票庄考略. 上海:上海商务印书馆. [收录于山西财经大学 晋商研究院主编. 2008. 晋商研究经典文库(全五册), 山西票庄考略分册(根据商务印书馆 1937 年版重印). 北京:经济管 理出版社.]

Djankov, Simeon, Rafael La Porta, Florencio López de Silanes and Andrei Shleifer. 2003. Courts. *Quarterly Journal of Economics* 118(2): 453–517.

Dong, Hai; 东海. 1917. 山西票号.银行周报, 1917(7:8). [收录于山西财经大学晋商 研究院主编. 2008 晋商研究经典文库(全五册), 晋商研究早期论集(一)分册. 北京:经济管 理出版社.]

Fan, Chunnian; 范椿年. 1935. 山西票号之组织及沿革.中央银行月报 1935(4:1). [[收录于山西财经大学晋商研究院主编. 2008. 晋商研究经典 文库(全五册),晋商研究早期论集(一)分册.北京:经济管理出版 社.]

Goetzmann, William and Köll, Elisabeth. 2005. A History of Corporate Governance around the World: Family. In Randall Morck, ed. *A History of Corporate Governance around the World: Family Business Groups to Professional Managers.* Chicago: University of Chicago Press.

Golas, Peter 1977. Early Ch'ing Guilds. In G. William Skinner, ed. *The City in Late Imperial China*. Stanford: Stanford University Press.

Gompers, Paul, Ishi, Joy, and Metrick, Andrew. 2010. Extreme Governance: An Analysis of Dual-Class Companies in the United States. *Review of Financial Studies* 23(3):1051–1088.

Gu, Cheng; 顾诚. 2003. 南明史. 北京:中国青年出版社.

Han, Yefang; 韩业芳. 1921 单行本.调查山西票号记. 1937 载中央银行月报 1937(6:5) [收录于山西财经 大学晋商研究院主编. 2008. 晋商研究经典文库(全五册), 晋商研究早期论集(一)分册.北京:经济管理出版社.]

He, Qiutao; 何秋涛. 1860. 朔方备乘, 卷 46.

Hou, Zhaolin; 侯兆麟. 1936. 近代中国社会结构与山西票号- 山西票号历史的 正确认识. 中山文化教育 馆季刊, 1963 冬季号 :1151–1162. [收录于山西财经 大学晋商 研究院主编. 2008. 晋商研究经典 文库(全五册), 晋商研究早期论集 (一)分册. 北京: 经济管理出版社.]

Huan, Kuan; 桓宽.[汉]. 盐铁论.

Jensen, Michael and Meckling, William. 1976. Theory of the Firm: Managerial Behavior, Agency Costs and Ownership Structure. *Journal of Financial Economics* 3(4): 305–360.

Jensen, Michael and Murphy, Kevin. 1990. Performance Pay and Top-Management Incentive. *Journal of Political Economy* 98(2): 225–264.

Ji, Chengming; 吉成名. 1996 论唐代盐业政策与王朝的兴衰.河北学刊, 1996(3).

Jie, Zunsan; 颉尊三. 1944. 山西票号之结构.单行本成文于 1936, 后收 录于卫聚 贤之山西票号史 (1944) 的附录出版. [收录于山西财经大学晋商研究院主编. 2008. 晋商研究经典文库(全五册),晋商研究早期论集(一)分册.北京: 经济管理出版社.]

Jun, Shi; 君实. 1917. 记山西票号记.东方杂志 14(6): 72–82.

Kirby, William. 1995. China Unincorporated: Company Law and Business Enterprise in Twentieth-Century China. *Journal of Asian Studies* 54(1): 43–63.

La Porta, Rafael, Florencio Lopez-de-Silanes, Andrei Shleifer and Robert Vishny. 1997. Trust in Large Organizations. *American Economic Review* 87(2): 333–338.

La Porta, Rafael, Florencio Lopez-de-Silanes and Andrei Shleifer. 2008. The Economics Consequences of Legal Origins. *Journal of Economic Literature* 46(2): 285–332.

Li, Hongling; 李宏龄. 1917. 山西票商成败记.单行本成文于 1917, 后收录于卫聚贤之 山西票号史 (1944). 的附录出版. [[收录于山西财经大学晋商研究院主编. 2008. 晋商研究经典文库 (全五册), 晋商研究早期论集(二)分册.北京: 经济管理 出版社.]

Li, Weiqing; 李渭清. 1937. 山西太谷银钱业之今昔.载中央银行月报. 1937(6:2). [收录于山西财经大学 晋商研究院主编. 2008. 晋商研究经典文库(全五册), 晋商研究早期 论集(二)分册.北京: 经济管理出版社.]

Liang, Xiaomin; 梁小民. 2007. 小民话晋商. 北京:北京大学出版社.

Liu, Jiansheng, Zhang Peng, Zhang Xinlong; 刘建生,张朋,张新龙. 2007. 浅 析西口在北路贸易中的历史地位. 中国经济史研究. 2007(4).

Liu, Shangxue; 刘尚学. 1937. 山西平遥县票庄记.载中央银行月报. 1937(6:5). [收录于山西财经大学 晋商研究院主编. 2008. 晋商研究经典文库(全五册), 晋商研究 早期论集(一)分册.北京:经济管理出版社.]

Lu, Guoxiang; 陆国香. 1936. 山西票号之今昔.民族杂志(3)401–415. [收录于山西财经大学晋商研究院主编. 2008. 晋商研究经典文库(全五册), 晋商研究早期论集(一)分册.北京:经济管理出版社.]

Miyazaki, Ichisada. 1993. Chinese Civilization, History and Salt. *Complete Collection of Ichisada Miyazaki XVII*. Tokyo: Iwanami Shoten.

Morck, Randall, Andrei Shliefer and Robert Vishny. 1988. Management Ownership and Market Valuation: An Empirical Analysis. *Journal of Financial Economics* 20(1/2): 293–315.

Morck, Randall, Stangeland, David and Yeung, Bernard. 2000. "Inherited Wealth, Corporate Control and Economic Growth: The Canadian Disease?" In Randall Morck, ed. *Concentrated Corporate Ownership*. Chicago: University of Chicago Press, 319–369.

Negishi, Tadashi, ed.; 根岸佶(主编). 1907. 支那经济全书,第三辑第五编,山西票庄. 东京: 丸善株式会社.

Nenova, Tatiana, 2003. "The value of corporate voting rights and control: A cross-country analysis," *Journal of Financial Economics* 68(3): 325–351.

Oyang, Xiu, Qi Song, et al., eds.; 欧阳修、宋祁 等 (主编). 1060. 新唐书. 54. 食货志.

Peng, Xinwei; 彭信威. 1954. 中国货币史.上海群联出版社出版,上海. [Trans. by Edward H. Kaplan. 1994. *A Monetary History of China*. Bellingham: Western Washington University Press.]

Pérez-González, Francisco. 2006. Inherited Control and Firm Performance. *American Economic Review* 99(5): 1559–1588.

Smith, Brian and Ben Amoako-Adu. 1999. Management Succession and Financial Performance of Family Controlled Firms. *Journal of Corporate Finance* 5(4): 341–368.

Spence, Michael. 1991. *The Search for Modern China*. New York: Norton.

Stulz, René. 1988. Managerial Control of Voting Rights: Financial Policies and the Market for Corporate Control. *Journal of Financial Economics* 20(1/2): 25–54.

Sui Yuan Tong Zhi Gao; 绥远通志稿,卷 49.民国年间抄本

Thompstone, Swart. 2004. On the Banks of the Neva: British Merchants in St Petersburg before the Russian Revolution. *History Today* 53(12): 29.

Villalonga, Belen and Raphael Amit. 2006. How Do Family Ownership, Control, and Management Affect Firm Value? *Journal of Financial Economics* 80(2): 385–417.

Wang, Hongxu et al. eds.; 王鸿绪等(主编). 1789. 明史,食货志.

Wang, Yidian; 王夷典. 1998.日升昌票号.山西经济出版社,太原.

Wang, Yidian; 王夷典. 2001. 百年沧桑日升昌.山西经济出版社, 太原.

Wei, Juxian; 卫聚贤. 1935. 山西票号之起源.中央银行月报 1935(4:6). [收录于山西财经大学晋商研究院主编. 2008. 晋商研究经典文库 (全五册), 晋商研究早期论集(一)分册.北京:经济管理出版社.]

Wei, Juxian; 卫聚贤. 1937/1938. 山西票号之最近调查.中央银行月报, 1937 (3–7: 11–12), 1938(1–2). [收录于山西财经大学晋商研究院主编. 2008. 晋商研究经典文库(全五册),晋商研究早期论集(一)分册.北京:经济管理出版社.]

Wei, Juxian; 卫聚贤. 1944. 山西票号史.重庆: 重庆说文社 [收录于山西财经大学晋商研究院主编.2008.晋商研究经典文库(全五册), 山西票号史分册.北京:经济管理出版社.]

Xiao, Yuanjin; 萧源锦. 2004. 状元史话. 重庆:重庆出版社.

Xie, Yanxi; 谢赓禧. 1864 京饷宜解实银疏.

Yang, H.K. 1937. The Rise and Decline of the Shansi Native Banks. *Central Bank of China Monthly* 4(1): 1–6.

Yang, Lien-sheng. 1952. *Money and Credit in China, a Short History.* Cambridge: Harvard University Press.

Ye, Shichang; 叶世昌. 2002. 中国金融通史第一卷： 先秦至清雅片战争时期. 北京:中国金融出版社.

Zhang, Zhengming; 张正明. 1992. 明代北方边镇粮食市场的形成.史学集刊, 1992(3).

PART III

SHAREHOLDER RIGHTS AND THE GROWTH OF INDUSTRIAL ECONOMIES

A SHAREHOLDER LAWSUIT IN
FOURTEENTH-CENTURY TOULOUSE

William N. Goetzmann and
Sebastien Pouget

The milling companies of medieval Toulouse provide an opportunity to examine how one early manifestation of the corporate form grew out of feudal precedent. The historical roots of business companies are typically traced back to business partnerships and the Roman trading *societas*. This lineage has posed problems for legal scholars because it does not account for one distinctive characteristic of the modern corporation: the tradability of shares. Henry Hansmann, Reinier Kraakman, and Richard Squire (2006) argue that a precondition to share tradability is the characteristic of entity-shielding—the protection of the firm from claims against one of the shareholders. In their view, entity-shielding eliminated the need to assess the liabilities of potential shareholders. This, in turn, enabled companies to raise capital from a large pool of anonymous investors and to allow transfer of shares without approval.[1]

The historically documented trade in shares of the medieval Toulouse mill companies by 1350 suggests that the problem of entity-shielding was effectively resolved earlier there than in other European polities. While the Toulouse mill companies date from the eleventh century, they do not predate business partnerships such as Italian ventures set up for maritime trade. In addition they are contemporaneous with international Italian banking companies. The features that distinguish the Toulouse firms from these other early European examples are share transferability and a governance structure oriented toward shareholder rights.

In this chapter we discuss the feudal foundations of the Toulouse companies and the potential institutional basis for entity-shielding. We next trace the development of the governance structure of the Toulouse companies during an important period of institutional transition, focusing on a major legal proceeding in the fourteenth century that highlighted limitations in the governance structure and may have triggered important changes that, to the modern eye, look like the institution of a board of directors. Finally we discuss the political implications of the Toulouse companies. They emerged in the context of a strong urban tradition of governance by council, not unlike contemporaneous Italian city-states. We suggest that the Toulouse companies not only borrowed from earlier feudal precedents, but also were governed by a council-like structure of committee, as opposed to a single executive model. Given that one of the Toulouse mill companies survived as a public company into modern times and continues to survive as an enterprise, we consider the potential influence that the institution may have had on the development of the modern corporation.

Although the mill companies of Toulouse have long been known to scholarship, they have had relatively little influence on the history of the corporation. The important exception is Germain Sicard's definitive 1953 study, *Les Moulins de Toulouse*. His book is based on a complete analysis of the archives of the mills, and examines the mills from a number of different perspectives: as technological innovations, legal entities, investments, and potential historical precedents to the modern corporation. Sicard's study is the primary source of information for this chapter, and interested readers are referred to his work. (The original in French is available from the publisher, and an English translation is forthcoming from Yale University Press.) Although not specifically concerned with shareholder rights and activism, Sicard's work provides an extraordinary opportunity to study how external legal institutions such as courts as well as internal agency contracts supported shareholder rights in the late Middle Ages.

BACKGROUND

Situated on the Garonne river in the French Midi, Toulouse was a major regional center for grain milling and distribution from the eleventh century to the eighteenth century thanks to the construction of a large-scale hydraulic infrastructure: a wooden dam to regulate the

flow of the Garonne, floating mills anchored in the stream, and ultimately large-scale, stationary water mills along the riverbank. These
major investments were not undertaken as public works but instead
were financed by private enterprise. The mills were owned through
the medieval shareholding institution called *pariage* or *paréage*, which
allowed for the pooling of private investment capital and governance
on the basis of proportional ownership.

PARIAGE

Pariage was a feudal institution that allowed for mutual ownership
of a fief. Sicard proposes that it grew out of an egalitarian tradition
of inheritance and a corresponding weakness in primogenitor. Rather
than passing along seigniorial rights to the eldest child or dividing
actual properties among heirs, *pariage* divided the rights and responsibilities of the feudal fief among heirs. A property held in *pariage*
conferred the economic benefits to the *pariers* collectively and divided
them according to their respective shares (Sicard 1953, 157). Verzijl
(1970) emphasizes the political nature of *pariage*. The oldest extant
acte de pariage in the *Ordinances de France* is an 1155 agreement
between Louis VII and the abbot of St. -Jean of Sens for the protection of three villages and the sharing of feudal rights to benefit
from them (Jean Joseph Raepsaet 1838, 375). According to Verzijl,
many early *pariage* agreements were effectively exchanges of benefits
for military protection. The shares of the more powerful party were
hence not alienable, but typically the shares of the less powerful party
could be sold (Verzijl 1970, 325). The most famous surviving example of a political *pariage* is the state of Andorra, the co-ownership of
which was established in an act of 1278 between the bishop of Urgel
and the count of Foix, whose right has descended to the president of
the French Republic (Verzijl 1970, 325).

ESTABLISHMENT OF MILLING RIGHTS IN TOULOUSE

The *pariage* framework governing the mills of Toulouse was neither
so grand nor so strategic as the preceding examples. The rights held
in *pariage* in Toulouse do not concern the governance of a city or a
region, but rather concern the perpetual lease of the river. The institutional structure and presumably the legal definition of corresponding
rights and responsibilities and legal standing were adapted from feudal governance to the creation of a shared entity to pursue mutual
business interests.

This adaptation was likely a natural one. The property rights to use the river and its banks for mills and related activities, particularly fishing, derived from feudal law, and by the fourteenth century rights to the use of the banks of the Garonne had been conferred by political and ecclesiastical authorities to three different groups of mills referred to by their locations: the Château Nabonnais—the castle at the south end of the city, the Dorade—the oldest church in town whose name refers to its lavish gilt interior, and the Bazacle—once a shallow ford situated just downstream from the ancient city walls. Of these three, the Bazacle still survives as a physical and corporate entity, albeit now state owned. It is a functional electricity generating plant on the foundations of the medieval gristmill. Sicard identifies specific acts of feudal enfeoffment legally conferring mill rights in two locations in Toulouse: the first in 1177 for the Dorade, and the second in 1183 for the Château Nabonnais; the latter explicitly mentioned shareholders as *pariers* (Sicard 1953, 70–71). The count gave shareholders the property rights to the river banks in perpetuity in exchange for an annual payment from future proceeds of the mills.

Companies owning groups of mills were eventually formed through the consolidation of individual *pariage* partnerships operating mills in and along the river at their respective locations. At the Bazacle, *pariers* from various mills decided on June 23, 1369, to divide the profits from the mills according to a fixed sharing rule. Their expenses, however, were excluded from the agreement: common expenses such as dam repairs were still shared by the *pariers* of all the Bazacle mills but expenses related to a particular mill were incurred by the *pariers* of that mill only. This cooperative arrangement continued for three years until the consolidation of the Bazacle company—including both debt and equity—which occurred in 1372. This *de facto* incorporation occurred almost concurrently or immediately following the shareholder lawsuit that we study in this chapter and is arguably related to the uncertainties of governance and management revealed in the lawsuit proceedings.

SHAREHOLDERS

The *pariers* in the mills were entitled to a share of the yield of the mills according to their proportional ownership. Presumably the mill companies actually sold the annual output and distributed the monetary profits to shareholders. *Pariers* were also liable for periodic capital calls when additional investment was required. If they were unable to contribute their portion of new capital their shares were reclaimed by the company and sold to investors who could make the necessary payments. This occasionally happened in extreme circumstances—when milldams burst and major rebuilding was needed, for example. Shareholders thus enjoyed annual dividends and had to make occasional contributions, although it is not clear how profitable their investment actually turned out to be. Lacking good grain prices, Sicard was unable to calculate the returns to share ownership. One additional right of shareholders was the ability to sell their shares. A record of share prices for the mill companies in gold and in *livres tournois* is available for the period 1370–1571, and during that interval prices ranged from 100 to 500 g of gold. It is doubtless the earliest pricing information for a publicly traded company in financial history.

The social and political position of *pariers* is an important issue. How, for example, were the companies related to the political power structure of Toulouse? Shareholders typically belonged to the well-to-do bourgeois class of the city, which included lawyers, merchants, and occasionally financiers. While women had full shareholder rights—including the right to vote at annual meetings—they did not serve in administrative roles. Sicard reviewed the names of shareholders of the mills mentioned in the enfeodation documents of the late twelfth century and noted that these matched many of the names of the members of the Toulouse city council. He found little evidence that the mill shares were owned, for example, by millers. Rather, from the outset, the *pariers* were primarily suppliers of capital.

Shareholder lists from the fourteenth to fifteenth centuries document a broad range of *parier* professions: judges, merchants, carpenters, drapers, weavers, apothecaries, doctors, bakers, grocers, bankers, money-changers, silversmiths, priests, and nobility. Sicard estimated that the average *parier* had a net worth of 250–500 *livres tournois* at a time when the average price of a share ranged between 20 and 150 *livres tournois*. Thus a single share represented a significant portion of shareholder wealth and, in turn, the companies were run by well-to-do urban professionals.

Governance

By the late fourteenth century the three mill companies were holding regular annual shareholder meetings at which a set of two to four managers called *bailies* (related to the term "bailiff" in English) were elected from among the 60–90 or so shareholders to serve for a year. The aforementioned list of professions of *pariers* would suggest that even the elected *bailies* delegated day-to-day management of the milling operations, serving as overseers and managers rather than as operators.

The use of the term *bailie* is consistent with the institutional derivation of the company structure from feudal precedent. John William Donaldson (1852) traces the root of the term to the Latin *bajulus* or bearer. In the romance languages of southern France and Catalonia it came to imply a second in command—in effect the agent of the lord (Donaldson 1852). Interestingly, the first infeudation of the Dorade mills was actually granted by the *bailie* of the count of Toulouse to the shareholders. The count's *bailie* in the twelfth century thus clearly held a political office, and the use of the same term to denote the managers of the mill company implies that their role as servants of the owners of the fief—the shareholders—was similar to that of a *bailie* serving a feudal lord.

Interestingly, the selection of *bailies* from among shareholders addressed the classic agency problem. When managers are salaried, their interests may differ significantly from shareholders. In the modern era, this divergence in interests is addressed by conferring some equity ownership on management. Thus, when the fortunes of the company wane, the manager shares the pain of shareholders. Restricting management to the class of shareholders effectively aligned the interest of shareholder and manager in the same way as modern executive stock options—perhaps even better. It ignored, however, the potential need for managerial specialization and expertise. This problem may have been partly mitigated by the fact that *bailies* could be reelected for several years in a row. Thus a subset of shareholders who were good at managing the mills (about half) appeared to take turns fulfilling this role.

Bailies were responsible for the business operations of the company, including commercial and financial transactions. They could enter into bilateral contracts, approve real estate transactions, hire external contractors, and buy property as needed. They also sometimes served as the legal representatives of the firm in court proceedings; however, the mill companies also enlisted specialized representatives as needed. Sicard notes that occasionally shareholders appointed attorneys as their representatives in particular, but not only, to deal with cases at the Paris Parliament.

EVOLUTION OF THE GOVERNANCE OF THE MILLS

The administrative organization of the mill companies was in a state of flux during the late fourteenth century. In particular, the companies were in the process of consolidating semi-independent mills into larger associations. These changes were coincident with changes in governance practice. After 1374 the Bazacle company annually elected a set of *conseillers* or *conselhans* from among their ranks in addition to the *bailies* (Sicard 1953, 209). Sicard observes that the *conseillers* may have originally served an advisory function but by 1379 they had assumed oversight of the *bailies*—no important decisions could be taken by the *bailies* without the approval of at least four of eight *conseillers* (Sicard 1953, 210).[2]

The role of the *conseillers* further evolved in the early fifteenth century. It became customary for them to serve nonrenewable, one-year terms and for the *bailies* to serve as salaried employees of the firm for renewable one-year terms. The emergence of the *conseillers* might be related to the fact that it was probably very time demanding to manage the mills on a day-to-day basis. Up to the fifteenth century, *bailies* were *pariers* and did not receive extra compensation for the services they were offering to the mills. From the fifteenth century onward, *bailies* gradually became employees of the mills (and were no longer *pariers*) under the supervision of the *conseillers*, who were the representatives of the *pariers*. With this new structure, the mills had professional managers and representatives of *pariers* to check on them and oversee the main decisions. Evolution away from the use of *pariers* as *bailies*, however, introduced problems of agency.

Also by the fifteenth century, *conseillers* selected their successors and asked only for a vote of approval for their proposed slate at the annual shareholder meeting. The Bazacle company even had a particular arrangement for the staggering of the terms of the *conseillers*. Each year, two of the eight were selected by their peers to serve an extra year without being subject to shareholder approval (Sicard 1953, 213). The emergence of a staggered board may have reflected a need for some institutional continuity from one year to the next, rather than being a power play by the board to exert further control. Nevertheless, the modern experience with staggered boards suggests that it is a means to entrench board support of management by reducing the ease with which an entire set of board members can be replaced at once.

Another important administrative role that emerged in the late fourteenth century was the corporate treasurer, who was charged in general with the financial operations of the firm and particularly with cash transactions. The role is referred to as *receptor pecuniarum* (money receiver) in legal documents, as opposed to the designation *receptores bladorum* (grain receiver)—a role for which the term *baile* was then reserved (Sicard 1953, 210). The treasurer served an important auditing function. Sicard speculates that the distinct role of the treasurer of the medieval firm is preserved in the modern

French public administration practice of requiring treasurer approval of management expenditures.

In addition to dealing with the firm's cash income and expenditures, the corporate treasurer also evidently provided working capital to finance the mills' operations. Potential amounts of money lent to (or sometimes borrowed from) the companies by the treasurer were reimbursed to him on a yearly basis. In effect, corporate treasurers played an important financial role in providing liquidity in the absence of a formal and effective banking system. There also seems to have been a shareholder auditing function of the treasurer accounts—in 1381 two *pariers* oversaw the submission of the final accounts (Sicard 1953, 229).

THE LAWSUIT

A legal dispute occurred in 1368–1369 between the Bazacle mills and a Toulousian merchant. The records of the trial are in a volume, the *Liber Instrumentorum,* that was probably compiled in the eighteenth century from the original fourteenth-century documents. The volume includes, among other things, the transcript for the 1369 appeal trial in 88 folios. This transcript includes a copy of the 1356 debt contract as well as a copy of the transcript of the 1368 ordinary trial. We were fortunate to be able to consult this volume in writing this chapter.

The dispute centered on a debt of 25 *livres* incurred on May 24, 1356, on behalf of the Bazacle mill organization by Jean de Fulhenchis, Guillaume Salomonis, and Jean de Caussidières, three *pariers* of the mills (see figure 10.1). The loan was granted by a merchant from the "rue de la Tour" located close to the Bazacle mills.[3] The debt was incurred under the "mortgage and obligation" of the Bazacle mills in order to fulfill the necessities of the mills. For a number of years the loan went unpaid, finally precipitating legal action in the form of two lawsuits. These lawsuits allow us to understand the nature of these early firms as juridical personalities, and the legal framework by which the managers of the firms could enter into contracts that obligated the firm and pledged its assets.

Of immediate interest to legal historians is whether the dispute suggests that the Bazacle company was effectively recognized as a legal entity that could borrow in its own name. The fact that the defendants in the case where shareholders, and more precisely former *bailies,* and not the enterprise itself leaves open the question of whether the company by this time was a "juridical personality." This issue is complicated by the gradual development of the Bazacle mills into a unified entity following the period of the trial. Nevertheless there was no

Figure 10.1 Transcript of the debt contract of 1356 incurred in the name of the Bazacle company

ambiguity about the fact that the debt was incurred for the purposes of the company and not for personal use by the defendants.[4]

It is possible but unlikely that the debt was disputed because it preceded the formal consolidation of individual mill debts as a result of incorporation. The 1356 debt contract indicates that the debt was made in the interest of the Bazacle mills—more precisely for the necessities of the mills. This suggests that the *bailies* of the mills in 1356 were explicitly acting in the name of all the *pariers* and not only for the mills in which they possessed shares.

The amount in dispute was not trivial. The claim by the merchant Arnaud Albiges appears significant in comparison with the size of the company. The nominal value of the debt, namely, 25 *livres,* can be compared to the transaction prices of one *uchaux* (i.e., one share of the Bazacle mills that comprised around 90 *uchaux* at the time of the trial), namely, 20 *livres* in 1352 and 50 *livres* in 1363. The debt thus represents between 1.4 and 0.5 percent of the value of the Bazacle mill company.

The first court proceeding occurred in November 1368. At that time Albiges brought a charge against the 1368 *bailies* of the Bazacle mills before a local judge. To defend themselves, the 1368 *bailies* claimed that the 1356 *pariers* who contracted the debt were not *bailies* and thus could not commit in the name of the other *pariers*. This evidently was not true, as one of them, Jean de Caussidières, served as a *bailie* of the company when he incurred the debt in 1356.

The Bazacle mill company lost the case and appealed in May 1369 before the judge of the *Sénéchaussée* of Toulouse and Albi. This suggested that the law recognized that the firm managers had the right to obligate the firm and also that the debt was genuine. This time, two of the mills' *bailies*, Guillaume Helie and Bernard Proensal, acting as attorneys for the entire group of *pariers*, claimed that the *bailies* could not commit for the other *pariers* on specific issues without their explicit consent. This line of argument presented logistical problems, since shareholders only met in an annual meeting and no mechanism existed to provide for interim consultation. Sicard indicates that ten *pariers* appeared as witnesses in front of the court (Sicard 1953, 205). Six explained that they did not know if *bailies* could actually commit to a particular obligation for the entire group of *pariers* without their explicit consent. Three witnesses answered that *bailies* could not commit for the others without explicit consent but did not provide any evidence.

On the basis of other legal proceedings from before the case, Sicard argues that by the fourteenth century, *bailies* typically exercised broad powers of management, limited only to the extent that they could not alienate the capital of the firm or revise the company statues (Sicard 1953, 204). The question posed by the second trial is thus whether the law would continue to recognize these powers. Unfortunately, the final ruling of the second proceeding is not recorded, but Sicard suggests that the case was lost by the Bazacle mills.

The witnesses' testimony in this second case presents problems for Sicard's argument. Indeed, it is clear that *bailies* derived the right to commit for all the *pariers* from the consent expressed yearly at the occasion of a general assembly. This presumably was necessary and sufficient to give *bailies* enough power to manage day-to-day operations and would imply that shareholder consent was not required for specific business decisions. If the court struck down that right it left a fundamental problem for future management of the company.

AFTERMATH AND INTERPRETATION

The trial is significant for several reasons. Although it was not brought by shareholders against management, but rather by a creditor against shareholders, it raised the important issue of whether shareholder interests were properly protected by the governance structure of the quasi corporations in the 1350s. The trial addressed the fundamental question of who could obligate a company to pay a debt and under what circumstances they could do so.

It is important to recognize that the loan and the subsequent lawsuit occurred prior to the institutionalization of the *conseillers* as overseers of management. The first court's decision about the loan was unsatisfying from a governance point of view because it did not settle this issue of who has the right to indebt the firm. This is important because, if any shareholder could indebt the firm, this would have limited the viability of dispersed share ownership and made the financing of mill operations difficult. Ambiguity about whether a loan was actually an obligation is an obvious disincentive to a lender and would impair the ability to fund operations.

The adoption in 1374 of what amounted to a board of directors charged with oversight of management and the right to approve major decisions may have occurred in order to resolve this ambiguity. Although we have no record explaining the rationale for these institutional changes, it is tempting to interpret the *conseiller* system as a fix to the problem of direct shareholder oversight of management and an organizing principal for a chain of command for the operation of the company. The original *pariage* system, derived from the feudal relationship, implied that the *bailie* served as the direct agent of the feudal lord. A basic problem of the *pariage* structure is that its *bailie* serves multiple masters. As the lord's role was replaced in the *pariage* structure by a group of shareholders, a mechanism was required to express the interest of the principal. With a large shareholder base, such expression was infeasible. Thus a board came to serve an intermediate role as representative of the principal.

ENTITY-SHIELDING AND THE TOULOUSE COMPANIES

The sustained existence and operation of the Toulouse mill companies over centuries in a legal environment in which creditor rights were actively supported by the courts clearly suggests that the *pariage* system shielded the corporate entity from liabilities incurred by individual investors. The lawsuit does not challenge this interpretation as it established that the shareholders borrowed money for corporate purposes, not for their own benefit.

One of the greatest risks of enterprises that lack entity-shielding—such as partnerships—is the potential for a creditor of one partner to interrupt the business operation of the entity via a claim on the debtor's share of the partnership's assets. In the *pariage* system, it appears that the share—the *uchaux*—was recognized as atomistic: a

piece of property that carried the right of sale and even hypotheca-
tion, but not the right to attach underlying entity assets. Perhaps this
boundary is a function of the original intent of the *pariage* contract as
a means to avoid division of assets by interested parties and instead to
substitute a sharing of benefits. The entity-shielding nature of *pariage*
may also derive from the intent to limit the relationship of the *pariers*
solely to mutual enjoyment of an asset and not to any implied sharing of potential debts and obligations. That fact that the king and
other major feudal lords were involved in the early *parier* contracts
may have set a precedent that shielded the crown from obligations of
a co-owner.

TOULOUSE MILLS AND POLITICAL POWER

The governance of medieval Toulouse was distinguished from the
early twelfth century onward by a powerful city council that managed
most urban affairs. The town council was referred to initially as "The
Good Men," drawn from the class of knights and well-to-do burghers
of the city. It initially advised the feudal lord, the count of Toulouse,
on matters ranging from the courts to commercial practice to policing
and civil defense. The council later negotiated with the count to limit
his powers of taxation and conscription. The Good Men of Toulouse
in the twelfth century were drawn from a relatively small group of
powerful families within the town—like Venice, the city was effectively run by a lineage-based oligopoly. Their political position was
formalized in 1152 as "The Common Council of the City and the
Bourg" (John Mundy 1954, 32), after which time they had control
of the administration of justice and more importantly the power to
initiate and debate legislation, activities that ultimately led to effective
self-rule.

Meanwhile the counts of Toulouse retained an advisory council of
12, six of whom were lawyers and judges and six of whom were called
"chaptermen," who served as advisors to the count on town affairs
and appeared in legislative proceedings as witnesses. Mundy argues
that these chaptermen were actually chosen by the Common Council,
perhaps by informal election or under the influence of powerful family
clans, to serve a year's term from among the members of the Common
Council themselves (Mundy 1954, 40).

This strand of self-governance suffered in the Albigensian Crusade
of 1209–1229, during which the king of France and allies led a military campaign against the people of the Midi to stamp out the Cathar
heresy. For a period after the Crusade, the Common Council exercised relatively little power. Sicard notes that members of the council

were leaders of the resistance during the Albigensian Crusade and that members of the council were also among the mill shareholders. It was not until the mid-thirteenth century—following years of the Inquisition—that the council regained its independence and influence.

It is difficult not to construe the development of the Toulouse corporations as a natural outgrowth of self-government and rule by committee in the Midi. Evidence of this is clear in the governance structure of the companies themselves. Shareholders chose *bailies* from among their group, much as town chaptermen were chosen from among Common Council members in the twelfth century.

Perhaps more significantly, both *bailes* and *conseillers* were chosen in groups and ruled or advised by committee. Mills did not have singular CEOs, just as medieval Toulouse was not governed by a mayor—with the exception of Simon de Montfort's domination of the city following the Albigensian Crusade.

In the light of the development of political institutions in Toulouse, the mill companies might thus not be thought of as entrepreneurial ventures but rather as an organizational means to create valuable municipal infrastructure. In their organization and operation, mill companies resembled miniature versions of municipal government itself. As such, these early firms may also be taken as evidence of a shift in urban power into the hands of a business group that, after all, controlled much of the rights of the city's major asset, the Garonne.

The governance structure of the Bazacle company existed into the nineteenth century. Eventually *uchaux* were replaced by shares in a *société anonyme*—a modern corporation. The stability of the organization attests to the fact that it must have achieved an equilibrium that solved basic problems of agency and equitable treatment of shareholders.

CONCLUSION

The Dutch East India Company is traditionally regarded as the first modern corporation; however, the study of earlier organizations like the mill companies of Toulouse suggests the occasional emergence throughout European history of a corporate-like form to address the needs of capital-intensive enterprise. With dispersed investor ownership comes a set of governance challenges. Who will make decisions in the name of the company, how will their interests be aligned with shareholder interests, and how will they be monitored and the operations of the company audited? We think we have some idea about how to do this today. It is interesting to see that the people of Toulouse developed frameworks that look like separation of ownership and control, expert management incentivized by equity and oversight by a board of directors.

The experience of the Toulouse milling companies of the late Middle Ages provides evidence on how these governance challenges were addressed through the organic process of firm consolidations, shareholder lawsuits, and the development of increasingly specific managerial and oversight roles. Whether or not these institutions were adopted by later European companies is an open question, but equally interesting is the possibility that solutions to problems of agency in large firms may have been discovered independently as natural paths toward organizational equilibrium.

ACKNOWLEDGMENTS

We wish to thank Geneviève Douillard, archivist at the Archives Départementales de la Haute-Garonne, who was extremely helpful in helping us read the original documents.

NOTES

1. For evidence of entity-shielding and share transferability in Republican Rome, see also Ulrike Malmendier (2009).
2. Bernard Proensal, who was a *bailie* at the time of the 1369 appeal trial discussed in this chapter, appears to be a *conseiller* in 1376–1377 (see Sicard 1953, 235). This can be interpreted as an evidence for the fact that power migrates from the "managers" (the *bailies*) to the "board of directors" (the *conseillers*).
3. The merchant Albiges was living or working close to the Bazacle. It seems normal that a neighbor of the mills, who belonged to the same social class and probably knew the *bailies* or some *pariers*, provided these *pariers* with financing. What is more surprising is that the *bailies* and their successors sought to escape their obligation. In fact, they tried so hard that they were willing to go to court. This type of strategic default provides evidence of the difficulty of setting up a well-functioning financial market even in a pretty small business world in which social sanctions could potentially play a role.
4. As an aside, there is no claim or evidence that Jean de Caussidières, or the other 1356 *bailies* who indebted the mills, personally profited from the financial transaction, so the case was not about managerial misconduct. Nor does it appear that the shareholders of the company regarded his action as mismanagement. They reappointed him as a *bailie* in 1369 and 1370. This suggests that there was no real conflict between the *bailies* who indebted the mills and their successors or the other *pariers*.

Indeed, if the 1356 *bailies* had breached a disposition of their mandate, thereby penalizing the other *pariers*, it seems unlikely that these *pariers* or their successors would reelect them.

REFERENCES

Donaldson, John William. 1852. *Varronianus: A Critical and Historical Introduction to the Ethnography of Ancient Italy and to the Philological Study of the Latin Language*, Cambridge: Deighton, Bell, and Co.

Hansmann, Henry, Kraakman, Reinier, Squire, Richard. 2006. "Law and the Rise of the Firm." *Harvard Law Review*, 119: 1335 (2005–2006).

Malmendier, Ulrike. 2009. "Law and Finance 'at the Origin.' " *Journal of Economic Literature*, 47(4): 1076–1108.

Mundy, John. 1954. *Liberty and Political Power in Toulouse 1050–1230.* Columbia University Press, New York.

Raepsaet, Jean Joseph. 1838. *Œuvres completes*, IMPRIMERIE DE G. ANNOOT-BRAEGKMAN, electronic edition.

Sicard, Germain. 1953. Aux origines des sociétés anonyms: Les Moulins de Toulouse au Moyen Age, LIBRAIRIE ARMAND COLIN 103, Boulevard Saint-Michel—PARIS.

Verzijl, J.H.W. 1970. *International Law in Historical Perspective*, Vol. 3, p. 325. A.W. Sijthoff's Uitgeversmaatschappij, N.V, Leiden.

CHAPTER 11

CORPORATE GOVERNANCE
AND STOCKHOLDER/STAKEHOLDER
ACTIVISM IN THE UNITED STATES,
1790–1860: NEW DATA
AND PERSPECTIVES

Robert E. Wright and Richard Sylla*

The early United States based much of its financial development on European precedents modified to fit American circumstances and to take advantage of opportunities presenting themselves to a new nation. One area of financial development in which the United States most differed from European precedents was that of the business corporation. In Europe, corporations tended to be privileged monopolies, and there were relatively few of them. The first promoters of U.S. corporations may have had the European model in mind, but increasingly found themselves overwhelmed by democratic political forces that insisted upon the extension of corporate privileges to nearly all white males who desired them. It was in the United States, therefore, starting in the 1790s when about 300 corporations were chartered, that the old European idea of the corporation as privileged monopoly began to be transformed into the modern idea of the corporation as a competitive enterprise.

Between 1790 and 1860, U.S. state governments chartered some 22,000 corporations under special legislative acts and another 4,000 or so under general laws of incorporation. Assuming that exit rates

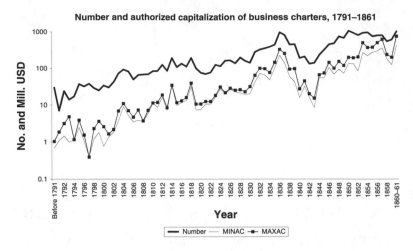

Figure 11.1   Number and authorized capitalization of business charters, 1791–1861

did not drastically differ between continents, by 1830 the United States had at least 15 times more corporations per capita than Britain did (Harris 2000, 288; Sylla 2009, 226–228). France, Germany, and Russia lagged even farther behind (Thieme 1961; Freedeman 1979; Owen 1991). "In no country," wrote Joseph Angell and Samuel Ames, the authors in 1832 of the first treatise on U.S. corporations, "have corporations been multiplied to so great an extent, as in our own" (Angell and Ames 1832). Available data, including our new database of all specially incorporated businesses chartered in America prior to the Civil War (summarized in figure 11.1, showing the number of charters issued each year as well as minimum and maximum authorized capitalizations), also show that early U.S. corporations attracted far more equity capital per capita than their European counterparts did.

Importantly, U.S. corporate development was a national phenomenon not limited to the seaboard, the non-slave states, and certainly not the few industrializing states in the Northeast (Kessler 1948). "Every state in the union," remarked Angell and Ames, "was an extensive manufacturer of home made corporations." New York State jurist James Kent, a contemporary of Angell and Ames, also observed that "the increase of corporations, in aid of private industry and enterprise, has kept pace in every part of our country with the increase of wealth and improvement" (Kent 1894; first published 1826–1830). The slaveholding states of the U.S. South by themselves chartered more corporations than any other nation, although the free states of the North chartered even more. As figure 11.2 shows, by

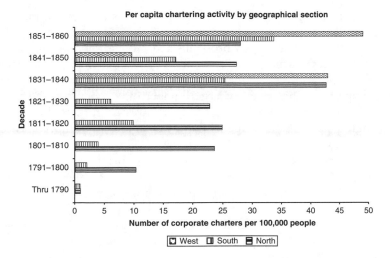

Figure 11.2   Per capita chartering activity by geographical section

the 1850s, if not the 1830s, entrepreneurs in the South and West chartered in per capita terms about as many corporations as did entrepreneurs in the North.[1]

The reasons underlying America's early corporate dominance remain contested. Perhaps, as the authors believe, the U.S. financial system and economy, jumpstarted by the ratification of the Constitution in the late 1780s and the growth-promoting policies of Alexander Hamilton in the early 1790s, were simply more dynamic and innovative than those of sclerotic European empires still burdened with the vestiges of aristocracy, mercantilism, predatory governments, and frequent wars (Wright 2008; Sylla 2009). Or perhaps, as others have argued (Lamoreaux 1995, 2004; Lamoreaux and Rosenthal 2005, 2006), European for-profit enterprises by the latter half of the nineteenth century, if not earlier, enjoyed access to a wider variety of organizational forms, such as limited liability partnerships, and hence had less need for the corporate form than their American counterparts did. Although the latter explanation may be plausible, it misses the fact that other organizational forms, including limited liability partnerships (Hilt and O'Banion 2009) and "sole corporations" (our research on early U.S. chartering has encountered quite a few "family" or small-enterprise corporations without dispersed public shareholders; Sylla and Wright 2009), were available to early U.S. firms. It also fails to explain why America's generally pro-growth legislatures would have (or indeed could have) blocked the development of noncorporate business forms had they been widely sought after by entrepreneurs.

ROBERT E. WRIGHT AND RICHARD SYLLA

Rather than try to resolve the issue here, we instead concentrate on the equally interesting question of how U.S. stockholders were able to mitigate principal-agency problems and protect their lawful claims upon corporate earnings. Some infamous episodes of managerial defalcation demonstrate that America's early corporate governance system was imperfect. The relatively large number of corporations founded and the substantial sums of equity capital invested in them, however, strongly suggest that managerial fraud was an uncommon occurrence and that corporate governance was usually adequate.

Specifically, we find that the following sorts of restraints on managerial or insider opportunism were built into the early U.S. corporate system to mitigate principal-agent problems:

- Corporate charters—legislative acts creating bodies corporate—delimited the geographical scope, capitalization, and acceptable activities of firms.
- Bylaws of firms, sometimes adopted at the behest of directors and stockholders, as well as charters, established rules and monitoring procedures that restrained managerial opportunism.
- The voting rules under which shareholders chose directors frequently were such as to protect the interests of minority shareholders from exploitation by insiders and large blockholders; in particular, so-called prudent-mean voting rules balanced the interests of blockholders and small investors.
- Sequenced payments for stock in corporate start-ups disciplined managements by providing subscribers to shares with a low-cost way of exiting if managers failed to perform according to expectations.
- Widespread local, regional, and national secondary trading markets for shares provided continuing venues for shareholder monitoring, exit, and entry.
- Dividend payments were regularly announced items of information that signaled to shareholders the conditions and operational successes of the enterprises in which they had invested.
- As both corporations and a body of corporate law grew *pari passu*, the U.S. common law-based judicial system created case-based precedents that resolved disputes and furthered corporate development.
- A free press not only regularly reported stock prices and dividends declared, but covered corporate developments and exposed abuses.

At this early stage of our investigation, we can only provide suggestive examples of these aspects of corporate governance systems and restraints on managerial/blockholder opportunism in the formative decades of the U.S. economy. Nonetheless, we think they help us to understand the rapid spread of the corporate form of business organization in those decades, which was substantially in excess of related developments in other nations. Economic historians continue to search for the sources of the economic dynamism that transformed the relatively small and newly independent country on the periphery of a European-centered global economy in 1790 into the world's largest national economy less than a century later. Being the first "corporation nation" very likely was one of them.

*   *   *

Americans created more corporations and a wider variety of them than classical economists such as David Hume, Adam Smith, and their followers (Taylor 1833, 36–37) thought prudent. Most famously, Smith argued that corporations presented two major problems, internal agency conflicts and monopoly. Agency costs arose from the fact that managers followed their own interests, which were often distinct from those of stockholders. "Being the managers rather of other people's money than of their own," he argued, managers did not watch over the business "with the same anxious vigilance with which the partners in a private copartnery frequently watch over their own." For corporations to be profitable, therefore, a government had to endow them with monopoly privileges, which were another "great enemy to good management" and economic efficiency. Smith therefore concluded that apart from the banking, insurance, and large public works (canals and water utilities), joint-stock companies were ill-advised (Smith 1776). Early American entrepreneurs did charter numerous banks, insurers, canals, and water utilities, but they ignored Smith's advice by incorporating a wide variety of other business types as well.[2]

Early U.S. business charters typically contained explicit restraints on agent opportunism. Some states eventually mandated the publication of corporate financial and ownership records. (By the 1840s, for example, many Maine corporations had to publish lists of their stockholders, which presumably allowed stockholders to more cheaply contact each other if they saw fit [Wright 2002b].) In addition, generally pro-growth legislatures and judiciaries along with freedom of the press provided rule of law and at least some transparency (Hartz 1948; Cadman 1949; Heath 1954; Hurst 1970; Horwitz 1977; Banner 1998).

Overall, however, government oversight of corporations was rather minimal compared with what it later would be; corporate law and related judicial decisions developed along with, and usually with some lag behind, the development of the corporation itself. In a study of how trading in securities, a new form of property two centuries ago, came to be regulated, legal historian Stuart Banner (1998, 245) notes:

The largest group of litigated disputes over securities transactions involved questions of how corporations were to be governed or when shareholders were to be liable for corporate debts. These cases were understood to belong to a new category of law, the law of private corporations, a category that did not exist (and could not have existed) until the corporation became a common form of business enterprise. This group of cases [in a footnote, Banner references 21 such cases with dates ranging from 1802 to 1859, with all but four in the 1840s and 1850s] produced doctrines that had no application where corporate stock was not involved, but those doctrines were less concerned with transactions in stock than with internal governance and the liability of shareholders for the debts of the corporation—in the classification scheme used by late twentieth-century lawyers, these cases raised questions of corporate law rather than securities law. . . .

Given the lag of corporate law and judicial decisions behind that of the corporation itself, early corporate stockholders had strong incentives to devise ways to protect their property. "It is a just political maxim," Hume once wrote, "that every man must be supposed a knave." Early corporate entrepreneurs, many of whom were also among the young nation's early political leaders, applied that political insight to business corporations by building a variety of checks and balances into public share offerings and governance processes (Wright 2002a).

Before going public, some early U.S. corporations had significant operating histories as sole proprietorships, partnerships, or unincorporated joint-stock associations. Most, however, did not. Mere start-ups were able to raise capital by selling scrip, or call options on their shares, directly to the public without the aid of investment banks, of which there were few in the early decades of U.S. history. That "installment" mechanism served to minimize opportunism on the part of incorporators (company founders) because subscribers only partially capitalized companies until their managers began to show tangible business results. In some instances, subscribers stopped paying installments on their stock because they believed that the company was not making sufficient progress or had deviated from the business plan laid out in its prospectus (Anon. 1800; West Virginia Iron Mining 1837). But the effect of this check on poor corporate performance was limited because many charters specified that a failure to meet installment payments would lead to a forfeiture of one's stock.

Before the twentieth century, information disclosure by corporations was selective and optional rather than full and mandatory. The quantity of information shared with stockholders was certainly less than it is today, but the quality was arguably better. Directors and managers expected that large stockholders would want to inspect the corporation's operations frequently (Beverely Family Papers). Many company officials learned that sharing information with stockholders, whether mandated by the charter or not, was a good idea because it made stockholders less suspicious of management. The Lancaster and Schuylkill Bridge Company, for example, shared financial statements with stockholders. The managers went into such detail regarding the bridge's construction that they felt it necessary to apologize, "... feeling themselves bound to give the Stockholders a faithful account of their proceedings, it became equally obligatory on them to conceal nothing" (Lancaster and Schuylkill Bridge Company 1814, 1:394).

Early nineteenth-century corporate charters were usually quite restrictive pieces of legislation. That led some early economic historians to argue that charters had a "crippling" effect on business (Livermore 1939, 258ff.), an unwarranted conclusion in light of the relatively large number of corporations now known to have incorporated. The restrictions written into charters probably made investments in corporations by "outsiders" more rather than less attractive by limiting managerial opportunism. Typically, special acts of incorporation limited businesses' geographical scope, capitalization, and acceptable business activities. In addition to shielding society from corporate predation, such strictures protected stockholders by lawfully limiting the scope of managerial discretion. The directors of the Schuylkill Permanent Bridge Company in Philadelphia, for example, had to obtain the permission of the stockholders to refinance the company's existing debts by issuing convertible bonds. To increase support for the proposal, the directors voluntarily published an audited financial statement of the company's revenues and expenditures (Schuylkill Permanent Bridge Company 1807).

Corporations that needed to change one or more major features of their charters could do so by gaining legislative approval. Charter amendments were common in almost all states and outnumbered original charters in some states, especially the older and more commercially active ones. Charter amendments were effective checks because they were transparent and took some time to enact, providing stockholders time to learn of the proposed change(s) and to decide whether or not to protest management's proposed amendments. Often, as with the New York and Boston Railroad Company, stockholders had to approve charter amendments before they took effect (New York and

Boston Railroad 1850, 4:179). The amendment process also provided legislatures with an ability to monitor developments in corporations seeking them.

Corporate bylaws provided additional safeguards. Those of the Washington Mutual Assurance Company of New York, for example, limited the company's investment to New York City banks, the Jersey Bank, and U.S. government bonds. That corporation's bylaws also required the treasurer and other corporate officers to post large performance bonds. Its bylaws also specified the acceptable length of policies, coverage limits, fees, downpayments, and the like, presumably to prevent the managers from engaging in self-dealing or special dealing (Washington Mutual Assurance 1809). To ensure that all stockholders who wanted to attend the annual stockholders meeting could do so, the bylaws of the Franklin Manufacturing Company of Richmond specified that directors had to give ten days notice of the location of the meeting held the first Monday of each April (Franklin Manufacturing 1834). To prevent election rigging, the bylaws of the Bank of Virginia stipulated that the directors had to appoint three stockholders to serve as election judges (Bank of Virginia 1836, 2:244).

In most cases, shareholders had to assent to changes in bylaws before they became effective. The Dedham Bank of Massachusetts, for example, allowed the directors to make bylaw emendation recommendations, but they had to be approved at a stockholder meeting before they took effect (Massachusetts 1815, 1:421; South Carolina Canal and Rail Road Company 1828, 2:20). The bylaws of the Great Falls Manufacturing Company also could not be amended except at "a legal meeting, at which a majority of the Stock is represented" (Anon. 1841).

In some companies, an additional set of regulations for the internal management of the board remained the exclusive purview of the directors (South Carolina Canal and Rail Road Company 1828, 2:18). Even here, however, additional safeguards were sometimes put in place. Directors of the Bank of Virginia, for example, could change the "regulations for the interior management" of the bank only if "regular notice" of the "proposed alteration" was "given at a previous meeting" of the board (Bank of Virginia 1836, 2:252). That check prevented a quorum-sized cabal from drastically changing the board's governance without the input of absent members. The bank's bylaws also held the bank's directors responsible "in their several individual capacities" to the extent that they authorized dividends that exceeded the bank's profits (Bank of Virginia 1836, 2:242).

Stockholders who disliked bylaw, charter, or other governance changes were at liberty to exit by selling shares. Shares in even the

smallest corporations in the least commercial states traded, sometimes over considerable distances. Local sellers who could not find a
counterparty buyer on their own could turn to regional brokers who
specialized in matching buyers and sellers. Corporate officers sometimes acted as informal dealers in their company's shares. Even if
not formally listed on an exchange—and most stocks then, as now,
were not so listed—the shares of many larger corporations traded
so frequently in the broker-dealer markets of Boston, New York,
Philadelphia, Baltimore, Charleston, SC, New Orleans, and elsewhere that their prices were regularly quoted in local newspaper lists.
The number of such "listed" corporations grew consistently over the
antebellum period and was already considerable by 1830. All else
equal, shares with lower par values traded more actively than shares
with higher par values. Median (and average) par values decreased in
nominal (and real) terms in the first few decades of the nineteenth century, from $225 to just $50, making shares more attractive to a wider
range of investors (Wright 2002b, 2009; Sylla and Wright 2009).

In lieu of selling, disgruntled early stockholders could also fight
corporate decisions in various ways. In law, as well as by common
understanding, they were the company's owners and hence had a great
deal of authority. In most instances, only a small number of them were
required to call a special stockholder meeting at which their grievances
could be aired, inquiries made, and investigatory committees formed.
For example, any 20 shareholders who owned at least 600 shares in
the South Carolina Canal and Rail Road, that is, $60,000 or about
8.5 percent of the authorized capitalization of $700,000, could call a
stockholder meeting (South Carolina Canal and Rail Road Company
1828, 2:18). The result of such emergency meetings was often the formation of a committee charged with investigating and reporting back
to the shareholders (e.g., Anon. 1851). For example, the stockholders
and bondholders of the Philadelphia and Reading Rail Road Company commissioned such a committee composed of "parties in every
way qualified to judge" the road's finances and physical attributes
"and having no interest whatever in the property" (Philadelphia and
Reading Rail Road Company 1846, 3:382). The company's officers
complied by laying before the committee "promptly and without
reserve, the books and papers of the office." According to the committee, the officers "tendered to us every assistance in their power, and
showed at all times, a disposition to promote a free and full inquiry"
(3:384). Replying to a 15-point interrogatory, the committee even
inspected the physical rails along the 94-mile long route and made
recommendations about how to improve the corporation's accounting
practices and capital structure (3:385–389, 413–424).

Tellingly, in the late eighteenth and early nineteenth centuries corporate governance lapses were reported to stockholders and not to government regulators, of which there few (Wright et al. 2004, 1:xvi). In 1801, a former cashier blew the whistle on the Columbia Bank by publishing a two-page open letter to stockholders showing that the directors had borrowed on shaky security some seven-eighths of the bank's $400,000 capital, and that the intrinsic value of the bank's stock was about 50 percent of par (Hanson 1801). Over 30 years later, long-serving bank president Charles Sigourney warned stockholders that his cashier, a Mr. Beach, had turned roguish. Unable to steal from the bank due to Sigourney's diligent monitoring, Beach engineered a takeover of the presidency by duping stockholders out of their proxies. Once in control of the bank, Sigourney warned, Beach would make large, risky loans to himself and his family to finance their mercantile and land speculations (Sigourney 1837). In 1847, a stockholder in a rival railroad tried to persuade Boston capitalists not to aid in the revival of the Portsmouth and Roanoke Railroad (in Virginia) by pointing out that local investors, who had much greater knowledge of the company, its route, and the commercial situation in the region, "have so little confidence that they risk little or nothing" in the venture (Virginian 1847, 4:89). In 1855, an assistant cashier of the Mechanics Bank of New York caught his boss stealing and immediately brought the matter before the board. The cashiered cashier retaliated by accusing the president of malfeasance, but the president laid the matter to rest with an open letter to stockholders (Knapp 1855).

Scrips, charters, charter amendments, bylaws, markets, and stockholder activism and monitoring protected shareholders from three major forms of corporate malfeasance, namely, expropriation by managers, by directors, or by blockholders (large stockholders). Other checks aimed at more specific targets. The so-called prudent mean voting rule, first proposed by Alexander Hamilton in the charters he drafted for the Bank of New York in 1784 and the Bank of the United States in 1790, for example, was designed to mitigate agency problems between large and small shareholders (Sylla 2005). Rather than empower small holders over blockholders by authorizing one vote per shareholder, or turning control over to blockholders by following a one vote per share rule, about 20 percent of early corporations took a middle route and provided nonlinear voting rules. For example, stockholders in Pennsylvania's Allegheny and Conewango Canal Company received one vote per share up to two shares, one vote for every two shares thereafter up to ten, one vote for every four shares up to 30, one vote for every ten shares up to 100, and no votes thereafter. An additional 5 percent of early corporations allowed one vote per share but capped the maximum number of votes any one shareholder could cast.

Prudent mean voting rules and caps were more common early on, but waned in the decades before the Civil War. Why they gave way to one vote per share over time is an open question, but it may have simply gotten too easy to subvert them as voting by proxy (or not at all) became increasingly common.

The main function of voting was the selection of the board of directors. Directors sometimes engaged in managerial functions themselves, but more often they were primarily responsible for making strategic business decisions and then selecting and monitoring managers to oversee daily operations. In financial services companies such as banks and insurers, directors also provided managers with information regarding the creditworthiness of potential borrowers, the risks posed by insurance applicants, and so forth (Bodenhorn 2002; Wright 2002b). Ceteris paribus, more directors meant more information and also more monitoring of managers. It is not surprising to find in figure 11.3, therefore, that financial services companies had more directors on average than did nonfinancial corporations.

*   *   *

Many of the companies that suffered from major governance breakdowns before the Civil War appear to have been of middling size and extent, as contrasted with either quite large or quite small corporations. These middling-sized corporations had stockholders who were spread pretty wide geographically and their share prices may have been listed on the exchange or in the newspaper. But they were not at the time of the malfeasance considered important stocks. In a sense, they fell into the gray area between the small, local company and the large corporation with an active, liquid share market.

Typically, enough of the stockholders of bridge companies, small manufactories, and the shorter turnpikes or canals lived close enough to the business to monitor it at low cost. If they detected trouble, they could easily and cheaply meet with enough other stockholders to take action. In 1845, for example, 20 of the Norridgewock Bridge's 30 stockholders lived in Norridgewock, Maine, and undoubtedly regularly used the bridge to cross the Kennebec River. Three other stockholders lived in nearby towns, two lived further afield, and the location of five could not be ascertained. The two-thirds of stockholders who lived in town also accounted for almost exactly 66 percent of the bridge's $5,205 of outstanding stock, so they undoubtedly had enough clout and interest to monitor bridge operations closely.

In very large corporations such as the first Bank of the United States (1791–1811), the second Bank of the United States (1816–1836), and the bigger canal and railroad systems, by contrast, stockholders

242

Sector	Agriculture, fishing, mining, oils, quarrying	Financial services: banking, exchanges, insurance, etc.	Manufacturing, construction, and drainage	Mixed sector enterprises: banks and railroads, etc.	Other services: entertainment, education, hotels, resorts, trading, etc.	Transportation, navigation, bridges, canals, harbor facilities, railroads, turnpikes, etc.	Utilities: electricity, gas, telegraph, water
No.	535	2,320	1,073	240	393	6,119	438
High	16	56	16	17	24	36	17
Low	2	1	1	1	2	1	2
Med.	6.00	9.00	5.00	7.00	5.00	7.00	6.00
Avg.	6.54	9.87	5.60	6.68	6.28	7.31	6.00

Figure 11.3 Number and Distribution of Directors by Business Sector, 1790–1860
Note: This table is missing data from several states in addition to New York and Maryland.
Source: Sylla and Wright 2009.

were extremely dispersed geographically and largely unknown to each other. In particularly dire circumstances they tried communicating with each other via newspaper advertisements and pamphlets. Most corporate information regularly available to stockholders, however, took the form of dividend payments (Baskin 1988). By carefully monitoring dividends and stock prices, stockholders in large, actively traded corporations could keep close tabs on their investments and, if necessary, take corrective action.

Consider, for example, Maine's Portsmouth, Saco, and Portland Railroad. Almost 72 percent of its 315 stockholders, owners of 86 percent of its $868,500 capital stock, lived outside Maine, spread from Boston to Charleston, SC. Only 14 of them resided near the terminus in Portsmouth, New Hampshire, and they accounted for less than 2 percent of the company's capital. The few Maine stockholders were spread thinly, and surprisingly few resided in Saco or Portland (Wright 2002b). The company's stock traded frequently enough in Boston, however, to make the newspaper price lists from the time of the railroad's completion in the early 1840s through at least the mid-1850s (Sylla, Wilson, Wright 2004). Unsurprisingly, the railroad survived the antebellum period (Coolidge and Mansfield 1859, 1:289, 309) and the Civil War (Anon. 1871).

The stock of numerous gas light companies also traded frequently enough to discipline management and promote good governance. A committee charged with investigating the history of gas light companies for potential investors from Nova Scotia claimed that it "cannot find any instance on record of the failure of Gas Companies... but on the contrary, have ascertained from undoubted sources, that in every instance (where judiciously managed) they have been a source of great profit to the Stockholders." A Boston gas light company had paid 12 percent dividends (on the par value of shares) for a dozen years, pleasing stockholders so immensely that they only parted with their shares at a great premium. Similarly, New York's gas light company traded at 45 percent above par and Baltimore's at 35 percent, on dividends of 8–10 percent of share par value plus sizable annual additions to surplus (Halifax Gas 1840, 3:177). In the Midwest and South, many gas light companies also did well by following the sound governance principles of engineer-manager-consultant John Jeffrey (Wright 2009).

Shares in several Pennsylvania coal mining companies were typically owned by short-term speculators and Philadelphia capitalists, well protected by limited liability, who invested only a small portion of their wealth in any one concern. As a result, the capitalists did not monitor their investments carefully, especially those whose main activities took place about 100 miles to the north. Some observers believed that such investors were regularly fleeced by speculators puffing and subsequently selling the stock (Taylor 1833, 44–45, 56–57). Episodes matching such a description are discernible in the fluctuations of published share prices of the Lehigh Coal and Navigation Company and, to a lesser extent, the North American Coal Company, but they were infrequent and could also be explained by the industry's cyclicality (Wright 2005, 175–176; Anon. 1881, 48–49). Although perhaps occasionally duped by speculators, early investors were able, collectively, to keep the directors and managers enough on task to prevent failure of the companies. The North American survived at least into the late antebellum era (Anon. 1856) and the Lehigh company was still in operation in 2010 after emerging from bankruptcy in 2004.

In many medium-sized companies a combination of eyeball and market monitoring occurred, with large stockholders living at a distance communicating with agents, business associates, and relatives who lived close by the bank or corporate headquarters. Robert Beverely of Virginia, for example, kept close tabs on the Northern Virginia banks and insurers in which he had invested by corresponding with his brother Peter Randolph Beverely, William Hodgson, Francis Corbin, and others. The network shared information about which banking companies made numerous, short, safe loans to the best borrowers, and which made a few, large, risky loans to insiders; which were headed by roguish directors who owned little stock, and which were directed by men of property, standing, and ability. Network members also discussed the reasons why some large stockholders could not garner enough support to gain election, which institutions faced hostile takeovers by cabals gathering proxies, and the like. Share prices, dividends, and informal balance sheet information, especially the perceived quality of loans and risks, also circulated among the correspondents.

Nevertheless, governance was a constant struggle because many of the stockholders, including Beverely, resided "in the Country" and hence were rarely fully informed of the latest corporate election machinations or business upheavals. Only by placing his brother Peter on the board of Columbia Insurance, for example, was Robert able to mitigate insider claims adjusting and other shenanigans by shipper-directors who for their private gain verged on running the company into bankruptcy (Beverely Family Papers).

Unsurprisingly, casual monitoring by small stockholders sometimes fell short for medium-sized corporations because too many stockholders were too remote from the location of the core business activities. When the Maine Stage Company shut its doors in 1849, with a book value of $15 per share, its 600 shares (par value $100 each) were owned by 50 different stockholders spread from Augusta and Durham to North Yarmouth and Brunswick. Most lived in Portland (Maine 1849, 52–53), but the company's headquarters were apparently in Brunswick, where the stockholders met the directors in August 1850 to "transact such business as the interest of the stockholders may require" (Anon. 1850). The reasons for the corporation's exit are not clear, but technological obsolescence was not among them as stage coach lines continued to run in Maine for at least several more decades (Anon. 1883).

Early America's biggest corporate governance failures required two factors: a knave able to borrow well beyond his means (assets), and medium-sized companies inadequately monitored by either small shareholders or securities markets. As Mark Twain once quipped, history rhymes rather than repeats. The early history of U.S. corporate governance scandals rhymes repeatedly. "Every instance, without exception, which has yet occurred, of a bankrupt Bank," Phoenix Bank president Charles Sigourney astutely noted in 1837, "has grown out of the overweening confidence of stockholders in some one individual" (Sigourney 1837, 3:112). The same held for other types of corporations as well, as histories by Hilt (2009), Kamensky (2008), Davis (1917), Kindleberger and Aliber (2005), Wright and Cowen (2006), and contemporary commentary (Johnson 1834; Poultney 1834) attest. Later scandals right down to the early twenty-first century—the Bernard Madoff one comes to mind—perhaps indicate that there is a certain timeless quality to what Mr. Sigourney observed in 1837.

*   *   *

Despite its birth from a Mother Country that largely disdained corporations, the United States in the first half of the nineteenth century became the world's first corporation nation. It was the first country that proved able to decrease the agency costs inherent in the corporate form sufficiently to make corporate charters that were widely demanded by business entrepreneurs appeal also to numerous outside investors who purchased and traded company shares. It did so by building checks and balances into corporate charters, bylaws, and other corporate statutes, specifically the sale of call-option-like scrips, prudent mean stockholder rules, and sector-appropriate numbers of directors. Stockholder activism played a key role as well, especially in the smallest and largest corporations where monitoring was relatively inexpensive due to direct observation of company activities or share prices. A free press, evolving corporate law, and a judiciary attuned to decisions that would help the economy to grow also contributed to the corporation-nation outcome.

The biggest governance failures appear to have occurred in mid-sized corporations that were too large for individual stockholders to monitor yet too small for the securities markets to effectively discipline. As a result, they were vulnerable to knaves willing to break bylaws, charter restrictions, oaths, and regulations and to provide false or deceptive information, including unwarranted dividends.

Corporations, governments, and investors counterattacked known threats. Neither investors nor companies nor governments, however, developed foolproof strategies for anticipating and preventing new forms of defalcation; these instead initiated and perpetuated a cycle of crisis and response.

To this day, governments and financial regulators continue to play a costly variation of the game Whack-A-Mole. Occasionally a knave (such as Bernard Madoff in our time) gets whacked, but another soon pops up in an unexpected area such as rogue trading, stock-option backdating, subprime mortgage origination, or Ponzi scheming. The problem today is that government regulatory authorities have undertaken to perform most of the whacking, and it simply is not clear that regulators whack as quickly, as hard, or as smart as conscientious stockholders (or properly incentivized institutional investors on their behalf) and short-sellers would (Sloan 2009).

No doubt there are good historical reasons why shareholder activism and monitoring have given way to more government-sponsored regulation of corporate affairs. But something may have been lost as shareholders gradually ceded the monitoring responsibility to government agencies. The rapid growth of corporations throughout the United States from 1790 to 1860, a period in which governments had vastly less oversight of corporate affairs and finances than they do now, may testify to the possible benefits of less, rather than more, governmental regulation in promoting more active and responsible behavior by individual shareholders and groups of shareholders.

NOTES

*Robert E. Wright is the Nef Family Chair of Political Economy at Augustana College in South Dakota. Richard Sylla is Henry Kaufman Professor of the History of Financial Institutions and Markets in the Department of Economics at the Stern School of Business, New York University.

The authors wish to thank the Stern School of Business, New York University; the Berkley Center for Entrepreneurial Studies; the Ewing Marion Kauffman Foundation; the National Science Foundation under Grant No. 0751577, "U.S. Corporate Development, 1801–1860"; and the Millstein Center for Corporate Governance and Performance for research support. Timothy Guinnane, Jonathan Koppell, and other participants in the "Origins of Shareholder Advocacy" conference held at the Yale School of Management in November 2009 helped us to tighten our focus and strengthen our argument. Any opinions, findings, and conclusions expressed in this chapter are those of the authors and do not necessarily reflect the views of the National Science Foundation, other institutional sponsors, or individuals named here.

1. Here the South includes Alabama, Arkansas, District of Columbia, Florida, Georgia, Kentucky, Louisiana, Maryland, Mississippi, Missouri, North Carolina, South Carolina, Tennessee, Texas, and Virginia.

    The Northern states were Connecticut, Delaware, Illinois, Indiana, Maine, Massachusetts, Michigan, New Hampshire, New Jersey, New York, Ohio, Pennsylvania, Rhode Island, Vermont, and Wisconsin.

    The West was composed of California, Colorado, Iowa, Kansas, Minnesota, Nebraska, New Mexico, Oregon, Utah, and Washington.

2. Specifically, we identify the following types of companies in our database: agricultural companies; commercial banks; boom companies; breweries and distilleries; bridges; canals; cemeteries; construction companies; dams; delivery companies; docks, piers, wharves, and other harbor companies; drainage, hydraulic, and levee companies; educational institutions and libraries; entertainment companies; exchanges; ferries; fishing companies; gas utilities; hospitals; hotels; ice companies; insurance companies; land companies; lumber companies; manufacturing companies; mining companies; mixed commercial navigation and transportation companies; oil companies; parks; power generation companies; printers and publishers; quarrying companies; railroads; telegraph companies; thrifts; trading companies; turnpikes; warehouses; and water utilities.

REFERENCES

Angell, Joseph, and Ames, Samuel. 1832. *A Treatise on the Law of Private Corporations Aggregate*. Boston: Hilliard, Gray, Little & Wilkins.
Anon. 1800. *Extracts from the Resolutions of Stockholders on the Delaware and Schuylkill Canal Navigation and the Procedure of the Managers Thereon in Order to Carry the Same into Effect*. Philadelphia: n.p.
Anon. 1841. *Several Acts of Incorporation and By-Laws of the Great Falls Manufacturing Company*. Great Falls: Light Press, W.D. Crockett in Wright et al. 2004, 3: 179–200.
Anon. 1850. "Maine Stage Company." *Portland Daily Advertiser* (August 9, 10, 12, 13, 14).

Anon. 1851. *Report of a Committee Appointed to Investigate the Affairs of the Staunton and James River Turnpike Company*. Scottsville: n.p.

Anon. 1856. "Real Estate." *Boston Daily Atlas* (October 10, 25, 27).

Anon. 1871. "A Railroad Struggle in Maine." *New York Times* (February 5).

Anon. 1881. *History of Schuylkill County, Pa. with Illustrations and Biographical Sketches of Some of Its Prominent Men and Pioneers*. New York: W. W. Munsell.

Anon. 1883. "New England Gleanings." *Boston Journal* (April 25).

Banner, Stuart. 1998. *Anglo-American Securities Regulation: Cultural and Political Roots, 1690–1860*. Cambridge: Cambridge University Press.

Bank of Virginia. 1836. *An Act for Incorporating the Bank of Virginia ... With the Rules and Regulations for the Government of the Bank*. Richmond: J. Warrock in Wright et al. 2004, 2: 207–252.

Baskin, Jonathan Barron. 1988. "The Development of Corporate Financial Markets in Britain and the United States, 1600–1914: Overcoming Asymmetric Information." *Business History Review*, 62: 199–237.

Beverely Family Papers. Virginia Historical Society. Richmond, Virginia.

Bodenhorn, Howard. 2002. *State Banking in Early America: A New Economic History*. New York: Oxford University Press.

Cadman, John. 1949. *The Corporation in New Jersey: Business and Politics, 1791–1875*. Cambridge: Harvard University Press.

Coolidge, A. J. and Mansfield, J. B. 1859. *A History and Description of New England: General and Local*. 2 vols. Boston: Austin J. Coolidge.

Davis, Joseph S. 1917. *Essays in the Earlier History of American Corporations*. New York: Russell & Russell.

Franklin Manufacturing. 1834. *By-Laws of the Franklin Manufacturing Company of Richmond*. Richmond: T. W. White in Wright et al. 2004, 2: 181–190.

Freedeman, Charles E. 1979. *Joint-Stock Enterprise in France, 1807–1867: From Privileged Company to Modern Corporation*. Chapel Hill: University of North Carolina Press.

Halifax Gas. 1840. *Report of the Provisional Committee Appointed by the Stockholders of the Gas-Light and Water Company to Ascertain the Whole Cost of Erecting Gas Works for the Town of Halifax*. Halifax: John Munro in Wright et al. 2004, 3:165–178.

Hanson, Samuel. 1801. *To All Whom They May Concern, Stockholders As Well As Others*. Washington: n.p. in Wright et al. 2004, 1:115–117.

Harris, Ron. 2000. *Industrializing English Law: Entrepreneurship and Business Organization, 1720–1844*. New York: Cambridge University Press.

Hartz, Louis. 1948. *Economic Policy and Democratic Thought: Pennsylvania, 1776–1860*. Cambridge: Harvard University Press.

Heath, Milton. 1954. *Constructive Liberalism: The Role of the State in Economic Development in Georgia to 1860*. Cambridge: Harvard University Press.

Hilt, Eric. 2009. "Rogue Finance: Life and Fire Insurance Company and the Panic of 1826." *Business History Review* 83: 87–112.

Hilt, Eric and O'Banion, Katherine E. 2009. "The Limited Partnership in New York, 1822–1858: Partnerships Without Kinship." *Journal of Economic History* 69: 615–645.

Horwitz, Morton. 1977. *Transformation of American Law, 1780–1860.* Cambridge: Harvard University Press.

Hurst, James Willard. 1970. *The Legitimacy of the Business Corporation in the Law of the United States, 1780–1970.* Charlottesville: University Press of Virginia.

Johnson, Reverdy. 1834. *Reply to a Pamphlet Entitled: "A Brief Exposition of Matters Relating to the Bank of Maryland."* Baltimore: J. Lucas and E. K. Deaver in Wright et al. 2004, 2: 75–180.

Kamensky, Jane. 2008. *The Exchange Artist: A Tale of High-Flying Speculation and America's First Banking Collapse.* New York: Viking.

Kent, James. 1894 (first published 1826–30). *Commentaries on American Law* 4 vols. New York: Banks and Brothers.

Kessler, William G. 1948. "Incorporation in New England: A Statistical Study, 1800–1975." *Journal of Economic History* 8 (May), 43–62.

Kindleberger, Charles P., and Aliber, Robert. 2005. *Manias, Panics, and Crashes: A History of Financial Crises.* Fifth edition. Hoboken: Wiley.

Knapp, Shepherd. 1855. *Letter to the Stockholders of the Mechanics' Bank from Shepherd Knapp in Reply to the Defence of Francis W. Edmonds, Their Late Cashier.* New York: H. Anstice & Co., in Wright et al. 2004, 4: 263–275.

Lamoreaux, Naomi. 1995. "Constructing Firms: Partnerships and Alternative Contractual Arrangements in Early-Nineteenth-Century American Business." *Business and Economic History* 24: 43–71.

Lamoreaux, Naomi. 2004. "Partnerships, Corporations, and the Limits on Contractual Freedom in U.S. History: An Essay in Economics, Law, and Culture," in Kenneth LiPartito and David Sicilia, eds., *Constructing Corporate America: History, Politics, Culture.* New York: Oxford University Press.

Lamoreaux, Naomi and Rosenthal, Jean-Laurent. 2005. "Legal Regime and Contractual Flexibility: A Comparison of Business's Organizational Choices in France and the United States During the Era of Industrialization." *American Law and Economics Review* 7:28–61.

Lamoreaux, Naomi and Rosenthal, Jean-Laurent.2006. "Corporate Governance and the Plight of Minority Shareholders in the United States Before the Great Depression," in Edward Glaeser and Claudia Goldin, eds., *Corruption and Reform.* Chicago: University of Chicago Press.

Lancaster and Schuylkill Bridge Company. 1814. *Report of the Managers of the Lancaster and Schuylkill Bridge Company.* Philadelphia: Office of the United States' Gazette in Wright et al. 2004, 1: 385–401.

Livermore, Shaw. 1939. *Early American Land Companies: Their Influence on Corporate Development.* New York: The Commonwealth Fund.

Maine. 1849. *Documents Printed by the Order of the Legislature of the State of Maine During Its Session A. D. 1849.* Augusta: William T. Johnson.

Massachusetts. 1815. *An Act to Incorporate the President, Directors, and Company of the Dedham Bank*. Dedham: Gazette Office in Wright et al. 2004, 1: 403–424.

New York and Boston Railroad Company. 1850. *Address of the Board of Directors of the New York and Boston Railroad Company to the Stockholders and Friends of the Road*. Middletown, Conn.: n.p. in Wright et al. 2004, 4: 175–190.

Owen, Thomas. 1991. *The Corporation Under Russian Law, 1800–1917: A Study in Tsarist Economic Policy*. New York: Cambridge University Press.

Philadelphia and Reading Rail Road Company. 1846. *Report of a Committee of Investigation into the Affairs of the Philadelphia and Reading Rail Road Company*. Boston: Eastburn's Press in Wright et al. 2004, 3: 379–440.

Poultney, Evan. 1834. *A Brief Exposition of Matters Relating to the Bank of Maryland*. United States: n.p. in Wright et al. 2004, 2: 67–74.

Schuylkill Permanent Bridge Company. 1807. *To the Stockholders of the Schuylkill Permanent Bridge Company*. Philadelphia: n.p. in Wright et al. 2004, 1: 155–62.

Sigourney, Charles. 1837. *To the Stockholders of the Phoenix Bank*. Hartford: Case, Tiffany & Co. in Wright et al. 2004, 3: 97–114.

Sloan, Robert. 2009. *Don't Blame the Shorts: Why Short Sellers Are Always Blamed for Market Crashes and How History Is Repeating Itself*. New York: McGraw-Hill.

Smith, Adam. 1776. *An Inquiry into the Nature and Causes of the Wealth of Nations*. London: W. Strahan and T. Cadell.

South Carolina Canal and Rail Road Company. 1828. *By-Laws of the South Carolina Canal and Rail Road Company*. Charleston: James S. Burges in Wright et al. 2004, 2: 13–30.

Sylla, Richard. 2005. "Comment," in Randall K. Morck, ed., *A History of Corporate Governance Around the World: Family Business Groups to Professional Managers*. Chicago: University of Chicago Press.

Sylla, Richard. 2009. "Comparing the UK and US financial systems, 1790–1830," in J. Atack and L. Neal, eds., *The Origin and Development of Financial Markets and Institutions, From the Seventeenth Century to the Present*. Cambridge: Cambridge University Press.

Sylla, Richard, Wilson, Jack, and Wright, Robert E. 2004. "America's First Securities Markets, 1787–1836: Emergence, Development, Integration." National Science Foundation, Grant no. SES-9730692. Data available at: http://eh.net/databases/early-us-securities-prices.

Sylla, Richard and Wright, Robert E. 2009. "U.S. Corporate Development, 1801–1860." NSF Grant No. 0751577.

Taylor, George. 1833. *Effect of Incorporated Coal Companies Upon the Anthracite Coal Trade*. Pottsville: Benjamin Bannan in Wright et al. 2004, 2: 31–66.

Thieme, Horst. 1960. "Statistische Materialien zur Konzessionierung von Aktiengesellschaften in Preussen bis 1867." *Jahrbuch für Wirtschaftsgeschichte*, No. 2, 285–300.

Virginian. 1847. *A Letter Addressed to Those Capitalists of Boston Who Are Invited to Take Stock in Purchasing and Reviving the Portsmouth and Roanoke Railroad in Virginia.* Boston: Samuel N. Dickinson in Wright et al. 2004, 4: 85–111.

Washington Mutual Assurance Company of the City of New York. 1809. *The Washington Mutual Assurance Company of the City of New York: Charter, Bye-Laws, and Rates of Insurance.* New York: T. and J. Swords in Wright et al. 2004, 1:163–186.

West Virginia Iron Mining. 1837. *Prospectus of the West Virginia Iron Mining and Manufacturing Company.* Richmond: n.p. in Wright et al. 2004, 3: 133–163.

Wright, Robert E. 2002a. *Hamilton Unbound: Finance and the Creation of the American Republic.* New York: Praeger.

Wright, Robert E. 2002b. *Wealth of Nations Rediscovered: Integration and Expansion in American Financial Markets, 1780–1850.* New York: Cambridge University Press.

Wright, Robert E. 2005. *The First Wall Street: Chestnut Street, Philadelphia, and the Birth of American Finance.* Chicago: University of Chicago.

Wright, Robert E. 2008. *One Nation Under Debt: Hamilton, Jefferson, and the History of What We Owe.* New York: McGraw Hill.

Wright, Robert E. 2009. "Corporations and the Economic Growth and Development of the Antebellum Ohio River Valley." *Ohio Valley History* 9 (Winter): 47–70.

Wright, Robert E., Barber, Wray, Crafton, Matthew, and Jain, Anand, eds. 2004. *History of Corporate Governance: The Importance of Stakeholder Activism.* 6 vols. London: Pickering and Chatto.

Wright, Robert E. and Cowen, David J. 2006. *Financial Founding Fathers: The Men Who Made America Rich.* Chicago: University of Chicago Press.

CHAPTER 12

ORIGINS OF "OFFENSIVE" SHAREHOLDER ACTIVISM IN THE UNITED STATES

John H. Armour and Brian R. Cheffins

INTRODUCTION

Carl Icahn, 1980s corporate raider and currently operator of Trian Partners, a major activist hedge fund, spelled out his business philosophy in a late 1970s memo to prospective investors in his initial investment partnership:

> It is our contention that sizeable profits can be earned by taking large positions in "undervalued" stocks then attempting to control the destinies of the companies in question by: a) trying to convince management to liquidate or sell the company to a "white knight"; b) waging a proxy contest; c) making a tender offer and/or; d) selling back our position to the company.
>
> (Stevens 1993)

Others subscribed to what Icahn's biographer labeled the "Icahn Manifesto" well before Icahn himself. During the 1950s and 1960s, a key aspect of the business model of Hunt Foods, led by Norton Simon, was to search out and buy into companies in which the stock price was low and the potential value of their assets was high. According to Simon's *New York Times* obituary,

> Mr. Simon was perennially on the outlook for promising investments, and over the years he bought interests in dozens of companies. He would look

for companies whose profits were being held down by stodgy executives and whose stock was undervalued and widely held. When he spotted a likely target, he would buy stock, generally quietly, sometimes on his own, sometimes through the Hunt Company. Then, armed with a substantial block of shares, he would start telling management what it should do to improve operations.

(*New York Times*, June 4, 1993)

The investment philosophy Icahn and Simon put into practice will be familiar to those who follow contemporary developments in corporate governance. Icahn's hedge fund was one of a highly publicized cohort of hedge funds operating in the 2000s that sought to profit by "offensively" buying up sizeable stakes in target companies and agitating for changes predicted to unlock shareholder value. The fact that the "offensive" form of shareholder activism in which hedge funds engage has historical antecedents implies the underlying strategy has constituted over time a viable approach to profiting by investing in shares. But for how long? Has offensive shareholder activism been a constant with U.S. corporate governance back through time? Or is it merely a recent phenomenon? If so, why? Why didn't potential antecedents to Norton Simon, Carl Icahn, and today's activist hedge funds seek to pursue the superior risk-adjusted returns that could potentially be obtained by buying up sizeable stakes in public companies and agitating for change?

In this chapter, we address these questions, focusing on U.S. public companies in the first half of the twentieth century. In so doing we are exploring largely uncharted waters, as there is virtually no secondary literature on shareholder challenges to incumbent management teams for this period (Stigler and Friedland 1983, 237). The year 1900 is a logical departure point for our inquiry, as by this point in time industrial companies had begun to transform equity markets formerly monopolized by railway securities. We use 1950 as the end point because the narrative is much better known thereafter, with various "white sharks" challenging incumbent directors of public companies in a series of highly publicized proxy battles in the 1950s and with academics such as Henry Manne theorizing about a takeover-driven market for corporate control by the mid-1960s (Manne 1965, 110; Fraser 2005, 431).

The foundation for our analysis is a hand-collected list of proxy fights we have compiled by carrying out searches of major daily newspapers. For the proxy contests we have found, we have classified the nature of the shareholder insurgency along a number of dimensions, including whether the activism was "offensive" in the way we use this term or was "defensive" in the sense that the shareholders involved were protecting interests arising due to a preexisting stake in the company. The investors engaging in offensive shareholder activism stand out as the obvious forerunners to Norton Simon, Carl Icahn, and today's activist hedge funds, as they took up sizeable positions in companies in which they lacked a prior stake and agitated with sufficient vigor to end up involved in a proxy battle.

Our searches reveal that offensive shareholder activism was by no means unknown during the first half of the twentieth century. However, often the objective of the exercise was quite different from today's activist hedge funds. Activist hedge funds are collective investment vehicles run by fund managers who prefer not to tie up capital in the form of majority or sole ownership of companies and instead anticipate profiting as minority shareholders when shareholder returns improve due to changes management makes in response to investor pressure (Armour and Cheffins 2009, 6). In contrast, only rarely did collective investment vehicles engage in offensive shareholder activism during the first half of the twentieth century. It was much more common for an "offensive" activist to own or operate a business enterprise in the same or a related industry as the target, implying a key objective of the intervention was to capitalize on interconnections between the activist's existing business interests and the target company.

The opening section of the chapter describes the dataset that provides the departure point for our analysis of offensive shareholder activism during the first half of the twentieth century and identifies in a general way the practitioners of this corporate governance strategy. We then outline why collective investment vehicles of the era rarely adopted the tactics deployed by today's hedge fund activists. Next, we discuss practitioners of offensive shareholder activism who had preexisting business interests with their intended targets. The focus then shifts to the interrelationship between offensive shareholder activism and the market for corporate control during the first half of the twentieth century. The chapter concludes by drawing parallels between our study and present-day corporate governance arrangements.

OVERVIEW OF DATASET

To our knowledge there have not been any empirical studies of shareholder activism occurring in U.S. public companies during the first half of the twentieth century. To gain a sense of what occurred, we carried out searches of seven major newspaper in the *ProQuest Historical Newspapers* database to identify instances in which a shareholder of a public company solicited proxies from fellow shareholders to try to obtain directorships or otherwise influence corporate policymaking.

On the basis of our searches, we compiled a dataset of 286 proxy fights arising from 1900 through 1949 (Armour and Cheffins 2009b, 5). Not all activism is created equal (Cheffins 2008, 392). Activism can be termed "defensive" when a shareholder who, after acquiring a stake in a company, relies on shareholder rights to take rearguard corrective action. An example in a modern context is where a pension fund owning shares in a public company becomes dissatisfied with a particular aspect of the company's corporate governance and seeks to correct matters by putting a resolution before the shareholders advocating change. In contrast, "offensive" shareholder activism is characterized by an investor lacking a meaningful stake in a company building one up with the intention to agitate for changes to correct failures by management to maximize shareholder returns. This is the brand of shareholder activism engaged in by hedge funds that captured headlines in the mid-2000s.

On the basis of our assessment of the nature of the shareholder activism involved with proxy challenges in our dataset, 61 out of 286 instances (21 percent) qualified as "offensive," an average of 1.22 incidents per year. As with proxy contests more generally, instances of offensive shareholder activism were considerably more common in the 1930s and 1940s than in the opening decades of the twentieth century (figure 12.1). Offensive activism was particularly conspicuous by its absence in the 1920s, with only a tiny number of challenges being launched despite the aggregate number of stocks traded on the

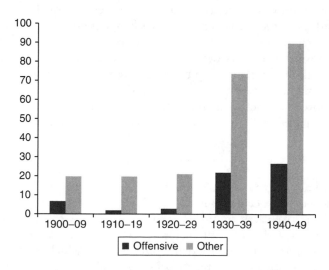

Figure 12.1   "Offensive" activism incidents, 1900–1949

New York Stock Exchange, New York's Curb exchange, and regional stock exchanges increasing from 682 in 1900 to 970 in 1915 and to 2,659 in 1930 (O'Sullivan 2007, 523).

In 37 of the 61 instances of offensive shareholder activism in our dataset, an individual acting in a personal capacity took the lead. On seven occasions the lead activist was a nonfinancial corporation. With the remaining 17 instances of offensive shareholder activism, the main protagonist fell into the "financial" category, which we deemed to encompass stockbrokers, investment banks, and institutional investors, including investment companies, the antecedents to today's mutual funds.

In only seven of the 17 instances in which the lead activist was "financial" did a collective investment vehicle resembling in any way today's hedge fund activists take the lead. On the first two occasions, both occurring in 1930, Otis & Co., an investment bank dominated by financier Cyrus Eaton and sponsor of Continental Shares, a major investment company, led the charge, with the targets being Gulf States Steel and Youngstown Sheet and Tube. Otis and Eaton were forced to walk away from Continental Shares in 1931 as Eaton's financial empire was sideswiped by the Depression (Gleisser 1965, 39). Next, Atlas Utilities, an investment company, used a recently acquired ownership stake and a proxy fight to secure in 1932 representation on the board of a rival investment company, Reliance International Corp (*New York Times*, March 31, 1932, 31).

In 1936 Phoenix Securities Corporation, an investment company that had as its investment philosophy in the mid-1930s "to buy up 'sizeable blocks' of stock of 'poorly managed' corporations and companies in 'fertile' industries" (*New York Times*, November 19, 1936, 39), launched two proxy contests that received press coverage. One involved an unsuccessful attempt to secure board seats at Standard Investing Corporation, another investment company, and the other was a successful attempt to secure board representation at Loft Inc., a candy manufacturer (*New York Times*, November 19, 1936, 39; *Wall Street Journal*, March 12, 1936, 11). Finally, Graham-Newman Corporation, an investment trust confounded by famed "value investor" Benjamin Graham that focused on "special situations" involving smaller companies that were cheap on the numbers, participated in an unsuccessful 1947 campaign to obtain board seats of Bell Aircraft and in 1948 solicited proxies from shareholders of New Amsterdam Casualty Co. to gain backing for a resolution proclaiming the company's dividend payouts were too small (*Wall Street Journal*, April 12, 1948, 12; Schloss 1999, 1; Henriques 2000, 92–93). Otherwise, investment companies did not step forward in an "offensive" style to challenge management in any other proxy contests that generated press attention.

Our dataset does underestimate to some degree offensive shareholder activism occurring in U.S. public companies during the first half of the twentieth century. We know from aggregate data in Securities and Exchange Commission (SEC) annual reports covering from 1943 to 1949 that our dataset does not encompass all instances in which a dissident shareholder in a public company solicited proxies from fellow shareholders (Armour and Cheffins 2009b, 6). Moreover, offensive shareholder activism does not necessarily result in a proxy battle. An example of this scenario involved Cyrus Eaton and utilities magnate Samuel Insull (McDonald 1962, 279; Wasik 2006, 166). Eaton, having founded Continental Shares in 1926 as a medium through which to invest in shares, "[s]wiftly, silently, shark-like . . . began acquiring enormous holdings" (McDonald 1962, 279). In 1927 and 1928 Eaton targeted Insull's utilities empire, quietly buying large blocs of shares in key firms in the complicated corporate pyramid Insull had created. Eaton's exploits do not form part of our dataset because he refrained from launching a proxy battle and indeed shied away from making any overt effort to challenge Insull, saying publicly he believed Insull was a top-flight utility operator. Nevertheless, Eaton worried Insull sufficiently for Insull to set up his own investment trusts, Insull Utility Investments and Corporation Securities, to buy up enough shares to reestablish firm voting control. In 1930, Insull's investment trusts engaged in what became known in the 1980s as "greenmail," buying up all of Eaton's holdings in the Insull companies, which had a stock market value of $50 million, for $56 million.

While there no doubt were instances of offensive shareholder activism during the first half of the twentieth century our proxy contest dataset does not capture, we anticipate that we have not missed much of the story. In order to obtain relevant background information on the strategies of activists, we ran further ProQuest newspaper searches on the names of those investors who led the proxy battles identified in our dataset. At least for those shareholder activists who were "repeat players," these searches should have identified noteworthy instances of activism that did not involve proxy contests and thus were not in our dataset. This indeed was how we initially encountered reports of Cyrus Eaton's successful "greenmailing" of Samuel Insull. Overall, however, our background research on shareholders who initiated proxy contests uncovered very few instances of offensive shareholder activism unaccompanied by a proxy battle.

There no doubt were practitioners of offensive shareholder activism who managed to avoid becoming sufficiently entangled in publicized proxy battles to appear in our dataset, meaning that the foregoing search strategy would have yielded nothing on them. As a cross-check against this possibility, we identified from the secondary literature major stock market "operators" of the opening half of the twentieth century who were not already included in our dataset and carried out searches of the *ProQuest Historical Newspapers* database and the relevant secondary literature to track down potential instances of shareholder activism otherwise unaccounted for.[1] This methodology failed to uncover additional noteworthy instances of offensive shareholder activism, save for two proxy contests not in our original ProQuest proxy contest dataset and a handful of 1920s interventions by the seven Fisher brothers, usually thought of as a unit, who collectively possessed a fortune of over $200 million after selling the Fisher Body Corporation to General Motors (Thomas 1967, 124).

Before buying into a corporation the Fisher brothers customarily made an elaborate study of it to ensure it met their investment criteria (Patterson 1965, 38). After deciding to proceed, the Fisher brothers would often buy up a sufficiently sizeable minority stake for them to feel justified in asking for representation on the board. Using this approach, the Fisher brothers secured board representation at Texas Corporation, an oil company; Mexican Seaboard, another oil company; the New York Central railway company; and Postal Telegraph and Cable Company, the chief subsidiary of International Telephone and Telegraph (Sparling, 1930, 168). Since the Fisher brothers do not appear in our proxy contest dataset they apparently were able to secure board seats by negotiation rather than having to resort to a proxy contest. Nevertheless, the Fisher brothers caused "consternation in several quarters" with their forays outside the automobile industry (Sparling 1930, 171). The Fisher brothers thus were offensive shareholder activists despite not being in our dataset. We anticipate, however, that they had few peers.

WHY WAS INSTITUTIONAL INVESTOR LED OFFENSIVE SHAREHOLDER ACTIVISM A RARITY?

Hedge funds, currently the dominant practitioners of offensive shareholder activism, commenced 20 of the 46 contested proxy solicitations occurring in U.S. public companies in 2007 and 31 of 56 for 2008 (Georgeson Shareholders 2008, 48; 2009, 46; Armour and Cheffins 2009, 22). In contrast, we found only seven instances throughout the

entire first half of the twentieth century in which a collective investment vehicle engaged in offensive shareholder activism that resulted
in a proxy contest.

The discrepancy is particularly striking because regulatory obstacles to activism were less potent than they are currently. For instance,
while Securities Exchange Commission rules that impose detailed fil-
ing requirements on an activist shareholder seeking to obtain support
from neutral shareholders by soliciting proxies currently constitute
a potential deterrent to activism, there were no rules at all prior to
1935 and regulation was rudimentary before the mid-1950s (Armour
and Cheffins 2009b, 29). Similarly, the Investment Company Act of
1940 (54 Stat. 789) and the Investment Advisers Act of 1940 (54
Stat. 847), which introduced a package of safeguards to protect U.S.
investors from misleading and dishonest practices allegedly engaged
in by investment companies in the run up to the 1929 Wall Street
crash and are often credited with discouraging regulated investment
companies—known as mutual funds—from engaging in activist investing (Gilson and Kraakman 1993, 985; Roe 1994, 102), were only in
force for the final decade of the opening half of the twentieth century.

Why, then, was institutionally led offensive shareholder activism a
rarity as compared with the present day? The discrepancy was due in
part to there being a greater number of public companies now than
there were during the first half of the twentieth century. However,
given that there were over 2,600 publicly traded companies by 1930 as
compared with 4,600 companies being listed on the New York Stock
Exchange and NASDAQ as of the end of 2007 (Armour et al. 2009,
687), there must be more to the story.

The most obvious circumstance in which offensive shareholder
activism will make sense is where a potential activist ascertains that a
company is "underperforming" and that it will be feasible to prompt
changes in financial policy or strategic direction likely to increase
shareholder returns. For those inclined to proceed in this manner,
the first step will be finding potential targets, and search costs help to
explain the dearth of collective investment vehicles engaging in hedge
fund – style activism during the first half of the twentieth century. It is
currently possible for anyone with a computer terminal and a subscription to mainstream data providers to gain instant access to detailed
financial data and substantial background information on thousands
of publicly traded companies. Matters were very different during the
first half of the twentieth century, as investors could only rely on basic
price information provided promptly through stock tickers and on
more detailed sources where a time lag was inevitable, such as official
reports of corporations, financial manuals, advisory and forecasting

services, brokerage house advice, and the general and financial press (Twentieth Century Fund 1934, 127).

Similarly, while investors nowadays can typically assume publicly available information is credible and reliable since disclosure is governed by detailed legal rules, there was no such guarantee during much of the period covered by our dataset. Instead, federal regulation of disclosure by public companies was only introduced by the Securities and Exchange Act of 1934 (48 Stat. 881). On the other hand, since 12 of the 22 instances of offensive shareholder activism in our dataset that occurred during the 1930s were initiated before the S.E.C. disclosure regime kicked into operation in 1935, it is unclear whether S.E.C. regulation caused the search costs associated with offensive shareholder activism to drop markedly.

Once a potential target has been found, a potential shareholder activist has to determine whether stepping forward is likely to do any good. Feasibility of change will hinge partly on legal arrangements. Shareholder rights are of particular significance, meaning in this context legal rules governing the scope shareholders have to determine the composition of the board, to exercise a veto over board initiatives, to counteract the advantages management has in securing shareholder support through the solicitation of proxies, and to gain standing to bring a suit challenging alleged managerial wrongdoing. Corporate law, which is enacted at the state level in the United States, has traditionally constituted the prime determinant of shareholder rights along this dimension, and activism should be easier to execute if shareholders acting collectively have substantial legal scope to arm-twist and ultimately replace incumbent directors. To the extent this is correct, the general trend over time during the first half of the twentieth century should have been for U.S. corporate law to discourage offensive shareholder activism.

In the nineteenth century in many respects state corporate legislation was restrictive, in the sense that those with managerial authority lacked *carte blanche* to pursue policies they favored. For instance, corporations typically could not repurchase their own equity, could not own shares in other corporations, and could not issue equity without offering it to existing shareholders on a pro rata basis. Over time, state legislatures, envious of financial advantages gained by states with liberal corporation statutes—most prominently New Jersey and then Delaware—abolished these restrictions (Levy, 1950, 154; Buxbaum and Hopt 1988, 119). Furthermore, shareholder approval requirements associated with amendments to the corporate constitution and with mergers between corporations were made markedly less strict. By 1910 competition between the states was lively and effective, with the result being that corporate statutes became increasingly lenient regarding the management of business corporations. A critic of the trend observed in 1937 that states following Delaware's lead had "created a system which not only is adapted to cope with the rapidly changing conditions of the business environment but also in consequence thereof, is liable to great abuses. The individual shareholder now has a 'pig-in-a-poke'. His old vested rights are now gone or going" (Rutledge 1937, 305). This implies that those inclined to engage in offensive shareholder activism could not count on corporate law to provide them with substantial leverage as they agitated for change.

As with shareholder rights (or the lack thereof) under corporate law, the ownership pattern in U.S. public companies likely discouraged offensive shareholder activism during the first half of the twentieth century. Dispersed stock ownership is typically a precondition for offensive shareholder activism, due to the fact those agitating for change are unlikely to be able to make credible proposals when a company has a shareholder who controls a sufficiently large block of votes to veto unwelcome shareholder resolutions. Adolf Berle and Gardiner Means famously declared in their 1932 classic, *The Modern Corporation and Private Property*, that a separation of ownership and control was a hallmark of large U.S. corporations (Berle and Means 1932), which implies there should have been a wide range of potential targets. However, the fragmentary evidence available implies diffuse share ownership remained the exception to the rule throughout the first half of the twentieth century.

Data compiled by Edward Herman on share ownership in 40 of the largest U.S. corporations as of 1900 suggest that at the turn of the twentieth century "management control," implying full-scale dispersion of share ownership, was largely unknown in even the biggest industrial companies and existed in only a minority of leading railway companies and utilities (Herman 1981, 67). In *The Modern Corporation and Private Property*, Berle and Means maintained their findings concerning the 200 largest U.S. nonfinancial companies demonstrated "there are no dominant owners, and control is maintained in large measure apart from ownership" (Berle and Means 1932, 110). However, a majority of the companies dealt with in Berle and Means' study (112 out of 200) fell outside their "management controlled" category and only 21 of those that qualified did so on the basis they met Berle and Means' primary test of management control, namely, lacking a shareholder having an ownership stake of 20 percent or more (Berle and Means 1932, 90). The Temporary National Economic Committee (TNEC), which also focused on the 200 largest U.S. nonfinancial corporations in a 1940 study of ownership patterns, indicated similarly fully diffuse share ownership was the exception to the rule. Less than one-third of the 200 companies lacked a "center of control," which the TNEC deemed to exist either where there was a sizeable concentration of equity (i.e., 10 percent or more of the shares) in the hands of one or more identified dominant groups or where the dominant group lacked a substantial minority stake but had managerial representation and remaining shareholdings were highly dispersed (Goldsmith 1940, 103).

Comparing Herman's evidence with Berle and Means' and the TNEC's, there likely was a trend in favor of diffuse ownership during the opening decades of the twentieth century. This may help to explain the greater prevalence of offensive shareholder activism in the 1930s and 1940s as compared with previous decades. However, given that larger firms are more likely to have dispersed share ownership than their smaller counterparts (Demsetz and Lehn 1985, 1155), even during these decades it likely was the case that among the full range of public companies only a small minority would have lacked a major blockholder and thus would have been an obvious target for an offensive shareholder activist.

Even once an investor minded to engage in offensive shareholder activism has found a suitable target, there are additional obstacles. One is that transaction costs will need to be incurred buying up shares and then likely incurred subsequently when the stake is sold. Over the past 40 years share dealing costs have dropped markedly due to deregulation and technological advances, thus creating greater scope for profitable shareholder activism (Armour and Cheffins, 2009, 14). Matters were much different during the first half of the twentieth century.

Until the 1970s, members of the New York Stock Exchange adhered to a comprehensive scheme of fixed minimum broker commissions that meant broker fees were generally much higher than they were after deregulation (Stout 1995, 611). In addition, there was a federal stock transfer tax in place from 1898 to 1902 and from 1914 to 1965, with the base rate being increased from 2 cents per share on no par value stock to 4 cents in 1932 and again to 5 cents in 1940 (Stout 1995, 635; Shultz 1946, 224). New York State introduced a similar tax in 1905, which initially generated sufficient revenue to pay for a quarter of the expenses of the state, and the tax rate was increased in 1933 from 2 cents per share to 3 cents per share for stock selling below $20 per share and 4 cents per share for stock selling at more than $20 (Shultz 1946, 224). Correspondingly, during the first half of the twentieth century, an investor minded to rely on the stock market to accumulate a sizeable stake in a target company had to be prepared to incur nontrivial transaction costs.

Financing constraints can act as a further obstacle to offensive shareholder activism because potential activists adept at finding suitable targets may well lack the spare capital needed to buy up sufficiently sizeable stakes to obtain genuine voting clout and to generate meaningful profits in the event of a successful intervention. One way a shareholder activist can address this obstacle is by raising capital from investors willing to back an investment fund with a suitable mandate. Today's activist hedge funds in effect rely on this approach. As the twentieth century opened, however, there was a dearth of equivalent institutional options.

Investment companies, often referred to as investment trusts, were in the United States the earliest form of investment vehicle established purely for the purpose of collective investment in numerous securities (Fowler 1928, 1). Correspondingly, they would have been the obvious institutional medium through which offensive shareholder activism could have been attempted. However, while the oldest U.S.-based investment company can be traced back to 1889, only four had been established by 1907 (Fowler 1928, 4). Matters had changed by the late 1920s. From 1927 through 1929 the number of investment companies operating grew from 120 to 279, and assets under management mushroomed from $1.8 billion to $6.3 billion, only to fall in tandem with the stock market crash to $2.5 billion by 1932 (S.E.C. 1939, 39). Still, investment companies were typically unlikely candidates to engage in shareholder activism. Like modern mutual funds, most of the investment companies of the 1920s pursued a diversified investment strategy (Fowler 1928, 20; S.E.C. 1939, 39). This was a pattern ill-suited for offensive shareholder activism because a diversification policy precludes "betting" the sizeable amounts of capital on potential targets required for offensive shareholder activism to make sense.

A potential exception was a cohort of investment companies known as "finance companies," (Livermore 1930, 432) or to use the label developed by the Securities and Exchange Commission in an exhaustive study of the investment company industry in the late 1930s, "management investment-holding companies" (S.E.C. 1938). This sort of investment vehicle "concentrated its investments to an extent sufficient to permit it to exercise control or influence over the management of its portfolio companies" (S.E.C. 1938, 29), but not so much as to constitute voting control of the shares. Finance companies thus were concentrating their investments sufficiently to open the way for buying up appropriately sizeable stakes in individual public companies to engage in offensive shareholder activism. On the other hand, as investment companies grew to prominence in the late 1920s there was little or no incentive for finance companies to market themselves as "activist." The enthusiasm for investment companies was so robust that those promoting them could attract plentiful capital almost regardless of the specifics of the investment strategy. There correspondingly was little need to market a finance company on the basis that management would add value by searching out underperforming companies, taking large stakes, and agitating for change.

If before the 1929 stock market crash investment companies lacked incentives to market themselves as activist investors, during the 1930s their power to act in the necessary fashion was greatly reduced. The industry was dominated at that point by "closed-end" funds that relied on leverage, created primarily by issuing bonds and preferred stock to purchase a portfolio of common shares, to magnify returns for investors during the stock market boom of the 1920s (Fink 2008, 10). The leverage that magnified returns in the 1920s had the opposite effect in the 1930s, compounding the losses end investors suffered.[2] Because the investors in closed-end funds could not compel redemption, there typically was no option but to sit and watch as values plummeted. This shattered investor confidence in closed-end funds, meaning that while they traded at significant premiums over underlying asset values in the 1920s, during the 1930s they traded at a substantial discount (Fink 2008, 15).

While the outsized losses suffered by closed-end funds did much to discredit the investment company sector, "open-ended" diversified mutual funds, where the fund was open to redemption on demand by investors, typically were able to at least match stock market trends in the wake of the Wall Street crash and thus performed well in comparison (Fink 2008, 17). Correspondingly from the mid-1930s onward almost all investment companies launched were of the mutual fund, open-ended form.[3] The open-ended form is not conducive to offensive shareholder activism because potentially illiquid investments such as influential blocks of shares pose considerable problems if investors demand their money back in times of poor performance and thereby impose a "liquidity squeeze" on the fund. Correspondingly, market trends associated with the Wall Street crash of 1929 were one of a series of deterrents to offensive shareholder activism by collective investment vehicles.

OFFENSIVE SHAREHOLDER ACTIVISM AND PRIVATE BENEFITS

The list of obstacles to offensive shareholder activism just catalogued is not an exhaustive one. Another constraint is that an investor engaging in shareholder activism will not capture all of the benefits generated

from orchestrating change. More specifically, while successfully exe-
cuted offensive shareholder activism might well generate benefits for
all shareholders, those who initiate matters will only receive a fraction
of any upside because they will own only a fraction of the target company's shares. An exception, however, is where activist shareholders
can secure private benefits from interventions they undertake, which,
by definition, do not need to be shared with other target company
shareholders (Rock 1994, 1002).

A scenario in which an activist shareholder can quite readily generate private benefits through intervention is where the shareholder
is a dominant player in a business enterprise operating in the same or
a related industry as the potential target. The interconnection creates
the opportunity for the activist shareholder to orchestrate dealings
designed to divert benefits from the target company in favor of the
activist's other business ventures. More benignly, synergies may be
achieved by an affiliation between the target and the activist's existing business operations. The existence of such synergies will mean the
activist's efforts should generate benefits for all shareholders in the target company, not just the activist, but there will still be a private benefit aspect because the firm with which the activist is closely associated
will reap benefits in which stockholders of the target will not share.

J. Paul Getty's prolonged 1930s activism campaign against
Tidewater Associated Oil Company, a firm specializing in oil refining and distribution, illustrates how anticipated synergies could act as
a catalyst for offensive shareholder activism (Hewins 1961, 101–2).
At the beginning of the 1930s the Getty business empire focused
on California-based oil production and Getty wished to invest in
an established oil refining company that badly needed crude oil and
had shares selling at a bargain price. Tidewater fitted the bill. Getty
thought Tidewater and the Getty companies would both benefit from
an alliance. As Getty said "(Tidewater) would gain friendship and
the support of two large independent producers; economies would
be effected; and the Getty interests would benefit from a community
of interest with a large refining and marketing organization" (Hewins
1961, 102).

Getty's Tidewater intervention was by no means an isolated incident. Instead, there often was an interconnection aspect with instances
of offensive shareholder activism during the first half of the twentieth
century. For instance, in 1921, Malcolm Chace, who was a dominant player in hydroelectricity and textiles in the northeast United
States, built up a sufficiently large stake in International Paper Co. to
secure election to the board in 1922, with a key consideration being
that International Paper owned many valuable water power sites (*Wall*

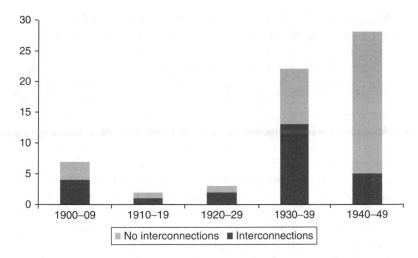

Figure 12.2 Interconnection and offensive shareholder activism, 1900–1949

Street Journal, April 28, 1922; *New York Times*, July 17, 1955). Likewise, in 1934 Fredrick Prince built up a sizeable stake in meatpacker Armour & Co. and then relied on proxies to achieve board control, with a primary motive apparently being to secure influence over a key customer of the Chicago Union stockyards, which Prince controlled (*Chicago Daily Tribune*, December 14, 1933, 25; *New York Times*, February 3, 1953, 25). Overall, the 1940s aside, in a slight majority of proxy contests in our dataset that involved offensive shareholder activism there was a substantial overlap or connection between the business activities of the target company and the business interests of the activist shareholder (figure 12.2).

OFFENSIVE SHAREHOLDER ACTIVISM AND TAKEOVERS

Practitioners of offensive shareholder activism can adopt various tactics to secure desired changes, ranging from quiet persuasion to public confrontation. A particularly forceful strategy is the one Fredrick Prince adopted with Armour & Co., this being obtaining decisive influence over corporate policymaking by winning control of the board in a proxy contest. Achieving boardroom dominance by seeking the backing of unaffiliated stockholders implies an activist's stake was insufficiently large on its own to give the activist the license to pass desired shareholder resolutions. Gilson and Schwartz provide an apt label for this method of securing control of corporate policymaking, this being a "transfer by vote" (Gilson and Schwartz 2001, 783).

An insurgent shareholder seeking board control can foreclose the need to lobby neutral shareholders to obtain proxies by adopting a more forthright technique for obtaining corporate control, this being carrying out a takeover transaction designed to result in the acquisition of a majority of voting shares. Applying Gilson and Schwartz's terminology, there will be a "transfer by sale" rather than a "transfer by vote" (Gilson and Schwartz 2001, 790). At first glance, it might seem takeover bids would crowd out offensive shareholder activism completely as a corporate governance technique. One consideration is that a successful offensive shareholder activist must, even with full-scale board control, split gains generated thereby with other shareholders due to owning only a minority stake.[4] In contrast, a party who launches a successful takeover bid and then buys out all remaining shareholders will be able to secure all post-acquisition gains from improvements in shareholder return (Macey 2007, 767).

Takeover bids also might be expected to crowd out offensive shareholder activism because of simplicity. In the case of a cash-based takeover bid, shareholders can simply take what is on offer, exit the company, and not worry about what the bidder does after obtaining control. In contrast, when an insurgent shareholder uses a proxy contest to try to gain access to the board or execute a full-scale transfer by vote, a complicating feature will be signaling credibly to shareholders that they will be better off under a new regime (Sridharan and Reinganum 1995, 57; Bebchuk and Hart 2001, 2). If shareholders cannot observe directly the managerial attributes of shareholder insurgents but anticipate—quite sensibly—that the average quality of potential rivals is worse than incumbents, the rational strategy will be to opt for the status quo. Shareholders will also justifiably be skeptical of claims insurgents make of superior managerial capabilities if the alleged shortcomings of the incumbents are not readily observable by way of publicly available accounting and market return information (e.g., because the alleged underperformance is a product of sins of omission in the form of overlooked new and profitable investment opportunities).

Takeovers, however, suffer from difficulties of their own. One is that, due to the fact those executing a takeover must be prepared to buy most, if not all, of the target company's shares rather than a mere minority stake, the financial outlay will be greater (Pound 1988, 1021; Bebchuk and Hart 2001, 16). Also, successful bidders end up, in investment terms, with many eggs in one basket. Activist investors sacrifice at least some of the benefits of risk spreading by building up sizeable stakes in the companies they target but successful bidders face the same difficulty in magnified form because they end up owning most, if not all, of the shares in the companies they acquire.

Though takeovers can sideline offensive shareholder activism the displacement effect will only be substantial if takeovers launched in anticipation of gains to be generated from replacing incumbent managers occur with some frequency. The received wisdom is that the "hostile" takeover bid was essentially unknown in the United States until the mid-1950s and did not become a mainstream transaction until the 1960s (Hayes and Taussig 1967, 136; Henriques 2000, 245), which implies that there would have been at best a minimal substitution effect during the first half of the twentieth century. In fact, a dataset of takeover incidents we have compiled suggests uninvited bids to secure voting control occurred with sufficient frequency to have a potential impact on offensive shareholder activism.

It is true that the tender offer, which involves a public solicitation of tenders of shares held by current stockholders and was the tactic frequently relied upon by corporate raiders from the 1960s onward, was virtually unknown during the first half of the twentieth century (Fleischer and Mundheim 1967, 317).[5] On the other hand, those minded to execute what Gilson and Schwartz term a "transfer by sale" could potentially do so without prior consent of management by engaging in a practice that became known as "sweeping the street," namely, buying a large number of shares quickly on the open market (Lipton 1987, 17). To get a sense of how often voting control was obtained in this manner, we carried out searches on the *ProQuest Historical Newspaper* database designed to track down instances occurring between 1900 and 1950 in which a party, acting without explicit consent from a target company's board, attempted to rely on the stock market to buy enough shares to obtain majority control (Armour and Cheffins 2009b, 70). We excluded from consideration mere rumors, instances in which privately negotiated purchases of shares were unsupported by significant open market operations, and cases in which the acquisition of shares was "friendly," in the sense the board of the target company endorsed a change of voting control. This left us with 82 separate instances between 1900 and 1950 in which a party sought to execute without explicit approval from those running a target company a transfer by sale by way of open market purchases of shares on the stock exchange, sometimes in tandem with private purchases negotiated with stockholders known to own a significant stake.

A decade-by-decade break down of our results reveals considerable variation (figure 12.3). Given that takeovers can sideline offensive

Figure 12.3 Bids for control using open market purchases of shares/offensive shareholder activism, 1900–1949

shareholder activism, one would anticipate that open market bids would be common during decades when activism was rare and that investors minded to build up sizeable stakes in target companies would opt for proxy contests when takeover bids were in abeyance. The data fit this pattern well, with the exception of the 1910s, when both offensive shareholder activism and takeover bids were rare. The market for corporate control thus apparently impinged to a significant degree on offensive shareholder activism during the first half of the twentieth century.

Why, though, did the number of bids for control using open market purchases vary substantially over time? General merger trends constitute an important piece of the puzzle. As figure 12.4 indicates, calculated on a decade-by-decade basis, bids of this sort were more common when there was substantial merger activity (the 1920s) and less common when there was not (the 1910s, 1930s, and 1940s).

The 1900s stand out as the one decade in which M&A activity fails to account to any significant degree for trends concerning bids for control using open market purchases of shares. Open market bids were considerably more prevalent during this decade than they were in any other decade, including the 1920s, when general M&A activity was at its height. The discrepancy can be attributed in large measure to railways. During the 1900s railroad companies constituted the target in a majority of open market bids but were of considerably less importance throughout the remainder of the first half of the twentieth century, including the merger-heavy 1920s (figure 12.5).

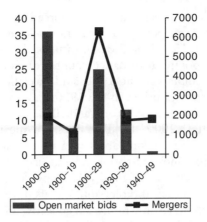

Figure 12.4 Bids for control using open market purchases of shares/merger activity, 1900–1949

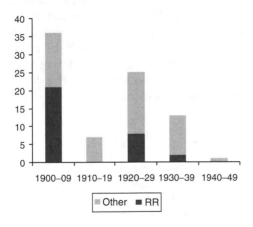

Figure 12.5 Targets of bids for control using open market purchases of shares, railroads, and other companies, 1900–1949

CONCLUSION

It is widely assumed that with respect to corporate governance historically "market control over the allocation of U.S. corporate resources stands out as a recent phenomenon" (O'Sullivan 2000, 70). Under this view, it was not until the 1980s that an "expansion and empowerment of the shareholder class" shifted "interest group power from managers to shareholders" (Hansmann and Kraakman 2001, 439). It was at this point, according to the received wisdom, that the norm of shareholder primacy achieved preeminence, fostered initially by the rise of the hostile takeover bid and reinforced in the 1990s by the growing influence and power of institutional investors (Deakin and Konzelmann 2006, 155). The rise of institutional investors, combined with a strong corporate governance counterreaction to the building of conglomerate empires in the 1960s and revelations of widespread corporate kickbacks and bribes in the 1970s, no doubt reshaped relations between executives, directors, and shareholders of U.S. public companies (Cheffins 2009, 1). This does not mean, however, that those running U.S. public companies in earlier eras were entirely insulated from investors inclined to take aim at firms with the intention of orchestrating changes designed to improve returns. The activist hedge funds of today lacked direct antecedents during the first half of the twentieth century, as only rarely did collective investment vehicles initiate activism campaigns. Nevertheless, our research into shareholder activism during this period has uncovered numerous instances in which investors targeted public companies and built up a sizeable stake with the intention of either launching a proxy contest or seeking to obtain outright voting control. Underperforming public companies no doubt have faced in recent times investor-driven discipline that is more robust than would have been the case during the period we have focused on. However, our research indicates the difference may have been one of degree rather than kind.

NOTES

1. The "operators" we investigated were Bernard Baruch, Arthur Cutten, the Fisher brothers, the Guggenheim family, Jesse Livermore, Michael Meehan, and John Raskob.
2. By 1937, the average dollar invested in leveraged investment company stocks in 1929 was worth 5 cents, whereas the non-leveraged dollar was worth 48 cents (Fink 2008, 17).
3. Investors briefly flirted with fixed trusts, which typically offered portfolios that did not change, but became more favorably disposed to "managed" funds after the stock market began to recover in 1932 (Fink 2008, 17). The proportion of total mutual fund assets under management in closed-ended funds was 95.4 percent in 1929, 57.5 percent in 1940, 25.8 percent in 1950, 10.9 percent in 1960, 7.8 percent in 1970, and 5.5 percent in 1980 (Baumol et al. 1990, 28).
4. According to a study of a sample of 100 proxy contests occurring between 1981 and 1984 in which around 60 were for control the dissidents owned 12 percent of the outstanding shares (Pound 1988, 237).
5. The rarity of tender offers is illustrated by a search of the *ProQuest Historical Newspapers* database focusing on the same seven newspapers as

we used for proxy contests. If "tender offer" is used as the search term and the dates are set to cover from the first half of the twentieth century there are only 43 "hits" and only one of these involves a contest for corporate control. See "First York Corp. Plans to Buy Large Block of Bell Aircraft Stock," *Wall Street Journal*, January 23, 1948, 14. Carrying out the same search for the 1960s yields 6,363 "hits" and for the 1980s yields 20,015.

REFERENCES

" 'Buying-Up' Policy of Trust Revealed," *New York Times*, November 19, 1936, 39.

"Casulty Firm Holder Seeks Proxies on Dividend Policy," *Wall Street Journal*, April 12, 1948, 12.

"Charles Guth Soliciting Proxies for Loft Meeting," *Wall Street Journal*, March 12, 1936, 11.

"Fredrick Prince, Financier, Is Dead," *New York Times*, February 3, 1953, 25.

"Inter'l Paper Election Considered Significant," *Wall Street Journal*, April 28, 1922, 2.

"Malcolm Chace, Financier, Dies," *New York Times*, July 17, 1955, 61.

"Norton Simons Businessman and Collector, Dies at 86," New York Times June 4, 1993, A22.

"Odlum is Elected to Reliance Boards," *New York Times*, March 31, 1932, 31.

"Prince Seeking Greater Power in Armour Co.," *Chicago Daily Tribune*, December 14, 1933, 25.

"Two Groups Fight for Trust Control," *New York Times*, March 3, 1936, 31.

Armour, John and Cheffins, Brian. "The Rise and Fall (?) of Shareholder Activism by Hedge Funds," *ECGI: Law Working Paper*, no. 136 (2009a): 6.

Armour, John and Cheffins, Brian. "Offensive Shareholder Activism in U.S. Public Companies, 1900–49" (unpublished working paper, 2009b): 5, 6.

Armour, John, Black, Bernard, Cheffins, Brian and Richard, Nolan. "Private Enforcement of Corporate Law: An Empirical Comparison of the UK and US," *Journal of Empirical Legal Studies* 6 (2009): 687, 706.

Baumol, William J., Goldfield, Steven M., Gordon, Lilli A. and Koehn, Michael F. *The Economics of Mutual Fund Markets: Competition Versus Regulation* (Boston: Kluwer Academic, 1990), 28.

Bebchuk, Lucian and Hart, Oliver. "Takeover Bids vs. Proxy Fights in Contests for Corporate Control," (2001) N.B.E.R. Working Paper 8633, 2, 15.

Berle, Adolf A. and Means, Gardiner C. *The Modern Corporation & Private Property* (New Brunswick, N.J., 1997, originally published in 1932).

Buxbaum, Richard M. and Hopt, Klaus J. *Legal Harmonization and the Business Enterprise: Corporate and Capital Market Law Harmonization Policy in Europe and the USA* (Berlin: Walter de Grutyer, 1988), 119–24.

Cheffins, Brian R. *Corporate Ownership and Control: British Business Transformed* (Oxford: Oxford University Press, 2008), 392.

Cheffins, Brian R. "Did Corporate Governance 'Fail' During the 2008 Stock Market Meltdown? The Case of the S&P 500," *Business Lawyer* 65 (2009): 1, 7–9.

Deakin, Simon and Konzelmann, Suzanne. "Corporate Governance after Enron: An Age of Enlightenment?" in John Armour and Joseph A. McCahery eds., *After Enron: Improving Corporate Law and Modernising Securities Regulation in Europe and the US* (Oxford: Hart Publishing, 2006), 155, 157.

Demsetz, Harold and Lehn, Kenneth. "The Structure of Corporate Ownership: Causes and Consequences," *Journal of Political Economy* 93 (1985): 1155, 1158.

Fink, Matthew P. *The Rise of Mutual Funds: An Insider's View* (Oxford: Oxford University Press, 2008), 10, 17.

Fleischer, Arthur and Mundheim, Robert H. "Corporate Acquisition by Tender Offer," *University of Pennsylvania Law Review* 115 (1967): 317, 335–336.

Fowler, John Francis. *American Investment Trusts* (New York: Harper & Brothers, 1928), 1–2, 20–21.

Fraser, Steve. *Wall Street: A Cultural History* (London: Faber and Faber, 2005), 431–32.

Georgeson. *2007 Annual Corporate Governance Review: Annual Meetings, Shareholder Initiatives, Proxy Contests* (2008), 48–49.

Georgeson. *2008 Annual Corporate Governance Review: Annual Meetings, Shareholder Initiatives, Proxy Contests* (2009), 46–47.

Gilson, Ronald J. and Kraakman, Reinier. "Investment Companies as Guardian Shareholders: The Place of the MSIC in the Corporate Governance Debate," *Stanford Law Review* 45 (1993): 985, 997–1003.

Gilson, Ronald J. and Schwartz, Alan. "Sales and Elections as Methods for Transferring Control," *Theoretical Inquiries in Law* 2 (2001): 783, 790.

Gleisser, Marcus. *The World of Cyrus Eaton* (South Brunswick, N.J.: A.S. Barnes, 1965), 39–40, 64–66.

Goldsmith, Raymond et al. *The Distribution of Ownership in the 200 Largest Nonfinancial Corporations*, T.N.E.C. Investigation of Concentration of Economic Power, Monograph No. 29 (Washington D.C., 1940), 103–105.

Hansmann, Henry and Kraakman, Reinier. "The End of History for Corporate Law," *Georgetown Law Journal* 89 (2001): 439, 453.

Hayes, Samuel L. and Taussig, Russell A. "Tactics of Cash Takeover Bids," *Harvard Business Review*, March-April (1967): 135, 136–137.

Henriques, Diana B. *The White Sharks of Wall Street: Thomas Mellon Evans and the Original Corporate Raiders* (New York: Scribner, 2000), 92–93.

Herman, Edward S. *Corporate Control, Corporate Power* (Cambridge, 1981), 67, Appendix B.

Hewins, Ralph. *J. Paul Getty: The Richest American* (London: Sidgwick and Jackson, 1961), 101–102.

Investment Advisers Act of 1940, 54 Stat. 847 (1940). Investment Company Act of 1940, 54 Stat. 789 (1940).

Levy, A.B. *Private Corporations and Their Control*, vol. 1 (London: Routledge & Kegan Paul, 1950).

Lipton, Martin. "Corporate Governance in the Age of Finance Corporatism," *University of Pennsylvania Law Review* 136, (1987): 1, 17.

Livermore, Shaw. "Investment Trusts in 1930," *Journal of Business* 3 (1930): 432, 434.

Macey, Jonathan R. "Too Many Notes and Not Enough Votes: Lucian Bebchuk and Emperor Joseph II Kvetch About Contested Director Elections and Mozart's *Seraglio*," *Virginia Law Review* 93 (2007): 759, 767.

Manne, Henry G. "Mergers and the Market for Corporate Control," *Journal of Political Economy* 73, (1965): 110.

McDonald, Forrest. *Insull* (Chicago: University of Chicago Press, 1962), 279–81, 287–291.

O'Sullivan, Mary. *Contests for Corporate Control: Corporate Governance and Economic Performance in the United States and Germany* (Oxford: Oxford University Press, 2000).

O'Sullivan, Mary. "The Expansion of the U.S. Stock Market: Historical Facts and Theoretical Fashions," *Enterprise & Society* 8 (2007): 523.

Pace, Eric. "Norton Simon, Businessman and Collector, Dies at 86," *New York Times*, June 4, 1993, A22.

Patterson, Robert T. *The Great Boom and Panic* (Chicago: Henry Regenry Co., 1965), 38.

Pound, John. "Proxy Voting and the Efficiency of Shareholder Oversight," *Journal of Financial Economics* 29 (1988): 237, 244.

Rock, Edward B. "Controlling the Dark Side of Relational Investing," *Cardozo Law Review* 15, (1994): 987, 1002–1003.

Roe, Mark J. *Strong Managers, Weak Owners: The Political Roots of American Corporate Finance* (Princeton, N.J.: Princeton University Press, 1994), 102–123.

Rutledge, Wiley B. "Significant Trends in Modern Corporation Statutes," *Washington University Law Quarterly* 22 (1937): 305, 337.

Schloss, Walter J. "Benjamin Graham and *Security Analysis*: A Reminiscence," in Janet C. Lowe ed., *The Rediscovered Benjamin Graham: Selected Writings of the Wall Street Legend* (New York: John Wiley & Sons, 1999), 1, 3.

Securities Exchange Act of 1934, 48 Stat. 881 (1934).

Securities and Exchange Commission (S.E.C.), *Report on the Study of Investment Trusts and Investment Companies, Part One: Origin, Scope and Conduct of the Study* (1938), 29.

Securities and Exchange Commission (S.E.C.), *Investment Trusts and Investment Companies: Report of the Securities and Exchange Commission, Part Two: Statistical Survey of Investment Trusts and Investment Companies* (1939), 39–52, 113–114.

S.E.C. *Annual Reports*, http://www.sec.gov/about/annrep.shtml (accessed April 10, 2009).

Shultz, Birl E. *The Securities Market and How It Works* (New York: Harper & Brothers, 1946).

Sparling, Earl. *The Mystery Men of Wall Street* (New York: Blue Ribbon Books, 1930), 168–170.

Stevens, Mark. *King Icahn: The Biography of a Renegade Capitalist* (New York: Dutton, 1993).

Stigler, George J. and Friedland, Claire. "The Literature of Economics: The Case of Berle and Means," *Journal of Law and Economics* 26, 237 (1983): 248.

Stout, Lynn A. "Are Stock Markets Costly Casinos? Disagreement, Market Failure and Securities Regulation," *Virginia Law Review* 81 (1995): 611, 634.

Sridharan, Uma V. and Reinganum, Marc R. "Determinants of the Choice of Hostile Takeover Mechanism: An Empirical Analysis of Tender Offers and Proxy Contests," *Financial Management* 24, no. 1 (1995): 57, 65.

Thomas, Dana L. *The Plungers and the Peacocks: 150 Years of Wall Street* (New York: Popular Library, 1967), 124.

Twentieth Century Fund, *Stock Market Control* (New York: D. Appleton & Co., 1934), 127–161.

Wasik, John F. *The Merchant of Power: Samuel Insull, Thomas Edison, and the Creation of the Modern Metropolis* (New York: Palgrave Macmillan, 2006), 166–169, 180–181, 189–190.

CHAPTER   13

CONTEMPORARY ISSUES IN
SHAREHOLDER ADVOCACY

Stephen Davis

By plumbing the earliest origins of shareowner advocacy in different
jurisdictions, authors in this book have laid groundwork for a new
branch of scholarship. We have seen similar births of fields. For instance, a fellowship of scholars in the history of economics began to
coalesce following a conference at the University of North Carolina at
Chapel Hill in 1974.[1] An academy focusing on the history of shareowner advocacy in capital markets may have begun at the November
2009 conference at the Yale School of Management where authors
first presented papers gathered for this volume. That would only be
fitting, as the event marked the four-hundredth anniversary of the first
recorded expression of investor advocacy. It is equally fitting that such
a field would emerge in a year noted for financial crisis. Findings drawn
from the research presented here not only explore underanalyzed
shareowner activism, they suggest lessons for scholars and practitioners seeking insights on how to reduce the risk of crises in the future.

Two dates mark the bookends of this volume: 2009 and 1609.
At the modern end, the financial crisis that engulfed world markets
in 2008 and 2009 put shareowners in a bind. They had lost great
fortunes in value, owing in part to portfolio companies with inatten-
tive corporate boards who were, in turn, enabled by lax regulators.
Some shareowners concluded that better corporate governance—
producing better managed risks and closer alignment of performance
with shareowner value—depends to a large degree on more vigilant
investors.[2] Yet the hard reality of budget pressures was, paradoxically,

forcing investment houses and research providers to slash, rather than build up, resources that enabled them to improve governance assessments.[3] The scene was being set for another round in one of the more dispiriting cycles of the capital market: investor impotence begetting management excess followed by financial losses for countless savers.

How do we break that pattern? Here is where a field of the history of shareowner advocacy can contribute. "Research into the institutional evolution of corporate governance is essential to understanding financial development," writes Andrew von Nordenflycht. "How *has* financial development occurred? How has entrenchment been overcome?" After all, chapters in this book demonstrate the sometimes eerie relevance of past experience. On January 24, 2009, media around the world featured headlines about corporate boards that had paid outsized bonuses to insiders, while leaving shareowners far worse off. Exactly 400 years earlier, on January 24, 1609, listen to a very familiar story. Consider "how badly the company's assets are being managed, and how every day needless and unnecessary expenses are being made, of great interest and to the detriment of shareholders," wrote Isaac Le Maire, the intrepid but controversial entrepreneur and investor, about the Dutch East India Company (VOC), the world's first publicly traded joint-stock company. Shareholders, he charged, were "less than happy with the authoritarian management and the use of the company's resources by the directors, who act as if they stand above even the Honourable Gentlemen Estates General, who do everything without consulting anyone, and who flout the company's charter by taking 2 per cent commission on all [outfittings], whereas they are allowed only 1 per cent, which they ought and should not do." Le Maire's initiative on that winter's day 400 years ago can now be recognized as the world's first recorded expression of shareowner advocacy at a publicly traded corporation.

Paul Frentrop, a scholar of financial history, while serving as the corporate governance chief at APG Investment Management, provided a fuller description of Le Maire's colorful struggles in a commemorative booklet.[4] For this research project, initiated by the Millstein Center for Corporate Governance and Performance at the Yale School of Management, he burrowed in the National Archives in The Hague, bringing to light Le Maire's original letter, which was known, as well as an accompanying memorandum, which had not been. Joost Jonker, professor at Utrecht University, labored to produce a translation of the Old Dutch Le Maire texts. Jonker then joined with Oscar Gelderblom and Abe de Jong in the chapter that sets out their interpretation of the 1609 clash.

Is there anything we can learn from the trove in the National Archives that can apply to twenty-first-century financial crises? For one, we can clearly appreciate, from this distance in time, how investors were then, as they are today, more likely to suffer loss if they were unable effectively to oversee how their assets were managed. One gains a vivid sense of such frustration in the Le Maire pleas.

Second, we can witness the powerful effects of shareowner activism—as well as the prospect of competition—on a corporate board bent on protecting its turf. In Le Maire's case, the impact was epochal. To gird its bid to secure monopoly control of a northern passage to China, a shipping route Le Maire wanted open to all traders—and especially his own company, the VOC hired the English explorer Henry Hudson to plant the company's flag in America. Through that step the VOC claimed what later became New York and, of course, its famous—or infamous—Wall Street.

Third, we can see how a government—in the 1609 context the United Provinces' Estates General—may be frequently drawn toward alignment with corporate executives over investors. This may happen because managers are more concentrated, better organized, more powerfully connected, and more richly resourced than shareowners. It is also the case that some companies grow so large as to virtually merge purpose with the state, or indeed may be founded explicitly to advance state interests. Gelderblom, de Jong, and Jonker argue that the VOC, while technically a private sector, joint-stock company, essentially served as an arm of the state: "An instrument for war and colonial conquest." The authors contend that this feature made the VOC *sui generis* and something of an evolutionary diversion in the history of public companies. But many governments since have found common cause between state interests and private enterprise. In the United States, Fannie Mae and Freddie Mac took on that character. So indeed did General Motors, AIG, and a legion of mega-banks all deemed by Washington so important that their failure in the financial crisis would wreck national havoc. Further study may posit that the VOC may simply have been an extreme case of such tacit alignment. But one feature appears common to cases in which government needs dominate: shareowners' interests get subsumed.

These initial lessons from Le Maire's saga demonstrate that study of the history of shareowner advocacy can serve more than academic curiosity. Looking back can help us better understand the origins of current structure and behavior as well as frame implicit challenges for the future. Indeed, scholars can now apply theories of corporate governance developed in our own time to past cases, casting a new light on developments. La Porta et al., for instance, found important relationships between regulation and finance.[5] These understandings can now be used to gain insights on how markets rose, fell, or stalled in earlier centuries. Fresh reflection can yield reevaluations of received wisdom. Le Maire, for instance, was long best known in the history of economics for being a pioneer of short selling. Applying a corporate governance lens gives us further insight. Yes, Le Maire—canny and indefatigable, but criticized for fraud and self-aggrandizement—developed investment techniques that bet on falling prices of VOC shares. But he appears to have done so in the context of a failure to achieve demands through what we might now term "engagement" with the company and the Estates General. Investors—both institutional and retail—can now better extract from the Le Maire story a modern question. Can they find means to avoid the trap they have hit time and again over four centuries and embed real, collective, sustainable ownership behavior into their investment approach at portfolio companies worldwide?

Lawmakers and regulators in the United States and the United Kingdom, interestingly, sought remedies to the 2008–2009 financial crisis by trying to break that ancient cycle and empowering owners. To see how, first step back to the Enron/Worldcom scandals at the dawn of the decade. Then, mandarins in the U.S. Congress concluded that fraud was the problem, and a conventional police-style response of fresh rules and regulations was the appropriate antidote. The Sarbanes-Oxley Act contained a raft of such measures topped by a requirement on the CEO to certify by signature that internal controls were functional, effective, and driving accurate reporting. Other jurisdictions imported similar, though often less restrictive, approaches. But the 2008–2009 financial crisis saw policy responses head in a different direction. To be sure, legislators focused on reshuffling systemic regulation and monitoring systemic risk. But steps designed specifically for corporations largely concentrated on reforms that promised vastly to increase the power of investors, more than market policemen, to serve as watchdogs.

In the United States, for instance, lawmakers led by Charles Schumer and Christopher Dodd in the Senate and Barney Frank in the House of Representatives framed statutes that would give shareholders and easier rights to nominate directors unsanctioned by a board. Other provisions were to grant annual advisory votes of confidence on pay policies.[6] And the Securities and Exchange Commission installed new disclosure requirements to allow investors more scrutiny of board leadership and executive remuneration structures.[7] In Britain, the Walker Review recommended, and the Financial Reporting Council drafted, a shareholder stewardship code designed to catalyze more investor engagement at corporate boards.[8] In Australia, the government's Productivity Commission introduced legislation that would hand investors unprecedented authority to sack whole boards that failed to respond to successive advisory votes against compensation policies.[9] In short, policymakers appeared eager to equip institutional investors with powers to serve as something of a "neighborhood watch" on corporate behavior and markets.

Investors, in turn, showed fresh interest in measures—not just those birthed by policymakers—that promised to amplify their voice in boardrooms. Tomorrow's Company, a London-based think tank, argued in a March 2010 report that "board-centric" governance typical of the United Kingdom should be replaced by "investor-centric" practices such as the Swedish model of investor nominations of corporate board members.[10] Recommendations drew immediate interest among investors, and helped fuel support for a CalPERS initiative to create a pool of shareholder-oriented board candidates, something already practiced in Italy by the Assogestioni, the professional investor body.

Through looking glasses provided by authors in this volume, we can now see that such impulses toward shareholder oversight are hardly new. William N. Goetzmann and Sebastien Pouget demonstrate that investors as long ago as the fourteenth century were devising intricate governance relationships, including a body of *conseillers* similar to a modern board of directors, to align their interests with those of enterprise managers. Determination to overcome what we now call the agency problem even sometimes brought shareholders to extremes. Randall Morck and Fan Yang show that in the early 1800s bank investors in China's Shanxi province installed contracts "permitting the enslavement of insiders' wives and children, and their relative's services as hostages," as a way to prevent managers from practicing fraud with shareholder capital. It worked, the authors report.

Nonetheless, a recurrent lesson is that investors, even when they enjoyed fulsome rights, have regularly found themselves outmaneuvered. This is particularly true for minority investors, or at companies grown "too large for individual stockholders to monitor yet too small for the securities markets to effectively discipline," as Robert Wright and Richard Sylla observe of the early United States. It is also especially true where the state is involved as a direct or indirect investor. One challenge therefore posed by the historical record is whether remedial measures to enhance effective shareholder oversight, whether contemplated by governments or by investors, have shared a common flaw of missing a key insight. Simply piling on rights will be meaningless if shareowners fail to exercise powers in an informed manner in the interests of beneficiaries. It may be that changing so insistent a tide requires still more ambitious reform involving a reengineering of key market structures.

Yale's Millstein Center sought to explore, in particular, whether changes in the architecture of investing institutions might be one route to effective ownership. The Center convened a roundtable in February 2009, in the thick of the financial crisis, and subsequently summarized participants recommendations.[11] Stewardship guidance offered by participants necessarily focused on collective investment vehicles that constitute the bulk of today's investment world. Advice included the following:

- *Funds should be held to as high a standard of accountability as they ask of portfolio companies.* In particular, funds should be required to disclose (a) their voting records, (b) fulsome voting and engagement corporate governance guidelines, (c) core values, and (d) their equity holdings. Such transparency may then provide opportunities for parties such as grassroots members and outside media to exercise informed scrutiny over fund behavior.
- *Trustee or oversight boards should be composed of members skilled in both fund issues and board dynamics.* Further, such fund boards should feature member representation with a clear structure of accountability—for instance, annual member votes for board members. Such bodies should also be free of conflicts of interest, and in cases of public sector funds, at arm's length from political control.
- *Trustees or fiduciaries should meet skill requirements and undertake trustee training, continuing education, and perhaps certification.* The Australian government set a model for such investor infrastructure when, in 2009, it allocated federal seed money to establish the Responsible Investor Academy.[12] The UK Pensions Act also requires standards of pension trustees; the Pensions Regulator even provides an interactive e-learning program.[13]
- *Fund trustees or fiduciaries should ensure that job descriptions for the chief investment officer and fund CEO include understanding and appreciation of environmental, social, and governance risks in investment portfolios.*
- *The private sector cannot on its own produce market-wide standards of transparency and accountability among funds.* National and state/provincial governments, where appropriate, may need to step in with legislation or regulation.
- *Fund scrutiny can be advanced by grassroots scheme members using social networking tools.* Nongovernmental social networking groups such as shareowners.org are attempting to advocate for citizen investors.[14] But the public sector may have ways to spur financial literacy. The U.S. Department of Labor, for instance, could require each plan it supervises to mount an interactive website enabling employees and retirees to review and comment on savings

arrangements. Web 2.0 now enables collective user-generated ratings of services from medical practices to restaurants. It would be possible to do the same with pension plans to spur a race to the top, and help regulators police. In some markets (e.g., the Netherlands) such ground-up scrutiny is subsidized by the public sector.

Some of these recommendations may find their way into policy and practice. But we may discover, as the field of the history of shareowner advocacy progresses, additional lessons buried in records to inform us on strategies that work or fail to strengthen ownership interests.

The 1609 affair—and other historical cases outlined here—also pose questions for governments around the globe. As Jonathan Koppell contends in the Chapter 1, the state is a special type of owner—with the sway to propel, retard, or destroy a corporation as minority investors cling on for the ride. Can governments draw a clear distinction between state and shareowner interests? Can they apply laws and regulations, both at home and across borders, that make for a truly level playing field rather than one tilted toward corporate managers? Can rules protect investors against fraud and abuse as well as against application of political influence? Conclusions from many of the studies in this volume show almost identical issues going back hundreds of years. Late medieval Venice, says author Yadira González de Lara, featured "the very same corporate governance problems we are facing today." Venice created "public gatekeepers" to constrain expropriation of investors. On the other hand, Thomas Hall shows that the Virginia Company of London, while a joint-stock company, foundered and lost investor capital—and squandered settler lives—when it bowed to political interference. Reza Dibadj finds similar features in France's eighteenth-century Compagnie des Indes: "There are striking parallels between the powerlessness of the company's shareholders and shareholders in today's large corporations, along with a similar eerie ambivalence about the role government should play vis-à-vis troubled enterprises." The 2008–2009 reinsertion of state ownership into Western spheres of commerce indeed keeps this question alive. History from the VOC to Fannie Mae seems to suggest that where ambiguity exists around the role of the state, investors face the potential for gain but at the cost of high risk.

It is perhaps surprising that comparatively little guidance exists on how the state or its agents should behave as an owner of listed companies. This is fertile ground for future research into history and practice. But there are examples of jurisdictions attempting to define parameters and objectives. The 2008 Santiago Principles set out first, very broad guidance on governance, stewardship, and disclosure for sovereign wealth funds around the world.[15] Some national and subnational public sector investment funds, notably the Florida State Board of Administration and Norway's Government Pension Fund-Global, have gone well beyond common standards in transparency.[16] Britain's twin state-sector agencies, the Shareholder Executive and UKFI, have sought to outline expectations of state behavior in rescued financial and other commercial institutions.[17] And the Obama administration, through an interagency taskforce led by the National Economic Council, produced ownership principles entitled *The Government as Shareholder*.[18] This reportedly drew policy borders to ward off political interference in commercial decisions. The document, however, was not released to the public.

These represent early efforts, in effect, to respond to cases in this volume that demonstrate the costs when such lines are not drawn. On the other hand, the very nature of government—and the way it may alter course with elections, crisis, and public pressure—means that even commendably explicit guidance may fail to supply materially greater comfort to capital players seeking to better manage risk.

Finally, the VOC experience of 1609 (along with other episodes described in these pages) prompts a test for today's corporations. Can their oversight boards find ways to draw value from investor engagement and accountability rather than retreat instinctively to defense? Boards are of course a central feature of governance; but they play very different roles depending on the jurisdiction and, especially, the characteristics of ownership. In the United States and Britain, with many public companies widely owned, the key challenge for boards is to balance sometimes competing investor interests while serving as a check on an often potent management. Almost everywhere else, where the state, enterprise, or family holds dominant stakes, the board's challenge is often to serve the blockholder while protecting minority investors from abuse.

History lessons in this volume demonstrate how readily boards may be swayed by dominant owners to the detriment of minority shareholders. Hall's Virginia Company of London is a prime example. The board chose to pay dividends to less-than-grateful English investors in the form of malarial swampland across the Atlantic. Yet it is the board rather than the tycoon that is, for the most part, the subject of authors exploring earliest corporate governance. They do not so much concentrate on the individual business leaders who, driven by greed and unchecked by directors, march a company to ruin. By notable contrast, contemporary accounts of Enron—in literature, film, and theater—heavily prefer to highlight errant executives over boards. Which perspective is right is arguable. But the scholars of governance history may have an advantage of distance.

The echo of historical concerns with suboptimal board oversight may be heard in modern times in many ways. One approach is to professionalize directors. Markets have grown whole industries devoted to the training and, sometimes, certification of board members. Another is to revise fiduciary duties of directors in ways that are meant to prompt more engaged participation. Class action lawsuits have multiplied in efforts to breach the formidable "business judgment rule," which normally protects boards from liability for unwitting errors. Policymakers, proxy advisors, and investor groups have advocated greater shareowner scrutiny of indicators from skill sets and track records of competence to independence, tenure, and attendance at board meetings. Experts are prospecting for ideas such as the Swedish nomination model mentioned earlier to achieve what Lucien Bebchuk and Jesse Fried have described as the objective of making boards "dependent on shareholders" rather than independent.[19]

In the United States, governance experts for years worked to promote the expansion of seats held by directors unaffiliated with management. The Sarbanes-Oxley Act and New York Stock Exchange and Nasdaq listing rules further advanced the concept with independence standards applying to audit and nomination committees. The position gained traction elsewhere, even without substantial in-market testing. The China Securities Regulatory Commission, for instance, moved to require that at least one-third of board seats at Chinese listed companies be held by nonexecutives. In the wake of the financial crisis, there was reason to forecast that advocates in the United States would turn their attention to board structure, and in particular to board leadership. For instance, the Chairmen's Forum, a new group incubated by the Millstein Center, issued a briefing and position letters advocating the model of independent nonexecutive chairmanship at publicly traded corporations.[20]

The history of shareowner advocacy, as it develops as a field of scholarship, may not instruct us in whether such initiatives will succeed in building sustainable corporations well aligned with the balance of owner interests. Nor will it necessarily illuminate clear paths to building corporations that serve society's best interests. But thoughtful probes into the archeology of governance can hope to provide perspective, temper hubris, and prompt consideration of fundamental forces at work when we mull reform. It is time, in short, for the history of corporate governance to have a future.

Notes

1. An account of the founding of the field may be found at www.historyofeconomics.org.

2. TIAA-CREF, for instance, issued a white paper in 2010 citing the need for greater investor vigilance. See www.tiaa-cref.org/ucm/groups/content/@ap_ucm_p_tcp/documents/document/tiaa01012041.pdf.

3. Deutsche Bank, Citi, and JP Morgan were among financial institutions that slashed corporate governance staffs in late 2008 (*Global Proxy Watch* XII-45, 46).

4. Paul Frentrop, Joost Jonker, and Stephen Davis, *Shareholder Rights at 400* (Amsterdam: APG Asset Management and Millstein Center for Corporate Governance and Performance-Yale School of Management, 2009). See also Frentrop, Paul. *A History of Corporate Governance 1602–2002* (Leiden: Leiden University, 2004).

5. La Porta, Rafael, Florencio Lopenz-de-Silanes, and Andrei Schleiffer, "What Works in Securities Laws," *Journal of Finance* 61, no. 1 (2006): 1–32.

6. See text of the final Dodd-Frank Act at http://frwebgate.access.gpo.gov/cgibin/getdoc.cgi?dbname=111_cong_bills&docid=f:h4173enr.txt.pdf.

7. See www.sec.gov/rules/final/2009/33-9089.pdf.

8. For the Walker Review, see www.hm-treasury.gov.uk/walker_review_index.htm. For the stewardship code, see www.frc.org.uk/images/uploaded/documents/Stewardship%20Code%20Consultation%20January%202010.pdf.

9. See www.pc.gov.au/projects/inquiry/executive-remuneration.

10. *Tomorrow's Corporate Governance: Bridging the UK Engagement Gap through Swedish-Style Nomination Committees* (London: Tomorrow's Company, 2010). See www.tomorrowscorporategovernance.com.

11. See Section G on Shareowner Stewardship at http://millstein.som.yale.edu/Policy%20Briefing%20No%206-Omnibus.pdf.

12. See www.responsibleinvestment.org/html/s02_article/article_view.asp?keyword=RIAA-RI-Academy.

13. See www.thepensionsregulator.gov.uk/trustees/trusteeKnowledge/index.aspx.

14. The author is a founder board member of shareowners.org.

15. See www.iwg-swf.org/pubs/gapplist.htm.

16. See www.sbafla.com/fsb/ and www.nbim.no/About-us/Government-Pension-Fund-Global/.

17. See www.shareholderexecutive.gov.uk and www.ukfi.co.uk.

18. *New York Times* June 1, 2009.

19. Bebchuk, Lucien and Fried, Jesse. *Pay without Performance: The Unfulfilled Promise of Executive Compensation* (Cambridge: Harvard University Press, 2006).

20. See *Chairing the Board* at http://millstein.som.yale.edu/chairmensforum.shtml#Briefing4.

INDEX